THE PASTOR'S
SANDAL PATH

THE PASTOR'S SANDAL PATH

Father Henry C. Schmidt

To order additional copies of this book, contact:
Xlibris Corporation
1-888-795-4274
www.Xlibris.com
Orders@Xlibris.com
68780

One bitter cold morning, as my Sandals were tramping through the knee-deep snow, a little snowflake spoke to me, and this is what it said: "I am so little and so insignificant. I don't even have a name. I am not big enough for anyone to ski or sleigh on or to become a snowman. I am unnoticed and my stay is so short. In fact, most people do not like me and wish that I would not even be here. How sad! So many are oblivious of God's masterpiece. For I am unique and the only one like me. And unknown to most people, I do much for them and the glory of God. But the greater sadness is that unlike me who sees my worth, they fail to appreciate themselves. Won't you help them? God made me, a tiny snowflake, with special care and deepest love and with a purpose in mind. He did the same for all his people. Help them to humbly acknowledge their greatness and graciously accept their littleness. For it is not what they are but who they are and their willingness to accept God's plan that brings them peace and happiness. Just look at me and see for I am God's masterpiece. If my short stay could accomplish only this, then my reason for being would be of eternal worth. Good-bye for I must go now."

As we begin this new year, hopefully we will listen to this snowflake. Remember, the Lord delights in all his creation, especially in us who are made in his image and likeness. All too often, we feel like the little snowflake, but persevere and trust in God. Our littleness is a big part of God's plan. Our weakness is God's strength. Our imperfection is the road of humility that leads to perfection. Forget what you are and concentrate on who you are—the beloved of God, and an heir to the kingdom. We are the "Great" "little" masterpieces called to *Life and love*. Thank you, "Little Snowflake" and *thank you, God!*

Father Henry Schmidt, January 17, 1999

On a cabinet in my office sits a frog perched and ready to hop, but it has been sitting that way for months; it never makes a move. How unlike the people of Little Flower Parish for they are always on the move! Have you noticed the many wonderful things happening around our parish and church, or the improvements that have been accomplished because of the great spirit of stewardship witnessed by many dedicated men and women? Thank God, they are not like my frog which never acts. My Sandals stand in awe of their generous witness of a stewardship way of life.

One day when walking along the edge of a pond, many frogs leaped into the water until the pond was alive with activity. This is how I see the "frogs" at Little Flower—some help with the school activities, some with the Vacation Bible School, others with the upgrading of the Quonset hut, some others with the church renewal or the habitat house or the St. John's Breadline, the ministries for the liturgies, and on goes the list. Some "splashes of the frogs" are noticed more than others, but every "frog" that leaps into the pool of activities is deeply appreciated and acknowledged by God. And I certainly am grateful for the involvement of the young and old and to whatever degree you are able to participate.

All too frequently we have a mistaken idea that we are not accepted; we seem different and so we hesitate to participate. Together let us work on acceptance. Acceptance is the answer to all our problems. When we are disturbed, it is because we find some person, place, thing, or situation—some fact of our lives is unacceptable to us, and we can find no serenity until we accept that person, place, thing, or situation as being exactly the way it is supposed to be at this moment. Nothing, absolutely nothing, happens in God's world by mistake; and unless we accept life completely on God's terms, we cannot be happy. We need to concentrate not so much on what needs to be changed in the world but on what needs to be changed in us and our attitudes.

So accept the call of Jesus, jump in the "pool" of parish life, and strive to use your differences to produce a "pond (parish) alive with activity" of faith living, sharing in the unconditional love of Jesus. Active frogs are happy ones. Be a happy "frog" and be active in our parish.

Father Henry Schmidt, July 11, 1999

Walking home late from the office, my Sandals were attracted to a beautiful firefly, better known as "lightning bug." A vast sphere of darkness is broken by the tiny flash of this summer beauty. With sadness, the little bug reminded me of the many little, but beautiful, things that go unnoticed because we are so "big" minded. Few appreciate the beauty of a "lightning bug," but they are quite aware of lightning with its graphic dramatic explosions.

So too with many ordinary events of life. But I want to share a few "lights" of my life this past week. The beautiful, simple, family-focused wedding prayerfully celebrated with only a best man and a maid of honor, no tuxedos, runners, or candelabras and with family members playing the music, the guests singing the songs, flowers arranged by family and friends, and no professional photographers, followed by a family-focused reception which included peanut butter and jelly sandwiches for the kids, along with a "kids corner" with toys etc., for them to enjoy while the adults dined, visited, danced, and enjoyed themselves.

Another was the celebration of a couple's sixty-seventh wedding anniversary along with their daughter and son-in-law's fortieth. This little light is extremely bright and a touching inspiration to me. I only wish that everyone could experience the deep faith-life of this couple's commitment, a commitment of love resulting from their weekly participation in the Eucharist.

I experienced another grace moment this week when our family celebrated the fiftieth Jubilee of my sister, Sister Henrianne, a Dominican sister. Like a lightning bug going from mission to mission, she spread the light of the Gospel News and shared her unlimited love with all that Jesus placed in her life on her journey of faith. Humbly and faithfully she has witnessed what each of us can do when our little light reflects the Light of Christ.

May the "lightning bug" remind us of our value, our mission, and our capability to change this dark world into a world of spiritual brightness, at least for a moment as does the little firefly. Together reflecting the love and light of Jesus, we reveal the way to eternal life. So little "firefly" lights the way!

Father Henry Schmidt, July 18, 1999

My Sandals spent an exciting, invigorating, and tiring week at the "Round Table" meeting and the "Jubilee Justice" gathering. During that week I experienced a visual affliction in my left eye. As problematic as it was, it was little when compared with the visual affliction of my inner spirit. When an Afro-American Jesus spoke to me, he said, "Free my people!" When a Native American Jesus spoke to me, he said, "Remove the yoke of injustice!" When a Hispanic Mexican Jesus spoke to me, he said, "Open your homes to my homeless!" And with tear-filled eyes I realized how weak I was. Prejudice, power, fear, and greed had silently and insidiously fabricated a Jesus to my liking, and who spoke a Gospel I found acceptable. But did I really know Jesus?

Our great contemporary prophet and martyr, Bishop Oscar Romero of San Salvador said, "A church that doesn't provoke any crises, a gospel that doesn't unsettle, a Word of God that doesn't get under anyone's skin, what Gospel is that? Very nice, pious considerations that don't bother anyone; that's the way many would like preaching to be. Those people who avoid every thorny matter so as not to be harassed, so as not to have conflicts and difficulties, do not light up the world they live in." There I stood convicted.

Then Jesus, a Chinese Sister, proclaimed as a clarion trumpet the unnerving challenge to become a true follower of his working for justice. Just as the angel, with both hands, pulled back the scales from the eyes of the blind Tobias, so the witnesses at these two world-changing gatherings began to remove the scales from the eyes of my soul. And I reached for colored glasses for I did not want to see what I saw, but a fourteen-year-old Jesus tossed them to the ground, as crowds of justice-seeking witnesses trampled them to pieces. I had to see the Gospel Jesus preached and lived equally—one of justice as well as charity. For a Gospel (or a Jesus) of charity without justice is comparable to a lighted stick of dynamite, slowly but steadily leading to destruction.

What is God's message for us today? Do we know Jesus? Does his Gospel afflict us? Now that I see, I need your support to live justly, act humbly, and love tenderly. Together let us live Jubilee Justice.

Father Henry Schmidt, July 25, 1999

My Sandals listened as the three roses on my desk spoke to me—two peace roses and one brilliant blood red. Sadly they remind me of life. They spoke of the many people working for peace, but amidst their efforts, inevitably there rises up some whose lives cause disturbance, destruction, and bloodshed.

At the Roundtable Symposium last week Jesus spoke these painful words: "I am the poor White, fooled and pushed apart, I am the Negro bearing slavery's scars. I am the Redman driven from the land, I am the immigrant clutching the hope I seek, I am the farmer, bondsman to the soil, and I am the worker sold to the machine. I am the Negro, servant to you all. I am the people—humble, hungry, mean—I am the one who never got ahead, the poorest . . ." There are many who go unnoticed, and those whom we pretend not to notice as we avoid them.

Perhaps you have seen the "lady at the pool" or the "lonely man" cooling his tired feet in the water outside our church. If you have, then you have seen Jesus. Did you recognize him?

The three beautiful roses on my desk are giving their all to please anyone who stops to "smell the roses" but most will quickly pass and fail to recognize or appreciate their beauty and sacrifice. The roses are well aware that along with their beautiful blooms and pleasant odor they present thorns, which prick and annoy those who are careless in handling them.

Likewise, Jesus reminds us that there is beauty even in his least. We must learn to handle them with loving compassion lest our careless handling will bring pain or distress.

My roses will soon be gone. Will I have gained from their gift? As my Sandals make their way down the path of life, will the "poor and lonely," the "least" become stumbling blocks or stepping stones to lasting Life? Will I gain from these gifts in my life?

May Jesus call each of us to look within our souls for that deep and holy love that sees him in all we encounter! May he make us disciples who dare to take the road less traveled with open arms and hearts, to create a path of justice and peace in our parish and homes! Let us all learn a lesson from the roses. Let us listen to Jesus.

Father Henry Schmidt, August 1, 1999

Did anyone see last week? I lost it. Time goes too quickly. Periodically, my Sandals see interesting "God signs" and this week I was moved by the following one: "Do you have any idea where you're going?"—God. Racing rapidly to the finish line caught in the rush of every day, it seems urgent that we determine where we are going.

On the table in the back of church I found a tiny bell, the remnant of the last wedding. This little bell symbolic of the call to a permanent marriage commitment specifically proclaims where they are going. Their faith journey must include Jesus.

In the next few weeks bells will be calling students back to school where effort will be made to prepare them for their going "in the world," but all walks of life eventually lead to the realization that "the world" is not the fulfillment of God's plan. So it is essential that each day we answer God's question: "Do you have any idea where you are going?"

Life like this past week is hurdling us into eternity. Don't lose the opportunity which Jesus offers you to use this life wisely witnessing the truth that you know where you are going. How carefully we plan life's goals and the manner of achieving them! So we are reminded of the need to be as foresighted in planning where we are going spiritually. That's the only goal that really counts and lasts.

Jesus sacrificed everything to reveal to us where we are going. He lived, loved, died, and rose to prove his teachings and left us the clear way, the truth, and the helps to life everlasting. From the moment of his birth to his return to his Father after his Resurrection, he had a clear view of where he was going and how to get there. What about us?

As followers of Jesus, we know well what is required of us. This past week the death bells tolled the call to eternal life many friends and members of our families. Those same bells will one day soon announce our final call to that place of peace, life, and love for which we have been created. Life is enhanced by the variety of bells announcing important events, grace-filled moments when Jesus speaks in the solitude of our hearts, "Do you have any idea where you are going?" What must we do to get there? Listen carefully to all the "bells" signaling his message to life.

Father Henry Schmidt, August 22, 1999

One morning as my Sandals meandered across the school playground, I was pleasantly surprised to see a group of interestingly formed white mushrooms. However, when I came by the same area the next morning, I was saddened to see that someone had come along and smashed God's beautiful work of art.

Gazing upon the fate of these gifts of God, I became disturbed by the similarity with which we treat God's greatest creation, people. Everyone is created in the image and likeness of God. Everyone is unique and beautiful. Still there are those who fail to see the beauty, and those who even seek to smash and destroy.

Sunday and Monday I shared in workshops that aim to unite us by creating small church communities. All too frequently we are divided by insignificant factors, which leads to tensions and destruction. We live as families and parishioners in such a busy and demanding world that we do not even know one another. Preoccupied with overwhelming expectations on our personal life, we do not have time to even listen to the needs of others. Worse still, we fail to make any connection with our faith or God's plan in our life.

It is my hope and prayer that together we can structure our parish where *the ordinary parishioners help each other connect everyday lived experiences with the great faith tradition of the church.* Our faith is our strength and our link with the God who knows all, loves all, and does only what is best for each of us. This is hard for us to see and accept when things don't go our way.

We don't know each other. Problems in families, school, parish, communities, or neighborhoods result because we do not communicate, listen, or connect these daily events with our faith.

Consequently what one or more see as a lovely "mushroom" and gift of God, others trample under foot and work to change or destroy, due to lack of understanding.

Being convinced that we are all special and have many similar likes and dislikes, let us strive to bring our faith into these situations. We are all ordinary people called to be church together. We cannot be church in any other way.

Father Henry Schmidt, August 29, 1999

13

Sunday afternoon, while sitting in Lincoln Memorial Gardens overlooking the lake and reading the documents for the National Bishop's meeting in Washington, DC, which I shall be attending this month, I was suddenly aware of the dichotomy of life. Behind me a huge flock of birds, like black leaves on a tree, were angrily chattering, while a beautiful white seagull silently hovered over the still lake water, undisturbed by the birds, me, or other passing strollers, intent only on the mission of getting food.

As we go through life, we will either imitate the chattering blackbirds disturbed by the accidentals of life over which we have no control, or we will continue on peacefully like the seagull pursuing the essentials of life over which Jesus has complete control.

My presence bothered the blackbirds and tossed them into complete turmoil, while the seagull went unbothered, fully attuned to the necessities of life. I am inspired and filled with admiration for you who keep your focus on Jesus as you live out your faith in spite of my leadership, and I ask forgiveness of those who, because of my imperfection, feel tested.

I can accept the reality that, because of misunderstandings or varying opinions, you find it difficult to support or celebrate at Little Flower, but I ask that you do not destroy Little Flower because of our differences by angry chatter, thus leading others away too.

During these trying days, when our church is being attacked from within and without, we need to unite in our efforts to attract people to the truths revealed to us by Jesus. Because Bishop Ryan upheld the teachings of Vatican II, he is being falsely accused, which is now leading to untold division and destruction. Let us not foster further division, but strive to accept one another and honestly resolve these accidental differences in a peaceful and mature manner, adhering to the words of Jesus "Peace I leave with you, my peace I give unto you: not as the world giveth, give I unto you. Let not your heart be troubled, neither let it be afraid."

As the silent, persistent seagull, together, we shall peacefully focus on our goal, Jesus, unbothered by the "chattering" or other passing distractions and attacks around us. I thank God for all the beautiful "seagulls" witnessing marvelous faith and testifying to the truth in our parish. Fly on guided by the Holy Spirit.

Father Henry Schmidt, November 7, 1999

With the last Thanksgiving turkey feather blown in the wind and the incredible onrush of the new millennium crashing upon us, I hope each of us will use the "quiet time" of Advent to examine our lives in search of opportunities to "put on Christ" in our daily witness of the Gospel message. We are all wonderful people, dearly loved by Jesus, needing the reshaping of the "clay" of our lives by the gentle hands of the "Master Potter."

In order to encourage us, I write the following: The song of life is silent—the mill is dead! Its body is decaying, and being carried away by the very stream that so faithfully had worked to nourish the huge giant, by turning the massive gears, now rusted and broken, which fed the insatiable hunger of the valley folks. And yet, in the silence, the air continues to echo the shocking words, "Murder—the mill was murdered," as nature strives to hide the evidence by a camouflage of weeds, briars, and saplings!

On my last visit, the valley was alive—people were gay and working together; the mill was humming, preparing the food of life; and flowers and birds added to the beauty of the valley, where peace and love could be seen and experienced. The kind and generous miller was revered and loved by all the people, for whom he worked tirelessly.

But soon an evil, worse than the plague, began its silent course of destruction, as a rotting apple, working from within and never affecting the beauty of the apple, until all ended in total destruction.

For the jealous Duke, seeing his people loving the kindly miller, who gave so much, more than him, demanded so much, began to propagate evil lies about him, and increased his mill taxes, hoping to destroy him.

How sad, and how evil, for the people needed the miller! And the Duke needed the people! But one by one, they began to leave, for the evil Duke had destroyed the peace of the valley; and soon the mill was dead.

The mill was dead! The mill was killed! So often good is destroyed, good people are maligned, and all because of jealousy. For some people can't stand to see others more popular, or do more for the community than they do and instead of trying to compete by doing good, they choose rather to destroy and ruin everything—themselves included—by smear campaigns, and by firing the furnace of prejudice and hatred.

There is a law, a law for all, a law from God, which states: "Thou shalt not bear false witness against thy neighbor," and the more beautiful counsel: "Thou shalt love thy neighbor as thyself, for the love of God." A church, a home, a community established on this foundation shall stand, grow, and guarantee peace, love, and prosperity; but the one which ignores this shall suddenly find—The Mill is dead!

Father Henry Schmidt, December 5, 1999

My Sandals are almost smoking from the fast pace these past few weeks. They are screaming "Stop." The somber words of John the Baptist "Prepare you the way of the Lord" are fading in the background because we are rushing so quickly through Advent. Already we are at the fourth Sunday of Advent. Have we found any time for "waiting"—waiting for Jesus to enter more fully into our busy lives? Blessed are you who found time to be renewed with the prayerful celebration of evening prayer and the special communal celebration of the sacrament of reconciliation. How powerfully present Jesus was as he revealed and renewed his love for all who participated!

Hopefully many of you will take/make time to gather for the Christmas Novena which is going on each evening at 8:30 p.m. We are busy people, but what is our business? We are a giving people, but what are we giving to our children, and to God?

During the past few weeks and in the coming week fortunes will be spent on "Christmas" giving, hours will be consumed in shopping and preparation for the holiday, and most everyone will be exhausted by the pressures of our times. But what happened to *Jesus*?

Some families have the practice of preparing their manger by placing a straw in it for every good act of kindness they do during Advent and removing one when they hurt one another. During this Advent, have we been more loving and accepting of one another? Have we participated as a family in the Eucharist each weekend? Do we gather with our children or spouses to pray? What have we sacrificed for the poor and less fortunate? If we have only been occupied with the material, then we may find that we have a beautiful surrounding for our "Crib" but have forgotten to place Jesus in the manger.

Jesus is waiting for us to make room in our lives so he can enter more fully in a real and personal way. What are we, and our children, waiting for this Christmas? We all enjoy gifts and the excitement of Christmas, but how quickly it passes and fails to satisfy!

Do we long for Jesus? Are we witnessing to our children and one another the value and importance of knowing and welcoming Jesus into our daily lives? This is contracultural, difficult, and so naive. But this is faith! We expect Jesus to give us peace, love, and happiness, and he will, but only if we ignore the "worldly" and give our lives to him.

Prepare the way of the Lord. Prepare a welcoming manger for Jesus, our Savior—your heart. Slow down! Reject the "peer pressure" worldly attractions. For Christmas is not a holiday, but a holy day. Christmas is Christ's Mass. Christmas is giving Jesus and not gifts.

Love one another as Jesus loves you. Forgive one another, over and over, seventy times seven, as Jesus teaches and witnesses. Be at peace, with that peace which Jesus alone can give. Then there is Christmas.

Rejoice and be glad! Have a blessed Christmas for unto us is born a Savior, Christ the Lord, who brings good news to the poor in spirit, forgiveness to sinners, and dwells with the humble. My gift to you is Jesus. Will you accept him? If you do, then you will give him back to me too. We wait together to be reborn. *Merry Christmas!*

Father Henry Schmidt, December 19, 1999

With snow covered Sandals, I gathered with young and old in a packed church for the 4:30 p.m. Mass to celebrate the birthday of Jesus. What excitement and joy in the eyes and actions of the little ones when Santa entered the church! Was that same emotion in the hearts of any of us when Jesus came among us in the manger of the altar?

Jesus chose to be born in a stable so the poor, humble, weak, and sinful would feel welcome, and come without hesitation or fear. Do we? Jesus was laid in a manger, a box of wood with a cross at each end serving as its legs. A manger is where animals come for food. Jesus is our spiritual food. The cross legs show the cross of salvation—one upon which Jesus died; the other, the gift of Jesus to all who are willing to die to sin and the world, take up their cross, and follow him to lasting life, peace, and love.

What a beautiful Christmas—snow, gifts, family gatherings—everything that we could ask for according to nostalgic worldly propaganda. But was Jesus truly there? Were the gifts, in excess, to cover over the lack of love? Were the families merely gathered or was there true sharing in prayer and compassionate caring, reconciliation, and recognition of Christ in one another?

The beautiful white snow which fell silently in the dark of night covered the ugliness of the earth and gave the appearance of newness and change, but it soon will melt and reveal the truth of a superb cover-up, with no substantial change in reality. Hopefully, Christmas will not be merely a coverup, a snow job, for a day or week, and then the ugliness of reality return as we settle back into the routine of life.

How disheartening to celebrate Mass, on the Feast of the Holy Family, the Sunday after Christmas, with a church so sparsely filled. The same Jesus, as in the manger, now present on the altar, was waiting to feed us, love us, bless our families, and to unite us in the peace. Has the "snow" of Christmas melted?

Our homes are to be a "greenhouse" of faith. Jesus sows the seed, through all of us, in our children and in one another, and relies on us to nourish them. As we approach the new millennium, let us resolve to *rebuild our home* into a place where we eat, pray, and share our lives as a family; where church, faith, and Jesus are more important than education, accomplishment, security, popularity, or wealth, and sports is a pastime and for fun, and not the pivot of our lives.

The world has stolen, from many of us, our home life, families, freedom, and even time itself by its overwhelming demands, thereby pushing Jesus, faith, and the spiritual life to the sidelines or out of the picture completely.

All the worldly things will pass, with the melting of the "snow of death" and what will remain? The twentieth century has passed, and what remains of lasting value from all twenty centuries is the presence and love of Jesus. God loves us and will always love us. Believe that—live in ways that witness your conviction, and commit this twenty-first century to Jesus. Together let us live in peace, hope, and love, longing for the fulfillment of life—union with Jesus now and forever.

Father Henry Schmidt, January 2, 2000

As my Sandals slowly meandered along the damp woodchipped path in Lincoln Memorial Gardens covered with the remains of the trees which once adorned our parish grounds, I was deeply moved as I gazed out over the ugly ice slowly returning into murky water because of the warm temperature. What a blessing to be alive!

The now weakening sun, slowly being choked as evening pulled it into the dense agitated clouds, seemed to join with a lone goose whose "cry from the wild" broke the silence of the woods. Do you appreciate life? What an awesome, prayerful moment!

Sitting on the bench beneath the naked trees, mindful and mind filled with the past, memories flashed within my head. Oh, how I disliked returning to school after Christmas, not because I did not like school, but because I did not understand Christmas! Because we were poor farmers, my parents were unable to give us "expensive" clothes or toys, and I dreaded being asked what did you get for Christmas? How sad! For my parents gave us siblings so much more than fancy, flashy things. They sacrificed far more than I realized at the time just to give us the necessities of life. But they gave us more than any material things could—they gave us true love, a family that prayed, played, and shared and a humble secure home. What a blessing!

This past week as my Sandals joined a small group of parishioners, we brought some love and compassion to the residents at St. Joseph Home. Oh, how they enjoyed our visit and singing! As we were leaving, I realized that little things have such powerful effects. A visit, a smile, a greeting, a song, a kind word, and so many other things we can all do for them or others. Why are we so loving and caring for one or two weeks surrounding Christmas? What about the rest of the year? It comes only when we truly appreciate life.

As we begin this new year, keep these thoughts in mind: Have you found someone to share your heart with? Are you giving to your family or community? Are you at peace with yourself? Where is Jesus in your life?

Are you unhappy? Many people are, because the culture we have does not make people feel good about themselves. We're teaching the wrong things. We're caught in the "first and best" syndrome. Secularism is more attractive than Catholic living. And you have to be strong enough to say if the culture doesn't work, don't buy it. Create your own; be with Jesus, who is life, as the pivot of all. As a parish family, may we make greater efforts to witness the blessings in our lives, always working for greater peace and harmony, striving for justice and longing for that greater union with life. Happy New Year!

Father Henry Schmidt, January 9, 2000

As my Sandals gathered with nearly a thousand people at the breakfast honoring Martin Luther King this past Monday, my eyes filled with tears as we sang "We shall overcome," and joined hands with people of various races and religions. How sad to see God's people divided because of prejudice! How hopeful to see so many people striving for unity and justice!

But my heart was even more painfilled when I realized how much division there is within our church over truly insignificant things. Divisions resulting because of differing opinions regarding the stations, the right-to-life monument, the length of Mass, cultural differences, the ways we offer to supplement our deficit of income, the increase of tuition, etc.

Is it not a bit ironical that the very purpose of all these projects, set up to preserve and foster a deeper faith, a greater appreciation of life and closer union with Jesus, have become causes of division. Maybe we need to refocus on where we have placed Jesus in our planning. Perhaps we might examine our reasons for instigating these causes.

"What would Jesus do in these situations?" continues to ring in my mind? Being a man of deep faith I trust in his plan. He has guided and preserved his Church for over two thousand years, and I am confident it will survive. But how are we cooperating in his plan of salvation?

I fail to understand our use or misuse of time—that precious gift of God. We manage to find time for all the pressing needs of society, but we seem to limit those dealings with Jesus which are beneficial for salvation. We make incredible sacrifices to better our positions or in the hope of attaining security for our children, while overlooking those which can truly guarantee them security and success in this life and in the next—the spiritual.

Where does discipline and spiritual accountability fit into our daily lives? We are so mesmerized by the seductions of the world which offer false satisfaction and fading crowns of glory that the true and lasting promises of Jesus fade and no longer hold the position of priority.

It is sad to see the evil of prejudice resulting from the malformed and misinformed, but we Catholics and followers of Jesus have no excuse. Jesus expects peace and harmony.

Family prayer and participation at the liturgy would be a good start. Faith and worship is not simply for our "elders" which seem to be the daily picture. The awareness that Jesus uses all of us, regardless of race, color, creed, sex, culture, age, abilities, or any other accidental differences in his plan of salvation might be a help in working together for the glory of God and for greater peace and unity. As we examine our personal lives, let us search for ways we can revitalize our faith, prioritize our goals, be more accountable for our actions, and live in his love.

In an inspiring book *Tuesdays with Morrie*, Morrie, who is preparing for death, makes a most profound statement: "Once you learn how to die, you learn how to live." We ignore death, we deny that "I" am going to die; we refuse to talk about it because we do not know how to die. Consequently, we do not know how to live. This failure is the font of our divisions. Oh, that we could learn how to die, so we could learn how to live!

Father Henry Schmidt, January 23, 2000

As my Sandals rushed into the Capitol rotunda this past Sunday, escaping from the cold, I thought of our youth minister, Ben Moss, and the bus load of young people who were among the crowds enduring the bitter cold in Washington, DC witnessing for the right-to-life. When Maria Johns, the keynote speaker, gave her testimony about "A Child of Hope" her unborn son, whom she was carrying while battling a most rare disease, it became quite evident that abortion of any sort is the fruit of a hopeless people. God alone is the giver of life, the preserver of life, and the controller of life. No one, humanly speaking, had any more reason to abort their child than did Maria, and few have witnessed as deep a trust in the plan of God as she did throughout her difficult and death-threatening pregnancy.

Later, on Sunday afternoon, I read in Henri Nouwen's book, *A Road to Peace*, a confirmation of that truth. He states, "Being neither an optimist nor a pessimist, Jesus speaks about hope that is not based on chances that things will get better or worse. His hope is built upon the promise that, whatever happens, God will stay with us at all times, in all places. God is the God of life."

Sunday morning while celebrating Mass in a small church, a tiny baby "sang" its praises to God in the only way it could—for the optimist it was a blessing, for the pessimist, a disturbance, but for me, a sign of hope. After Mass, I thanked them for coming as a family and encouraged them to continue to do so for God is the God of life, and he uses all stages and types of life for his glory. Do we see that? Do we believe that?

Marriage, friendship, sexuality, intimacy—all are in very deep crisis. Despair is on the rise. We, followers of Jesus, are called to be a people of hope. As Henri Nouwen says, "We cannot go around despair to hope. We have to go right through despair." We have to taste it and face it in order to perceive the hope that Jesus offers us. Rising from his place of despair, the tomb, Jesus says, "Love one another because I have loved you first." Despair in marriage, friendship, sexuality, and intimacy results from such an uncontrolled need of satisfaction that we are willing to do anything to fill it, even hurting or destroying each other. Hope enters when we are more willing to give than to receive, to love as Jesus loved. Hope builds on a love rooted in divine love.

Maria Johns was willing to give her life, if need be, for the life of her unborn son, because she believed that Jesus loved her and had a plan for her. Her hope was founded "upon the promise that, whatever happens, God will stay with us at all times, in all places. God is the God of Life." Jesus does not call us to be optimists, and he does not want pessimists; he empowers us to hope. Together let us journey from despair to hope.

Father Henry Schmidt, January 30, 2000

While walking to church early one morning, my Sandals paused as I stopped to enjoy the thrill of God's creation. Overhead I heard the "call of the wild," as numerous flocks of geese flew in V formation. Each time I hear their call and see them flying in their beautiful patterns, I am overwhelmed with an inner desire to fly and be free of the burdens of life.

Yes, we have much to learn from these splendid creatures of God. Their willingness to work together, to take their turn at leading and facing the hardships, their humble acknowledgment of their need to follow others in leadership roles, their continual crying out in support as they make their way through the elements of the seasons in search of shelter and food, and their compassion for one another in time of trouble, as well as their commitment till death.

Once the geese are gone and my Sandals realized that I cannot fly nor be free of the burdens of life, then I began to search how I can pattern my life after these marvelous creatures of God. What can I/we do to improve interpersonal conditions so we can work together in perfect formation so all are benefitting from our efforts? How can more parishioners be motivated to take on leadership roles for a period of time, and then humbly step aside to allow others to carry on the work they have begun? In what way can each one affirm and compliment the efforts of others, as we offer support on our faith journey which leads all to the sheltering arms of Jesus who longs to feed us with the Word and Living Bread? Do we see Christ in all who come into our lives and extend them the hand of compassion, and remain with them in person, in spirit, and in prayer as they face and work through their troubles? And how committed am I/we to remain faithful to Jesus? How sad it is to see and hear that Catholics, young and older, who have been so blessed by Jesus, as members of the Catholic Church, are now trying to satisfy their need in other churches! Why? How can partial truths and man-made gifts replace God's absolute truth and our God-given gifts of the Mass and the Sacraments?

These are the "geese" that are tired, burdened, and wounded. These are the "geese" we need to reach out to support, affirm, comfort, and nourish. These are the ones, as St. Paul states in this week's readings, we must witness to. St. Paul writes a letter to the people of Corinth to strengthen and motivate them to remain faithful to Jesus. We are to be living letters displaying to our families and neighbors that we truly believe that Jesus is our Lord and Savior; that our love for one another is greater than the wrongs that we might do to each other because we seek to imitate the love of Jesus; that we are striving for unity and togetherness in our families and parish; that our ambitions, personal development, and education will help all to come to know Jesus more personally; and that we are striving to develop a Stewardship way of Life.

We will never fly as the geese. We will never be free of burdens, but we can be "living letters" which inform the bothered, hurting, and wandering "geese" where the total truth can be found; that show the way that leads to lasting life; and offer love and compassion. Let our lives be "letters of recommendation."

Father Henry Schmidt, February 27, 2000

As my Sandals stood at the door of the church following Mass, a lady walked up to me with tear-filled eyes, and asked me, "How do you live with a miracle?" How blessed are the people of our parish for God has truly performed many miracles here, both spiritual and physical! How do you live with a miracle? In humble faith and deep appreciation for the incredible love of Jesus!

Many of you may have watched the TV series *"Touched by an Angel"* and experienced deep moving feelings, but I have seen real life people, who have been "Touched by Jesus" and experienced the powerful presence of Jesus. I am sure you have too. Praise God!

Very late Sunday night my Sandals carried my tired and weary body to bed following another *Growing in Forth Together* weekend. It was a "miracle" experience wherein over three dozen parishioners were deeply touched by the truth and healing grace of Jesus as he raised them to new life and a more personal relationship with him. What joy, love, community, and faith growth result from those two days! If you are looking for a new beginning, a meaning to life, or a way to refocus your life and goals, then take part in a *gift* weekend. No words can fully express the blessings. Come and experience a miracle in your life.

There are miracles of birth, healing, conversion, in nature, and so frequently that we become calloused and take them for granted. How sad! God blesses us every day with his marvels, and we hardly acknowledge his existence, much less his miracles.

But the greatest tragedy is our lack of believing he is present in the Eucharist. At every Liturgy, Jesus works a miracle—the most powerful of all—transforming bread and wine into his own body and blood, the Eucharist. *Jesus is present!* It is not a sign, a symbol, a reminder, the Eucharist is Jesus, alive, body and blood, soul and divinity. How do we live with this miracle?

Frequently I hear people speak of their distant travels hoping to see an apparition or miracle, only to return disappointed. We don't have to travel, and we need not be disappointed because someone has misguided us, for Jesus performs the greatest miracle at each Mass.

Living faith compels us to gather in church early to prepare to share with him who speaks to us in sacred scripture, and nourishes on the bread of life. Deep faith motivates us to bring our sacrifices, not only of money, but our sufferings, our sinfulness, efforts to reconcile, desires for perfection, to be offered in union with the sacrifices of Jesus. Convinced that Jesus is really, truly, physically present, we are distressed when it is time to leave. Can we believe this, or are we looking for signs and wonders?

I truly rejoiced with the lady, who "lives with a miracle," and I praise God with her, but I am more excited that Jesus loves her, me, and all of us enough to become a "living miracle" for each of us. The great question is "how do we live with this miracle?"

Father Henry Schmidt, March 12, 2000

As my Sandals sat at the big round office table following staff prayer, a robin crashed into the huge glass window. Surprised, stunned, and hurt it fell to the ground. But as God planned, it survived and later flew away. Why did God allow the bird to crash?

Perhaps our lives are a parallel. We are rushing through life, doing what we believe God has planned, when suddenly we crash into some totally unexpected obstacle, and are surprised, hurt, and confused. Why? Will it destroy us, or are we willing to face the problem and guided by Jesus, resolve the difficulty, and continue on reunited and stronger from the experience?

What is the "glass window" that abruptly curtails your "planned journey"? Look at the children lying stunned, hurt, or dying because their lives were misguided or unguided, now ending in tragedy. What a catastrophe to behold an increasing number of couples, being catapulted against the "window of surprise" due to irresponsibility of commitment! How devastating for parents whose children lie crumpled at the "window," the result of addiction!

The robin crashed and survived as a part of God's mysterious plan. Likewise, our difficult situations, shrouded in unfathomable mystery are permitted by God as faith-growth opportunities or grace occasions leading to a spiritual metamorphosis or a time to evaluate our priorities and to discern his will in our lives. With difficulty the Robin got up and continued on, faithful to the plan of God enduring the pain and committed to being a bird. Sad to say we are not as true to our God nor committed to our promises and responsibilities.

Such rationalization will only lead to more cruel, self-destruction, and family devastation. Crashing into the invisible "window"—God's plan for each of us can be a blessing in disguise, if we are willing to listen to Jesus who not only invites us to imitate him but witnesses how to endure such trials.

Jesus ascended to his Father so his spirit could be present in all our lives. That spirit, as he promised, empowers us to endure all trials to discern the healing solution best for both the individual and family, and enables us to willingly make the efforts to achieve the goal, which we know, is according to Jesus's plan. We, like the robin, can pick ourselves up, but we cannot fly away from those "windows" which alter our lives. That's a cop-out. We, with the help of God, must find a way to open the window to continue on together. Rationalizing the situation to avoid the truth will not bring peace, for the solution is contrary to the will of Jesus.

Mindful of Jesus's promise "I will be with you always," let us strive to avoid those "windows" of pain by greater honesty, communication, acceptance, forgiveness, and love so that true and just reconciliations may result, lives may be healed and uplifted, and Jesus may find room in our lives and homes. But if we crash into an unexpected "window," be not afraid, for Jesus promises to be with us always, especially in those difficult moments, if we welcome him. His solution is the only right one. His presence guarantees peace.

Father Henry Schmidt, June 11, 2000

23

A few weeks ago, while in East St. Louis, I, along with a group of friends, was rushing up the stairs to catch the Metro when suddenly someone paused to read the sign only to make us aware that we, in our rush, were going in the wrong direction. Luckily we noticed it in time and stopped. Realizing our mistake we turned around, descended the stairs, chose the correct path, and climbed up the steep stairs to the Metro, which brought us safely to our desired destination.

This incident exemplifies the reality that many are rushing through life and catching the wrong "Metro." They are longing for salvation, but in the rush they are not reading the signs and are being carried in the wrong direction.

One of the readings at the Mass a few days past stated that "days are coming, says the Lord God, when I will send a famine upon the land: not a famine of bread, or thirst for water, but for hearing the Word of the Lord." Those days are here!

The world today is plagued by the famine of physical hunger. Yet while millions are suffering from lack of food and water, a spiritual famine far surpasses the physical. Unknown numbers of people die each day because of the greed of the world leaders, the apathy of the rich, and the rush of many to catch the wrong "Metro." Tragic! But what about all those who suffer from spiritual famine? We Christians struggle to alleviate this catastrophe.

Conscientious and ambitious parents are rushing to get their children on the "Metro" of advancement in order to prepare them scholastically, socially, economically and financially. They need to stop and read the "direction" signs before it is too late! Otherwise they may achieve in the material world, but they will suffer spiritually.

I sincerely praise those parents who carefully read the "Metro" signs and travel with their families on the way that relieves spiritual famine. Just as there is no justification for such extensive starvation throughout the world, so too, there is even less excuse for the spiritual famine of which God forewarns us in the words of the prophet, which is rapidly ravaging the Christian world today.

There is plenty of food and water in the world for all if only we would heed the challenge of Jesus to feed the hungry, give drink to the thirsty, clothe the naked, shelter the homeless etc. Likewise, there is plenty of spiritual food for life if only we would live the challenge of Jesus to go forth and teach all nations. Our children are spiritually starving, craving to hear of Jesus, experience his powerful presence, and share his love, but we are riding the wrong "Metro." Get off now before it is too late. To starve and be deprived in this world because of physical famine is extremely painful but only for a time, while the ultimate effects of the spiritual famine are excruciating and eternal.

Witnessing to our children and to one another by praying together every day and worshiping as a family each weekend leads them to Jesus, the source of Life, and places them on the only "Metro" that eradicates spiritual famine. The fare for the "Metro to Life" is costly. Jesus paid with his life. What about us?

Father Henry Schmidt, July 16, 2000

Standing in front of the main building at Camp One Way, my Sandals beheld an impatiens plant about two inches tall, with one lonely red bloom squeezing up between the building and the cement walk, responding to the call of God to bloom where you are. Bearing in mind the living Word of Jesus who called each of us before the foundation of the world, I was greatly pleased to see these young people participating in the Exodus weekend, responding to his call to grow in faith, share his love and minister to his people.

Jesus calls each of us to love people and use things. Yet we frequently love things and use people. I dearly love Jesus, but it is so difficult to heed his instruction. When Jesus spoke to us this past Sunday, he told us to take nothing, no food or money, but only the absolute necessities and to trust in his providence as we proclaimed the Good News—that is loving people and using things for his glory.

Living in a world dominated by an excessive love of material things and using people mechanically to climb the ladder of success, it is extremely important that we focus on the summons of Jesus to a more simple lifestyle.

Pressured by modern society, we continually feel compelled to purchase a larger house, a new car, and work two jobs to acquire more gadgets for our homes, which we are unable to use because of lack of time, and live in constant fear of insecurity. Perhaps this is what Jesus was trying to help us avoid as he lived a life of detachment and simplicity, and prophesied "lay up treasures which rust cannot destroy and moths cannot devour." Loving one another, taking time to be with one another, and respecting each other is the only solution to counteract the destructive pace of our time. Appreciate who you are and why.

Not far from the tiny impatiens plant with its sole bloom in the middle of the yard were many other blooming plants, but they did not catch my eye as did that plant struggling to glorify God in its little way. Too often we try to impress people more with what we possess than with what we are. This ruptures or hampers our relationship with Jesus and causes division between families and friends as we fail to appreciate who we are and live in unreasonable fear of those who appear to have more. Jesus called the rough, simple, humble, sinful people of his day to follow and witness. He did not overlook the "least" in preference of the powerful and rich.

"Come, follow me, and I will make you fishers of men (all)" was Jesus's universal invitation to love and to minister. My Sandals stood in admiration of our parish youth and of Ben Moss, our youth director, as they prayed and prepared to accept their role in the church. Every one of us, empowered by the Spirit, has an important role in Christ's plan of salvation. As each of us prayerfully discern how and where Jesus is calling us to minister, let us encourage and welcome more of our young people to become actively involved in the faith life of our parish. They have much to give and are greatly needed. Responding to the call of Jesus, may God enlighten us to know what is the hope that belongs to our call!

Father Henry Schmidt, July 23, 2000

As my Sandals approached the office, I saw a little green hard rubber ball almost hidden in the grass. Reaching down, I picked it up and threw it against the walk, and it bounced high into the air. The more forcefully I threw it, the greater was its response. Over and over I tossed it, and entering the office I continued to bounce it, causing it to ricochet off the wall never losing its energy or resilience. Thus it showed its ability to adapt to cement, tile, plaster, or any hard surface. The stronger the resistance, the more it reacted. How like unto our lives!

Each of us, in the estimation of present-day society, is but a tiny, insignificant "little green ball" nearly hidden in the mass of humanity. Most of us will go unnoticed, by the rushing crowds, as we blend into the daily routine of life. But occasionally, society will notice and pick us up to test us. Then, with the power of Jesus, we too will show our true colors.

I have seen many "little green balls" bouncing around our parish, and I am inspired and motivated by their lives. Many elders of our parish give witness of deep faith and a solid prayer life amidst many difficulties and hardships, which come with age. These "pillars" of our parish enable Jesus to build a vitally living church. Daily they celebrate the Liturgy, and are nourished on the Eucharist and witness living faith in our community. Some hampered from time to time with debilitating illness, tossed hard against the walls of limitation, and they bounced back with incredible strength and cast out fear and despair, showing their true colors as faith-filled followers of Jesus.

If perceptive, we will notice other hidden "little green balls" of various ages and walks of life that rise to the occasion to carry out some difficult parish or community program. When others are ready to toss in the towel or buckle under pressure, they bounce forth with greater enthusiasm and muster up the resources to conquer the situation. Look around and notice the force targeted against such parish and community builders, and marvel at their adaptability to survive and flourish amidst growing rejection while branded as "social outcasts." Behold Jesus enfleshed.

I am not sure whether the little green ball I plucked from the soft grass was pleased or disturbed because I whisked it from its soft place of security. But one thing I am sure of is that it would never bounce left lying there or when tossed against something very soft. It was made to be tossed and bounced around.

We too were created by Jesus to live active faith and community lives built on solid family values. Enmeshed in today's standards of "free living, materialism, secularism, amidst a growing culture of death" every true follower of Jesus will be tossed and bounced around in such a dizzying fashion that we will need the empowerment of the Spirit to survive and not condescend to take the easy way out and lie in the soft muck of worldliness. We are meant to bounce off these temptations and witness the qualities of a faith-filled follower of Jesus, who made us "little green balls," bounces us to test our love and fidelity, and catches us in his outstretched arms of love. Everyone plays ball, but with whom? Hopefully with Jesus, our team coach.

Father Henry Schmidt, August 13, 2000

"Ready or not, here I come." Do you remember those words from "hide-and-seek"? When we were little and on the farm, the neighbor kids would gather, and we would play until too dark to see. Hearing those words, all who were hiding knew the search was beginning and so made their last effort to hide. Some who were found would cry, others would say I was not ready, while others would try to come up with some excuse that the game or hunter was not fair. Only the one or few who had managed to hide well enough to avoid discovery, or who evaded the seeker and ran home to the base were permitted to play the next game. So we try to play the game of life.

"Ready or not, here I come," says Jesus. This past week I shared in five funerals. Will the next one be mine or yours? I am not a morbid person, but I am afraid that we have come to view death as something which is "later" in life.

It appears that some of the "players," while hiding from God, run around doing a variety of things, thinking they have plenty of time to prepare for the "hunt," may find themselves discovered and not really ready for the "call." Will we be among them? Will we "cry" when we are found unprepared, claiming we were not ready, or that the "game" of life was not fair or some other flimsy excuse? Jesus gives each of us time—time enough to ready ourselves for his call. No one can complain that we were not given enough time and grace to "hide" from sin, and prepare ourselves through the living of our faith for the search—that final call.

From time to time, while playing "hide-and-seek," as kids, someone would try to change the rules of the game for their advantage, but then our parents would require that they remain the same for all. We live in a society today that tries desperately to change the rules of the game, but Jesus guarantees their permanence for each and every generation.

We can try to hide from God and live a jolly fun-filled free life ignoring the rules of the game, but we will be found. We can camouflage ourselves and pretend to be playing by the rules of the game, but when Jesus comes, it will do no good to claim we were not ready. We can proclaim that others had more time or better opportunities and life was not fair, but to no avail. For when Jesus calls our "Ready or not, here I come," he will respond to what he finds—the witness of our lives. We know the rules of the game, and we must live them.

In the game of "hide-and-seek," only the ones who hid from the "enemy," the hunter, until he gave up hunting or managed to run to the "safe spot" won the game. So too, all who listen carefully to the message of Jesus and avoid (hide from) sin by walking closely to him will make it to the "safe spot" heaven. No one knows how long the game is going to last. For some, the game is very short, for others it is quite long. But we all know the rules of the game, and they are the same for everyone. So be careful where you hide, and from whom you hide. Check how you are playing. Always be ready! For "ready or not, Jesus will come" again this week.

Father Henry Schmidt, September 3, 2000

27

Several weeks ago while walking the hills of Marquette Park, my Sandals rested to enjoy the beauty of God's creation. Looking up, I spied a beautiful hawk, gracefully gliding on the wind currents high up in a brilliant blue sky above the tree-covered hills looking over the country side for some moving creature to carry home to its young. The keen sight of the hawk in spying its prey at great distances, its gliding ability, the speed of its dive, and precision aim in chasing its victim is amazing.

The presence of the hawk, silently circling high in the sky, went unnoticed by nearly everyone. Still the hawk watched over all below, unaffected by the busyness of the rushing world, keeping an attentive eye on the situation and meticulously planning for the future.

What a marvelous analogy to the Holy Spirit. The Spirit of God hovers over the universal church, silently but truly concerned about the well being of each of us. Few of us take time to stop and look to God and consider how quietly and gracefully he watches every detail of our lives. The Spirit of God sees the total plan of our lives, and enters to share with us every moment of the routine and challenging facets encompassing our daily lives. He goes unseen by most due to their preoccupation with worldly things and oblivion of the ethereal. Still the Holy Spirit watches over each of us quietly maneuvering our journey of faith. The Holy Spirit, more alert to our situation than the keen-sighted hawk to the demands of its family and self-preservation sees our needs and proffers the solution with greater agility and ability than humanly possible.

Because of the multitude of worldly distractions, we fail to see the swift action of the Spirit in our lives, giving credit to some person or chance phenomenon, and frequently do not appreciate or recognize the precise solution to our need or problem predetermined by the Spirit.

Just as the high-flying hawk envisions the whole terrain and surveys the prospects determining the best outcome for its family, so too the Holy Spirit meticulously plans for every move in our lives, always seeking the best. Even when there is pain or disappointment, failure, sin, or death itself, the ultimate plan of the Spirit has our best interest in mind. We, however, must stop and look above the "beautiful trees" surrounding our lives, as I did in Marquette Park to view the graceful hawk, in order to see the beauty of the Spirit hovering in the incorporeal realms of God's eternal plan. We need to be open to the movement of the Spirit, and willing to accept whatever comes, if we are to draw good from these trying experiences in order for them to become opportunities of grace.

There is a sign on the wall of the parish office which summarizes well the working of the Holy Spirit in our lives: "Good Morning. This is God. I will be handling all your problems today. I will not need your help—so have a good day." And better still is the quote from St. Thomas More on the prayer card in my Breviary which states: "Never trouble your mind for anything that shall happen to you in this world—nothing can come but what God wills." The capability of the hawk is outstanding but the proficiency of the Spirit is infinite. Remember God loves each of us with an unconditional love and cares for us with infinite wisdom. *Trust him!*

Father Henry Schmidt, September 10, 2000

Several years ago, from time to time I would go out in a small sail boat to enjoy the quiet and beauty of God's nature. Each time I set sail, I was totally at the will of the wind. Sometimes I would nearly sit in the same spot and merely ride the waves due to the lack of wind. Then there were times when it was difficult to pilot the sailfish because of the overpowering winds. But once in a while, it was a perfect delight when the sun was bright, the breeze was cooperating, and the day was blessed in so many ways.

What a wonderful analogy Jesus made when he compared his Church to a boat, for it too seems to drift listlessly at times or be tossed and tormented by the storms of our present day as well as sail peacefully and directly on course at other times.

The size, shape, color, and other accidentals of the boat have some effect on the ride, but the wind, waves, pilot, and various outside influences have a greater bearing on the sail. Consequently, keeping an eye on the goal and persevering is most essential.

We don't change the message, the message changes us. The message is the Living Word of Jesus, which leads to salvation. Accepting the message necessarily changes us. For thousands of years the "boat," the Church, has been sailing around the world and touching the lives of every generation bearing the *same message*. In every generation, efforts are made to change the message in an effort to prevent change in us.

There are periods the "boat" seems to be drifting when only a few are active but the message remains embossed in our minds, and there are times when the "boat" is tossed so drastically that it nearly sinks, yet the message is still engraved in our souls.

Apathy and worldliness result when we lower our sails by closing our minds to the Wind of the Spirit, or take our eyes off the goal and we drift, slowly allowing the message to fade. Refusing to heed the Spirit acting in our lives causes rough water and dangerous sailing as we allow the wind to drive us swiftly against the rocks of destruction or futilely struggle to sail against the strong wind of truth only to capsize. So it is most essential that we keep our eyes on the goal, and stop trying to change the message.

The best sailing is when the sun is shining, the water is calm, the breeze is blowing gently, and all is at peace. So too, God's plan is for his "boat" to sail with his son shining in our lives, guided by the wind of the Spirit, and sailing on the peaceful waters of his message with our eyes constantly on the goal, the Will of the Father. This is a must when we all sail side by side forming the beautiful faith flotilla, the parish of Little Flower.

Unable to walk on water, my Sandals stand firmly in the "boat" trusting Jesus to calm the waters of our differences. Perhaps it is time we prayerfully pull ashore and allow Jesus to again speak to us the message of salvation. As a parish family, are we really growing in faith, spreading the faith, and seeking the true goal? Sail we will! But we don't change the message; the message changes us if we are to safely attain our eternal goal.

Father Henry Schmidt, October 1, 2000

As my Sandals walked across the cemetery following the burial, a leaf fell to the ground in front of me. That leaf would never have been noticed had it not fallen at that very moment. Yet God had a purpose for that leaf just as he does for each and every one of us and for everything that affects our life.

Jesus is forever trying to speak to us, and we fail to listen. Birthdays, baptisms, funerals, meetings, Fall Festival, prayer periods, and liturgies proclaim his message, but do we hear? As one who is totally deaf in one ear, I know how difficult it is to hear in many circumstances. Thus I have to make greater effort to hear the little voices around me.

"Every voice matters in the public forum. Every vote counts. Every act of responsible citizenship is an exercise of significant individual power. We must exercise that power in ways that defend human life, especially those of God's children who are unborn, disabled, or otherwise vulnerable." (U.S. Bishops, *Living the Gospel of Life*)

Jesus expects us to be good stewards of the gifts he has given us. He has given us the gift of life, and he relies on us to protect and defend our life and that of others. Your voice speaking out and your vote cast, guided by a moral conscience are as essential of a good steward, as the wise use of your money. You may be the very one who turns the flow of society. Your voice, vote, or stand could lead others to join in the renewal of our country.

If you find that difficult to believe, then return to my single falling leaf. It alone does not make a tree beautiful nor does it give shade by itself, but it alone caught my personal attention and led me to think about the importance of "little" things, and how they can begin a process with far reaching effects. And that one leaf joined with countless others certainly changed the appearance of the cemetery. One little drop of water united with others forms a mighty sea, as one little voice or act joined with others forms a mighty force for peace, justice, and the rights of all.

The voice of the small right-to-life group of Little Flower brought about the beautiful, useful memorial to Life. The leadership of a few parishioners united many in a successful community building and enjoyable Fall Festival. The single voice of a speaker at our Pastoral Council meeting has refocused the vision of Little Flower Parish. This happens over and over again.

Trees mighty and strong gain their beauty and life from their little leaves. Little Flower is a growing tree, stalwart and vigorous, rooted in Jesus, but it too must remember it's the "little" people that give it life, beauty, and character.

As we prayerfully consider our future, our priorities, our purpose and goal, let us be mindful of the need to listen to the children, the young people, the elderly, the unborn, the handicapped, and the dying, as well as the leaders. For your voice matters, your vote counts, your act as a responsible Catholic is the exercise of significant individual power to restore moral values to a suffering misguided world. Speak, vote, and act! Let your leaf fall where it will affect others.

Father Henry Schmidt, October 8, 2000

Sitting in the dark church early one morning, as the dawn began wrestling with night, my Sandals began to contemplate light. I am not afraid of darkness, but I certainly prefer light. Light is necessary for life.

Bombarded every day by a barrage of divergent lights, do we appreciate it, or take it for granted? What feeling do we experience? Certainly we react differently to the light of the TV, the light of the lamp at night, the computer light, the light of a full moon, the bright light of the operating room, the tiny light in a cave, or the brilliance of the midday sun. And the list goes on and on, but the most moving light for me is the light of a candle, not just any candle, but the sanctuary candle. The red glow of that candle animates my spirit in a way that no other light can. That light consoles my bothered soul, brings hope to my broken spirit, and warms my hurting person like a beacon directing a battered ship safely into port. It draws me to Jesus in the tabernacle, like a burning light attracts a moth, where I am convinced my dearest and most faithful friend waits for me. Whether wandering in a world of confusing lights, noises, and distractions, or drifting aimlessly through the bleak and frightening darkness of depression, that flickering candle beckons me to trust Jesus, the Light of the world, dwelling there and patiently awaiting me.

Believe that Jesus controls all and hope in his perfect plan. That is all that keeps me going. There are times when I am concerned about the straying and lost sheep as I see the dwindling numbers gathering for worship, and I become quite disturbed. Some days I feel like the lost shepherd walking alone, and question what I am doing, so I come before the light. Then the dazzling lights of the world with their false allusions pale before the flickering candle glowing in the silent darkness of the church. There the discouragement of my failures, misguidance, and poor management are transformed by Jesus as he shows me the way back to him and the flock. He will do the same for you if only you desire it and are open to the Spirit.

Don't get discouraged if nothing seems to be happening. Frequently I feel dry and empty. My daily prayers are so routine and filled with distractions that I am tempted to give up, but I will not for that is simply the working of the devil. Like that little candle flickering before the tabernacle, the Spirit of Jesus is burning within those who persevere. At times God lets us feel dry and empty in order to help us realize our total dependence on him. God is sometimes very close to us in his seeming absence. He always loves us and accepts us as we are, with all our limitations—even with our seeming inability to pray. A humble listening is a sign of love for him and a real prayer from the heart.

And God said, "Let there be light," and there was light. God saw how good the light was. May we appreciate how good and essential it is for all life, but especially the light which alone guarantees eternal life. Today, let Jesus be that light, and you will see good. Come before the flickering tabernacle light and pray, and the light will fill you with peace, give you hope, and lead to lasting love.

Father Henry Schmidt, October 15, 2000

One day this past week, while my Sandals stared into the waste barrel in the office, after the staff had cleaned the store room, God spoke to me, not verbally, but inspirationally. As I beheld objects being tossed away, which had been useful and advantageous in past years, it became evident that now they were no longer perceived valuable. What formerly was good, was now no longer useful and consequently being replaced. Only with difficulty are we able to adjust to change, but change will have its way every day and in every aspect of our lives.

Reflecting on this insignificant change, Jesus led me to delve more deeply into life experiences in order to perceive resolutions to more serious confrontations. He placed before my mind the analogy of a ship. Imagine a well-manned ship, piloted by a capable captain who had sailed for years and traversed the globe bringing supplies to satisfied customers much to his honor and the happiness of those involved in his service.

Then unexpectedly due to some unforeseen reason the ship runs aground and is in danger of sinking. When the alarm sounds, what value is there for the captain to blame anyone? What good does it do him to announce to the passengers that I have had an exemplary record of sailing? Why bring out the records or medals from successful expeditions? All are in peril, and now all depends on working together to survive, to save the cargo and the ship itself.

Our past records of success prove real only if we are able to draw upon them in solicitous ways to repair the unwanted and usually unwarranted damage threatening to sink our ship and destroy our lives. If we are unable to make the necessary changes to better the situation for all on board, then all will end in disaster.

Consequently each of us by looking over our lives is expected to determine the "grounding" reason or problem facing our parish, school, family, or friendships. Guided by Wisdom, mature enough to accept outside analysis, flexible to suggestions, humble enough to make changes that are in the best interest of all and realizing that "my way" is not the only way nor always the best will save all from destruction.

Over the years the church has experienced many changes. Despite it all, the church, guided by the Holy Spirit, has managed to survive. But for those who clung to the past, it brought disaster, pain, unnecessary and misguided division. The present church, guided by the Spirit, moves us to new and improved changes, thereby resulting in putting aside some of the accidentals of the past.

Popes, bishops, pastors, principals, teachers, and staff are constantly being replaced and thus changes result. Marriages, births, and deaths form the cycle of family life involving changes. No one is exempted from change as we walk our faith journey. But our openness to the Spirit, our willingness to reassess our means to a goal, our concern for the good of all is necessary if there is to be peace, harmony, and progress in our church, school, and family.

Have we run aground? Let's blame no one, but maturely, compassionately, and humbly search for the way Jesus wishes us personally to change to get back on course. Happy sailing!

Father Henry Schmidt, October 22, 2000

This past week, on two occasions when I was stretching a rubber band, it snapped. My Sandals are S-T-R-E-T-C-H-E-D and I am concerned. How far can they stretch before it all snaps? In the span of six days, I have eleven meetings after supper, not counting the busy day time schedule. I mention this simply to emphasize the need that we are all stretching too far. We are stretching ourselves dangerously in every phase of life, and some are snapping. Just as the rubber band would have been of service for a much longer time had I not extended it beyond its capacity, so too our lives could be more peace-filled and of higher quality if we relaxed, trusting in Jesus!

The "peer family" has stretched our lives and undermined our family life by its futile promises of happiness. Parents, stretching their days by working multiple jobs, are thus forcibly deprived of prime time with each other and their children. The financial s-t-r-e-t-c-h, oozes into our homes like a quiet fog, blinding our vision and forcing us to take foolish risks, which all too often end in tragedy. Consequently our "wants" have become our "needs."

The "famous sports idols" have become our role models, and our expectations and demands on our children to become the person we hoped to be, but failed to achieve, now run over their lives like caramel covering an apple so that we are unable to see that the apple may be spoiled, and the life we stressfully impose on them may stretch them and us beyond fame to stress, failure, and despair. Jesus assures us of peace and happiness when we choose "ideals" to pattern our lives, while warning of the hardships for those "idol" seekers.

"Mr. and Mrs. Knowledge" are also a constant source of stress. Certainly we should encourage and support quality education, but we all too often fall into the misconception that to "do your best, you have to be the best" and countless children are so s-t-r-e-t-c-h-e-d that they not only do not like school, but become so demoralized that they lose their motivation to even try.

Let us not be unaware of one of our most flagrant causes of stretching *meetings*. We not only have a super abundance of meetings, we have meetings to plan the meetings, followed by meetings to evaluate the meetings. It is time to ascertain who we are, where we are going, and what we are doing. Where is Jesus in our total life plan, and how does our faith fit into this whole vision? If you are overstretched, then Jesus is lacking. Pills and doctors merely lubricate the "rubber band" with temporary elasticity, misleading you to s-t-r-e-t-c-h further, until you snap.

If we must stretch our lives, let's stretch them to include daily Mass, quiet personal prayer, family prayer, daily prime time for family sharing, scripture reading, or searching into the truths of our faith. We find time for all the demands of society, only to reap the bitter fruit of stress and destruction. By prioritizing our time and listening to the wisdom of the Spirit, we can replace them with those which bring peace, harmony, and purpose in our life as we s-t-r-e-t-c-h to eternal life. S-T-R-E-T-C-H we will—carefully choose the way.

Father Henry Schmidt, October 29, 2000

A few weeks ago we turned our clocks back, and enjoyed the extra hour of sleep. This past Sunday, my Sandals went back in time as I visited New Salem with some friends. I usually do so a couple times each year to enjoy the slower pace and simple lifestyle.

Imagine the peace and quiet. As I wandered about on that beautiful autumn afternoon with the sun warming the village, the leaves rustling beneath my sandals, and the smoke rising from the cabin fireplaces, reminding me of the nearness of colder days, I was drawn to a group of small girls using their imagination and enjoying making cornhusk dolls. As we moved about the village, I encountered people dressed in clothes, living and working in the style of that era—baking and cooking in open fireplaces, washing wool which had been shorn from the sheep raised there, spinning it into yarn, dying their hand-spun yarn with various colors extracted from the plants and trees of the area and then weaving or using it in a variety of ways to make clothes. Some were making shoes by hand, others were husking corn, while the blacksmith produced utensils for use in the cabins and farming, and men made wooden barrels, buckets, chairs, etc. while enjoying the help and friendship of one another.

The harvesting was finished and preparations for the long winter were underway. There was a spirit of sharing and caring for one another and even with us visitors as we enjoyed corn popped in a big black pot over an outdoor fire and apple cider, heated and spiced to warm our hearts and bodies. From time to time soothing music played by an individual or a group of villagers on the instruments of Lincoln's Day floated across the field. A hard life indeed, but a life which encouraged everyone to develop their talents and imaginations to improve their lifestyle while living a slower pace and building a closely knit family and a supportive community.

How sad we have allowed the industrial revolution to destroy such a model lifestyle! Today a large number of people are so caught up in the rush to get ahead and to achieve convenience they no longer use their imagination—the art of cooking, sewing, using our time to develop our inner self and talents, or even enjoying the simple things of nature have slipped into oblivion.

When we find "time" on our hands we are either frightened or bored and consequently fill it with noise and busyness. What great joy and wisdom lie hidden and all too often is missed because we do not take time to really know our family or fail to help them use their talents! How difficult and lonely life becomes because we neglect to interact with our neighbors!

I know we cannot turn back the time, but we can reshape our lifestyle. Life is much simpler and more fulfilling when we have less material possessions. With fewer possessions, there is a greater need for people. Needy people develop friendships through sharing talents in support of the community.

If you want happiness and time to live, if you want peace and life eternal, then slow down and enjoy those around you, take time to pray and build a faith community. Get off the "fast track" and walk with Jesus.

Father Henry Schmidt, November 12, 2000

In the corner of my office there is a Christmas package (from last year), which I neglected to give for some mysterious reason. The wrapping shows a cuddly little bear sitting at the feet of Santa and waiting to be given to some loving child. That little bear is you and me. We are special gifts waiting to be given and accepted. Every day, I see little "bears" waiting to be given the opportunity to bring happiness to others, but they are just passed over. When will we recognize the potential of those neglected people?

As my Sandals made their way to the office, I saw little bushes of flowers fighting for their lives, tossed by the strong winds, withstanding the cold temperatures, offering their beauty to those passing by and hoping someone would notice and appreciate them. How rewarding to notice family members and friends making great sacrifices to bring beauty and joy to our lives.

The melodic rhythm of the morning rush-hour traffic was broken by the cawing of the crows that were systematically relaying information to others of the approach of danger, and the finding of delectable food in some neighborhood garbage bin. Over the years the crows have migrated from the cold woods into the cities to enjoy the warmth of the heated buildings, to avoid the fear of the hunter, and to partake of the ready supply of food. Could we not learn from them?

Our patroness, St. Therese, the Little Flower, reminds us that Jesus does not expect us to do great things, but to do little things well, for God produces well with very imperfect instruments. Whether we are a small package waiting to be opened to reveal the marvels of God's plan, or a small flower blooming along the pathway, or a "crow" offering the message of life, we are all special and have something to offer.

Each week as we gather for the Eucharistic Liturgy, many "packages" are left sitting in the corner as they are not present for the celebration. Huge bouquets of "flowers" go unappreciated because they are unable to withstand the winds and cold brought on by the enticements of our secularistic society and absent themselves.

Thus the work of the "crow" (all of us) comes into play. Instinctively they have come to realize the safety, warmth, and availability of food in the midst of city rather than fight the elements of the woods, always on the watch for the hunter, and continually searching for limited food often hidden by snow or ice. They have undergone a tremendous conversion of lifestyle.

Let us open those unwrapped lives about us and learn from them. Let us look at those wonderful people adorning our faith path and imitate them. Let us leave the dangers of the world and flee to the safety of the church. How inspiring it is to see those few faithful followers of Jesus sharing their time, talent, and treasures, those gifts of God, with others! How uplifting to encounter faith-filled parishioners who bring joy, beauty, peace, and happiness to all who walk the pathway of faith! But each of us, like the crow, must do our part to warn our families and friends of the dangers of our materialistic society confronting young and old alike, as well as to lead them to Food, Jesus, who alone assures protection and lasting Life.

Father Henry Schmidt, November 19, 2000

Last week when I stopped to see my brother and sister-in-law, my nephew was beginning his annual event of making fruitcakes for Christmas. What a mess! There were containers of sliced dates, chopped nuts, and colorful fruit pieces. There were bowls of sugar, flower, seasoning, butter, and pitchers of milk along with many other ingredients soon to be mixed together. There were pans of varying sizes in which the mixture was to be placed for baking, along with spoons, scissors, and a multitude of other utensils for this massive undertaking.

As I surveyed the table, countertop, and the stove covered with this intriguing conglomeration, I saw our parish as we must look to Jesus. What a mess! Not a mess that is bad, but rather the ingredients for a beautiful end product. The many ingredients of the cake are necessary. The ability to arrange them, and the correct time of baking etc. are also important if the end result is to be not only beautiful but tasty.

There are people in our parish or family that are a bit sticky like the dates, colorful like the fruit, flavorful like the nuts, sweet like the sugar, flexible like the milk, or unifying like the butter as well as those who add various seasoning of virtues as needed. Looked at separately, we are quite a mess, but carefully blended together we are molded in the plan (pan) of Jesus. Glazed with the love of the Holy Spirit, and baked carefully by the heat of our daily graced experiences, we become beautiful to the Father.

Just as my nephew used varying sizes of pans and multiple utensils for his cakes, so does Jesus use each of us in varying capacities, yet for specific purposes. Still the small as well as the large cakes were destined to become the same colorful, solid, delicious fruitcake. So we are all destined to glorify God regardless of our size, abilities, age, or vocation?

Last Sunday night as my Sandals gathered with one of the many small faith communities of our parish, this idea was clearly brought home to me as we prayerfully considered the many wonderful parishioners who, in their individual way, are adding magnificent and necessary components to the overall flavor of our parish. Individuals, families, or groups are helping to transform our parish into the living, loving family of Jesus.

I am deeply impressed and inspired by the way Jesus uses different people for his work and the outstanding "prophets" he has placed among us. How eloquently some of these prophets proclaim! The Good News—be they little children, teenagers, young adults, or our revered elders, it is so rewarding to be a part of the ingredients making Little Flower Parish the beautiful and nourishing "cake" that Jesus lovingly offers to his Father.

In order for this "cake" to come about, there are necessarily times when things appear to be one big mess, but as Jesus carefully blends us all together, the end result is worth all the mess. During these prayerful days of Advent, are we willing to be a part of the "mess of salvation"? Only when we allow Jesus to mess up our lives can he combine all the components in an orderly way to achieve the perfect result, the salvation of all. Come, join in the mess, lick the pans, endure the heat, and enjoy the taste of the perfect cake—eternal life.

Father Henry Schmidt, December 17, 2000

My Sandals approach the incredible feast of Christmas with sadness and joy. Sadness nearly overwhelms me as I repeatedly receive letters from my Palestinian friends living in the very area where Jesus, the Prince of Peace, was born and lived, informing me of the terrible atrocities confronting them day after day, and progressively worsening. But there is joy from the realization that these faith-filled people trust that Jesus will eventually bring them peace as well as the joy I experience from all who are praying daily and fasting each Friday for this to happen soon. Never underestimate the place you play in this plan for their freedom, peace, and justice, or how this fits into the overall plan of salvation.

The feast of Christmas is a time to appreciate the "little," for God uses the little to accomplish great things. Jesus was born in Bethlehem, too small to be among the clans of Judah, yet the Lord said, "From you shall come forth from me one who is to be ruler in Israel." Jesus was born of a poor, young Jewish girl who lived in a little town of Nazareth. Our Savior came, not as a powerful ruler, but as a weak little baby. Jesus was born in one of the smallest countries, amidst the little people, suffering from the power mongers of his day. And as a result, the "little" people, beginning with the poor shepherds were the ones who recognized him. They came to him and gave what they had in order to satisfy his needs. Are we "little" enough to do the same?

How sad that today so many, who are not "great" in the estimation of modern society, have come to feel they are useless! No one, nothing is useless. Everything that God has created has supreme value, especially you.

Take for example, the tiny snowflake. Who sees any value in this beautiful, unique, quickly passing creature of God? Few people even saw it pass through their life, and few realize the great effect it has in his overall plan. Nevertheless God created it special and sent it into our lives to bring beauty, and moisture so new life could abound. Size (power), length of time (age), visibility (fame), or accumulation (fortune), add nothing to our value in God's plan, and in fact, often are problematic. Still each tiny snowflake fulfills God's plan faithfully, and so can we.

The beautiful glistening countryside, reflecting the brilliant sun, began with a "little" snowflake. Only when joined with others did it visibly affect our lives. Each day is a composition of "little" seconds which form hours, days, and years allowing us to fulfill God's will. Together we praise Jesus for our littleness, and trust in the guidance of the Spirit to use us at the time and in the way he deems best for his glory and the good of his people.

The celebration of the birth of a little babe, Christmas, has become one of our greatest church feasts. We appreciate the "little" beginning of Jesus, which eventually brought us to the moment of salvation when he conquered sin and death as he rose from the dead. Realize that Jesus is and will continue to use your "little" to achieve his great plan of salvation. May each of us give our little, and unite to make a great Christmas—Christ in our midst! Have for yourself a "Merry "little" Christmas" and a lasting life of love.

Father Henry Schmidt, December 24, 2000

As my Sandals walked lightly on the snow making my way to the final evening of the Christmas Novena, I was reminded of a couple of the meditation readings, which cautioned us about missing Jesus. In our search for Jesus great care must be taken lest we miss him.

Advent was a time of preparing for Jesus, amidst a frantic nightmare of decorating, shopping, baking, and rushing to arrange for traveling or making sure the last-minute details were all in place for Christmas day.

Recalling that Jesus came amidst the rush of the census, when everyone was arranging for their personal benefits, and so they had no room for him, most of the people in their confusion, missed Jesus. Did you?

It is hard to slow down when all around us are scurrying about in response to the pressure of our materialistic society. It is even harder to recognize Jesus who comes in his mysterious ways into the lives of each of us.

Jesus seeks to enter our lives in the most inconvenient times and through the most unwanted people. Is he welcome? He was born in a cold, dark, smelly stable amid stinking animals with only a few street people present. Today he still tries to enter into our lives when people are unkind and cold to us—overpowering us and demeaning. Let him enter to bring warmth and love. Jesus seeks a place in the hearts of those who suffer from the total darkness, resulting from death of a loved one. Make room for the light of the world.

When I was in Israel, I visited the shepherds living in their tents with their animals, and I held one of the lambs; the smell was intense. Why would Jesus choose to enter this world in such a humbling way? Today, as never before, Jesus asks to enter into those "stinky" moments of your lives resulting from separation and divorce. Just as the sheep are the hope of the shepherds who live with them and care for them, so Jesus longs to enter into your "smelly" lives and bring you hope. Are we humble enough to overlook the fact that everything is not in perfect condition and allow him to share this "mess" and refresh us with his Spirit?

Sadly, since the "society" people of his day were too preoccupied, God sent the "street" people, the shepherds, to share the Good News of salvation. God saw goodness in these humble, needy, hurting outcasts and gave them life as they offered themselves. Do we see Jesus there too? If we are unable to see him in these people, the crib remains empty.

We have just celebrated Christmas, that great event in Salvation History, the birthday of Jesus. Hopefully everything was ready—the manger and crib, the tree up, the lights arranged outdoors, the gifts wrapped, the goodies baked, the meals arranged, and the cards mailed. But what about you? Did Jesus find room in your heart? Is your life still cold, dark, and stinky, then stand up, rejoice, and welcome Jesus, the Prince of Peace, the Light of the World, and let our Savior fill "the crib," your heart. Jesus is here. He misses you, don't miss him!

Father Henry Schmidt, December 31, 2000

Sometimes I feel like Rumpelstiltskin, the man who fell asleep and when he finally woke up things had changed so much he didn't know what was going on. It is hard to believe that Y2K has come and gone, Christmas is past, and this school year is half over. Wake me up before it is too late. We are beginning a new year filled with opportunities and blessings from God, but what will we do with them?

During these past few weeks, my Sandals have shoveled more snow than normal, which has remained on the ground for a longer period than we usually experience. While repeatedly removing the newest accumulation, I realized it is much like our life patterns. When the snow became a little dirty, it was covered over with a new layer, but the old dirt remained beneath. This temporary cover-up or pretentious renewal must eventually give way before new life will evolve; as winter gives way to spring, death is conquered by life. During this new year, let us resolve to stop covering up or excusing our faults and imperfections, and make the needed effort to achieve a real conversion in our lives.

Driving north these past few days clearly revealed the dangers of traveling on ice and snow-covered highways, as one beheld huge eighteen wheelers toppled on their side or worse, cars, trucks, and vans upside down or half buried in the snow in the medium and ditches. Apparently some fail to acknowledge the hazards of winter driving and recklessly rush to disaster, at times even fatal, just as many fail to listen to Jesus and carelessly live their faith.

Fresh falling snow is beautiful. A marvelous sight to behold as it gently and quietly covers over the ugliness of winter or glistens like diamonds in the glorious rays of the sun. But one also needs wisdom of maturity to enjoy this gift of God to move about safely and achieve our hoped-for destination. Is that not the same with life?

When God gifted us with life, he gave each of us a time period in which to get to know his son Jesus. He made life exciting and enjoyable. He placed the necessary helps, the Sacraments, the Mass, prayers, our parents and families and friends, and countless grace stations along the way. His competitor, the devil, then began to shower our lives with "snow" those beautiful and enticing temptations of life. Deluded by the "snow," which makes our wrong doings look less serious, we rush through life dangerously risking everything: loss of spouse, family, faith, friends, reputation, and even salvation itself. We trust the "snow" will cover our sin and make it look OK, but the "dirt," sin, is still beneath.

Jesus longs to be the center and pattern of our lives, our light and source of love, and our final goal. He is the son of God, the "sun" that melts away the "snow," reveals the truth and offers life. The "snow" will melt as we stand before our God. What will remain? For the faithful follower of Jesus, who carefully avoids the danger spots of the "snow," there will be fullness of life. May we make those essential changes, which empower us to clear the path and walk carefully with Jesus! It's time to shovel the "snow."

Father Henry Schmidt, January 7, 2001

39

Each day since Christmas, as I walk into the sacristy, I behold a little soft pink rabbit sitting on the table. When I took the crib figures from the closet before Christmas, this cute stuffed rabbit was found inside one of the figures. This rabbit was deprived of a place at the crib with the other animals simply because it's not our custom to have rabbits at Christmas, but at Easter.

Frequently, we miss the splendor of the unusual because we are programmed by custom and tradition. I'm quite sure that everyone would have noticed and questioned the presence of this pink rabbit had I placed it among the other animals gathered before the manger. When Jesus came among the people of his community, he was not welcome because he was looked upon as a "pink rabbit." He broke with tradition; he dared to be different. He was not accepted by those who upheld custom and tradition to a fault.

A King born as a baby in a manger, a powerful leader without any weapons, a man who respected and elevated the status of women, a high priest who offered his own life in place of the ordinary sacrifice, a person who welcomed and dined with sinners, one who loved everyone equally and unconditionally—this was not their custom and tradition—this was a class A "pink rabbit." Only a few welcomed Jesus. What a rewarding surprise resulted!

All too frequently, we fall into a pattern of life to which we become accustomed, or it becomes pleasing and fulfilling and we overlook the newness and usual experiences that God repeatedly offers to add beauty and excitement to the "ordinary." Look for those "pink rabbits."

What a delight to suddenly discover a child who sings or plays an instrument with great proficiency or an adult who brings a new dimension to the choir, the liturgy, or the parish life! How thrilling to welcome someone, into a new leadership role, who would have been overlooked because to all appearances they were "pink rabbits" and did not fit the customary scheme of action—breaking with tradition, daring to be different, rewarding surprises result!

As we begin a new year, we treasure the past accomplishments and are indebted to those whose sacrifices brought them to fruition, but there is an abundance of untapped wealth waiting to be identified and woven into our lives. Little Flower Parish is blossoming into a beautiful faith community encompassing a variety of cultures with differing gifts and practices of prayer and worship. What a marvelous font of spiritual blessings offered in the unusual! Let us readily welcome the new and different gifts of the Spirit as we invite these lovely people with their diverse customs and ideas to take an active role in our parish. Look around and notice the "pink rabbits" and encourage them to become involved in the faith life and leadership roles of our parish. Their presence is worth notice, but not to be questioned.

Everyone is special, unique, and has been blessed abundantly by God. Appreciating our personal friendship with Jesus, may we search for new ways to live A Stewardship Way of Life, appreciating that which is customary, alert to the unusual, and welcoming "pink rabbits" into our parish activities and faith life.

Father Henry Schmidt, January 14, 2001

Looking out the window on this dark and dreary day, my Sandals see piles of dirty snow, waiting to be obliterated by the heat of the sun or warm spring rain, trying desperately to cover the bare, black fields littered with dry leaves and other signs of death. But with eyes of a visionary, I can see the new life and beauty God is planning that will soon excite and revitalize our waning spirits.

This past Sunday, I joined in celebrating the ninetieth birthday of a "young" man who was surrounded by his family and friends. Also present were several of the men with whom he worked for years. With the eyes of youth, here was a man, old, useless, and perhaps even somewhat of a bother. True, he was not young in "age," but he was young at heart as he welcomed and celebrated life and his many blessings. What a delight to watch him joke and enjoy the interesting gifts he received!

The "snow," weather worn and not as pretty as in bygone years, was not waiting for the end. For he was a man still offering life and joy to all who crossed his path. In the eyes of a "senior," he was an example of aging with grace and dignity. Limited, but not stymied in his efforts to live, he continued to reach out and nurture new life while quietly and reverently preparing for the greater life to come.

As we patiently face these dreary winter days, hopefully we are not engulfed in an endurance contest, but rather are able to use this time to rest and rejuvenate our bodies and spirits for the rush of new life and activity resulting from the approach of spring.

Although each birthday reveals signs of aging, facing those piles of dirty snow, dead leaves, and barren fields, our aches and pains should not result in depression but a time of visualizing how we can still be of some value and help to others. We do not die because we grow old, but we grow old when we die. When we give up and fail to anticipate how God uses everyone, regardless of age or ability, then we die—mentally, emotionally, spiritually, and physically.

How rejuvenating to see, this humble "young" man celebrating his ninetieth birthday with so much life, as well as to observe the great number of "elders" of our parish witnessing their determination to minister, and function actively. Hats off to those who are working with our children in school; those who are cleaning our beautiful church each Friday; those who take part in the Young at Heart; those who actively participate in the various parish organizations; those helping with Meals on Wheels; those serving the community as "Care Givers"; those who join us for the morning Liturgies etc.

Society today tends to ignore and abandon anyone who is not young, beautiful, and talented. Let us encourage our young people to see the beauty and value of our "grand" people. Externally they may have diminished in beauty, but internally there is immense luster. Remember, beneath the aging melting snow, one can discover the fertile soil bursting with possibilities of new life. So life at nine, ninety, or ninety-nine is meant to be celebrated, shared, and reverenced. Every birthday is designed to be an advancement to that true and lasting life of heaven, eternal spring.

Father Henry Schmidt, January 21, 2001

As my Sandals stood before the office kitchen sink, waiting for the water to drain, I realized a remarkable comparison to people. We are a composition of faucets and drains. When both are in good condition, then all goes well, but when the faucet becomes clogged with lime, permitting only a trickle of water or gives rusty water trouble abounds. When the drain is clogged with garbage allowing the waste water to drain slowly or completely stop, then problems result.

God has made each of us to be a giving person, a faucet flowing with fresh, *life-giving* graces, and blessings. We must limit our outpouring of what should be done, or how it should be done. Even though it is good, if the sink is not large, like in our office, you experience an overflow. Remember sinks vary in size, so we have to regulate the inflow in order to give the drain time to dispose of what is coming in. So too, we must always carefully note the variances in the maturity of those to whom we are offering guidance or assistance. Gently and lovingly we are to supply the needs of others but not overwhelm them. Cautiously we must check to see if something has blocked their "drain" so they cannot properly receive what is being offered.

Likewise we must be careful that we are not offering rusty "water," due to our inability to accept those updated changes guided by the Holy Spirit in our church, for then no one will drink and complications will result. Also we must check our pipeline, our personal relationship with Jesus, to see if the line is clear and the pressure is good so we are able to give what he chooses to speak and witness through us. Failing this free-flowing relation with Jesus, we cannot supply our children and others with the needed help and guidance they require and rightfully expect from us.

God has made each of us to be a receiving person, but we are to be careful that we do not allow too much garbage to clog our "drain pipe," our minds, lest what we receive overflow and bring havoc into our lives and those around us. When we receive the Good News in the amount and at the times we need it and do not let things clog our drain, we become a well-functioning person. Fresh water from Jesus with the help of others to maintain well draining sinks guarantees the proper flow of grace, as well as the appropriate disposal of failures and sins in our lives.

We, like any sink, will receive garbage, and unless we have a "garbage disposal," in good working condition, we will certainly clog up. Consequently, we need to find ways to limit the garbage poured into our lives, and the means to dispose of it more efficiently.

Most do not like personal changes. However, sometimes it is necessary to replace the faucets and pipes bringing in clean water, and disposing of refuse. Ask Jesus to guide you in making such essential changes through prayer, the sacrament of reconciliation, and the guiding support of mature, humble, holy people.

So check your plumbing. Be a faucet flowing with clean, cool "life-giving water" to others as needed, and a sink to receive the truth, with an open drain and a functioning garbage disposal to prevent any blockage of grace. Trust Jesus, the plumber.

Father Henry Schmidt, January 28, 2001

Seeing our car in the lot with a flat tire, reminded me of Lent, that period of prayerful contemplation, which advocates us to do more than "giving up" things, unless it is sin and humbly focus on the unique person we are, abundantly blessed by our loving God.

What value or purpose do you see in your life? We live in a very competitive society which continually demeans us if we are not the first or the very best. As a result, it is very hard to love ourselves with a Christlike love. Yet Jesus loves each one of us unconditionally.

A beautiful car capable of fulfilling a variety of needs becomes useless due to a flat tire. Occasionally we are that flat tire. As a member of a family, we are essential to the total shared values and workings of the family. But failing to appreciate who we are and what we are capable of doing, we become as a flat tire, and we destroy the efficiency of the home life. We are also a vital part in the parish community, be it a big or a small function, the total performance depends on the quality of each part. Just as a beautiful car becomes useless due to a simple flat tire, so the faith life of a beautiful parish, established to respond to the needs of many, is lessened or stifled if we neglect our part. The parish cannot function properly if any part, as a flat tire, prevents it from moving forward. Little things play an important part in the working of the whole, be it a car, family, or parish—and those "little things" are you and me.

Jesus went out into the desert to fast and pray in order to prepare himself for his public life. His public life witnesses his openness to the will of his Father, and his willingness to sacrifice *all* for us. May we assess our goals and our special place in God's plan, as we check the four tires of a stewardship way of life—time, talent, treasure, and faith.

God, the giver of *time*, has granted us a period of life in order to know him, and those around us. Are we willing to take advantage of our Sunday Liturgy, Follow Me, GIFT, Small Faith Communities, Bible Studies, Koinonia, Promise Keepers, coffee and doughnut Sunday, etc., to attain a deeper understanding of Jesus and fellow parishioners, so the total parish faith life may experience a rejuvenation, as strangers become friends, and Jesus is seen as our special friend.

Gifted with various *talents*, we are invited by Jesus to share them, even without charge, to prepare other members of parish and family to function in a useful manner for the good of the whole, both around the parish church and school and among the parish families.

Possessions and *treasures* unshared are no better than a new car with a flat tire, for no one benefits. But to the one who shares generously and willingly, Jesus promises "a good measure, pressed down, shaken together, running over will be poured into your life; for the measure you give will be the measure you get back."

Faith in Jesus is the catalyst by which one lives a stewardship way of life. Such a believer realizes his uniqueness, potential, interdependence, and vital importance to parish, family, and self. Living faith assures us that we have a "spare tire," Jesus, as a replacement when one of the other three, time, talent, or treasure goes flat. Let this Lent be a time to check our "tires," and remember we all need to use the "spare tire" from time to time.

Father Henry Schmidt, February 18, 2001

This past week my Sandals were confronted with another problem as the sump pump in the rectory began malfunctioning. The pump could never stop running due to ice blockage in the line preventing the water from flowing into the yard, thus frustrating the pump and depriving the yard of life-giving water.

This is the last Sunday before Lent—a time when most everyone pauses to plan for a profitable Lenten season. A good time to check our grace sump pump. Are we allowing Jesus to pump life into us? Are we pumping that grace life into others around us or blocking the source or the pipe?

Every moment of our lives in the peace, love, and life of Jesus seeps into our souls, in the hopes that we will pump that life into our families, friends, and parishioners, but there may be a blockage, thus causing his grace pump to run endlessly by frustrating his work.

Little Flower Liturgy Team has chosen *Cultivating Our Relationship with Christ* as our overall theme for this blessed season. Everyone knows that in order to cultivate relationships there needs to be an open line of communication. We also realize that in cultivating a seed, there has to be an open line of water if there is to be life. So too, a line of spiritual water is essential for the life of our soul.

Jesus pumps life-giving grace into our souls through the Eucharist where we eat and drink at the table of the Lord; through the sacrament of reconciliation where we clean out clogged grace lines and through prayer, fasting and sharing with the poor.

There is no question in my mind that Jesus is abundantly pouring his grace life into our parish. However, it appears that some pumps are malfunctioning or some pipelines are clogged. This Lent, invite Jesus to come and check out the difficulty. Ask him to fix your pump and to remove whatever is clogging your spiritual lifeline to him, your family, and others. Perhaps you have drifted too far from Jesus, the "sun" who warms your spirit with the message of faith and consequently your pipeline has frozen.

Cultivating our relationship with Jesus means being open to the movement of his Spirit allowing him to lead us wherever he wishes, to prune us where needed, and to speak the truth as we listen with an open heart. All too frequently, the bitter coldness of people around us and the situations in which we must work and live gradually "freeze" us, closing off honest communication with Jesus. When that results, we cannot expect to cultivate a lasting, mature relationship with others.

Seeds die from bitter cold, lack of moisture, or lack of nourishment. Souls also need to dwell in the warming embrace of Jesus as he strengthens them on the nourishment of his Word, and supplies moisture through his body and blood. Spring is a time when farmers and gardeners break up the hard lifeless soil, plant the new seeds, and cultivate a special relationship with the new life. Lent is the spring of the Liturgical Year, when Jesus breaks up the hardness of our souls and plants the new seeds of love. Let him check your pump and thaw your blocked grace lines. May you *cultivate a renewed relationship with Christ!*

Father Henry Schmidt, February 25, 2001

Years ago, when I was young and working on the family farm, before we had tractors, my father farmed with horses, as did all the neighboring farmers. It would not be unusual to see pastures dotted with horses grazing, and it was normal each spring, summer, and fall to see them working the fields. It was the joy of a farmer to have a good "team" of horses, for even though many horses were working in the fields, few of them would work as a team. Individual horses all working in the same field often caused problems because one more powerful or energetic would outdo another and if the one planting worked faster than the one preparing the ground, it would be forced to stop, and time was wasted. It was essential when two or more horses were teamed together that they work harmoniously or great damage resulted to crops, and machinery, and the very life of the farmer was endangered. When two or more horses would work side by side as a team, they could accomplish much more and harmony would prevail. Likewise the farmer who had sons to "team" with him was blessed indeed, for while one prepared the soil, the other could be planting, when one was harvesting, the other could be hauling and storing.

It was sad to see the horses replaced by machines because with their passing, "team" work also disappeared and competition prevails. The biggest, fastest, most modern machines have divided most farmers, and only a few family farms are left where neighbors share work.

As my Sandals have served parishes varying in size, it has become evident that those parishes, where everyone worked as a team, grew in faith, developed a family spirit, experienced peace and harmony, and were blessed abundantly.

In many ways, our Little Flower Faith Community works together as a "team" and shares in the responsibilities, accountability, and blessings of our labors. We are gifted with an active parish and an exceptional school with many talented and sacrificing people witnessing faith and ministering to God's people with hard-working organizations and faith-building groups. Yet tensions and divisions from lack of team work damage our mission and hurt our people.

During the season of Lent, we are invited to look over our personal lives to discover how we are modeling our lives after Christ, who revealed to us the pattern of team work, as he shared with his apostles and disciples. Each time they neglected or refused to listen to him or work with him, problems resulted, and eventually it led to his very destruction.

We cannot work as individuals seeking our own goals, competing for recognition, striving for domination, and neglecting the feelings and needs of others any more than two horses not "team" trained could be expected to work in harmony. Disaster and destruction will result.

Being a "team" implies that we must work together, make concessions for our differences, overlook our imperfections, and discern the goal or mission which Jesus has designed for us. We are a team; each of us has much to give, have much we need; as a team we share our work in ways which benefit all. Peace, unity, and love abound when we "yoke" with Jesus, who says "My yoke is easy and my burden is light." Let him lead our team!

Father Henry Schmidt, March 4, 2001

Several years ago, I was driving home on an extremely dark and foggy night. After driving for some time, due to the density of the fog, I became disoriented. I knew I was on the right highway, but I was unable to see any recognizable signs to ascertain how far I had traveled. It was very unnerving because I never knew when a sharp curve or T-junction would suddenly confront me. Then too, I was unsure when an impatient driver would try to pass me or an oncoming car would approach. Nearly overwhelmed with a sense of helplessness and inability in deciding my future direction, all I could do was to remain on the highway and carefully continue on my journey trusting in the protection of Jesus. Only when I came to an intersection powerfully lighted could I determine what still lay ahead on my journey home.

It seems to me that some people on their spiritual journey are in a comparable situation. Aware that they are on the right road to salvation, believing the Catholic faith, they seem to be journeying in a dense fog. Unable to appreciate the marvelous signs of God's love, they continue on, hoping to arrive at their planned destination, while deprived of his friendship. Large numbers of people routinely neglect to gather and actively celebrate the liturgy, or regularly come late to Mass, or leave early because the "fog" of secularism blocks their clear view of what is happening. Blinded by the blurring fog of false security, they overlook the real presence of Jesus in the tabernacle and fail to perceive the *miracle* right before their eyes when Jesus changes bread and wine into his body and blood. Lives fogged over with busyness of the "jet" age, they seemingly are prevented from seeing the special gifts beneficial to the betterment of their spiritual life, be it the frequent use of the sacraments or participating in the special life-giving gatherings.

Driving in the fog is always dangerous because of unknown curves and the reckless driving habits of others, and a foggy spiritual life is also risky. The brighter the car lights, the more difficult it is to see clearly because of the glare. The greater the glaring lights of possessions, power, position, the less clearly we are able to see the light of Christ. Driving safely in fog demands care. Recklessness ends in disaster. Slowly we must extinguish the glare of the world in order to see the way Christ is leading, if we are to avoid spiritual disaster.

Be alert to the recklessness of those around you, who rush through the fog of life, lest they force you off the path or crash into you on your faith journey. Sudden stops may confront you when you approach a T-junction requiring you to alter your faith journey. Carefully pass through the fog of confusion and turn the way that leads you safely home to heaven and life with Jesus.

Lent is the time to examine our spiritual road map and to come out of the fog, so we can clearly determine the will of Jesus. Lent is the time to walk in the light and appreciate the beautiful blessings and graces on our spiritual journey. Follow Jesus, the true light, who clearly shows the way and offers the truth leading us safely home. Proceed slowly and carefully if you find yourself in a "spiritual fog." Stop if necessary and ask for help to clearly see Jesus. He is always there waiting just for you.

Father Henry Schmidt, March 18, 2001

46

FOR SALE! Regularly we read signs of yard sales, garage sales, store sales, and we are tempted to stop for a bargain. Usually it is not a bargain. But that is of little concern. But *who* is for sale is a great concern.

In the book of Genesis, we read of the most "costly" apple which the snake sold to our first parents as a bargain. That sale changed our lives for all times. Later we have the sale of Joseph, by his brothers, into slavery. This bargain also changed the lives of God's chosen people and his plan of salvation. Moving on, we have the sale of Jesus, by his close friend. Gradually the sale of *who* worsened until the ultimate devastation resulted. True, the sale of the apple and of Joseph affected our lives, but the sale of Jesus is shocking, beyond our comprehension. We condemn Judas harshly and find no excuse for his actions. But wait, be careful.

Time and time again, we still see people placing Jesus on the auction block, in our world of extreme competition, as we bargain with the lives of our spouses, families, and coworkers. We are disappointed in our first parents for their bargaining and frustrated at the brothers of Joseph for their jealousy, but it is baffling that we fail to recognize Jesus in the flea-bargaining we do to attain some personal "bargain." Forgetting who it is we are selling, we speak some untruth or exaggerate to put down some person in order to elevate ourselves falsely just to attain personal gain. When we did, we sold Jesus. That great bargain which was more important than sharing prime time with our spouse or family—was it worth the price we placed on our loved ones?

What is the bargain if we neglect to live a stewardship way of life and spend our treasures on material things while neglecting the spiritual? Look carefully at the bargains the world offers, and you will likely see that you are being asked to sacrifice the spiritual. When Adam and Eve bargained, they wanted to better themselves, but they ignored the will of God. Joseph's brothers, overcome with envy, hoping to get more of their father's attention, sold themselves into slavery. Judas, disappointed that Jesus was not establishing a powerful, worldly kingdom, decided to pursue his ends by another means, and ended in despair. There may be some good bargains in the world of material possession, but there is no justification for "selling" someone, no matter how insignificant, for then we are selling Jesus.

Lent is a good time to stop and see *who* is for sale in our lives. Politically, as we destroy our leaders by our smear comments, we sell Jesus. As Catholics, we unite to stop the sale of our teachers, leaders, personnel, and family members by the scathing criticism which undermines our moral foundation and ethical principles. Thus, we remove the "For Sale" sign from Jesus.

Our country is forever scarred by the horrible sale of the Afro Americans into slavery, and the painful annihilation of our Native Americans. Therein we sold Jesus. We cannot change our history, but we must protect our future. Jesus bore the "For Sale" sign to pay for our bargains. Together we are challenged to remove all *"Who is for sale"* signs.

Father Henry Schmidt, March 25, 2001

During this past week, my Sandals were confronted by two bishops, and I have been deeply tormented by both encounters.

The first was viewing the conversion of Archbishop Romero of El Salvador. A man who, satisfied with the lifestyle surrounding him and enjoying the pleasures and benefits of the rich, was slowly drawn into the pain of injustice afflicting the poor of his parish. Fighting for the rights of the poor resulted in incredible suffering for his people, priests, and self. The process of pulling away from the will of the government leaders and the upper class was as painful as the stripping of Jesus of his clothes. Standing up for the rights of the marginalized was comparable to Jesus carrying his cross, and rebuking the government and the powerful rich ended in "crucifixion," his death from the assassin's bullet while celebrating Mass.

His conversion deeply bothers me, because it is seemingly similar to mine or yours. What am I doing for God's least? All too frequently, I seem to be complacent with the situation and the lifestyle of our modern world. I try to avoid situations, which remind me of those experiencing a different social or economic level than mine. I give token donations, from my surplus, to various Lenten collections or needs throughout the year, but do little to change their situation. I must stop giving charity, assure justice, and provide them ways to improve themselves.

The second encounter was with Bishop James Walsh, who said, "To be a Missioner is to go where you are needed but not wanted; and to stay until you are wanted but not needed." Each of us is called by Jesus to be a missioner. How hard to respond to this call of Christ and leave my comfort zone! I need not leave my home, parish, or country to answer his call. I am to do it here and now in my home, school, parish, and community. It is much more gratifying to go where I am wanted than to go where I am needed. I am needed where there is injustice and suffering, and I am wanted and welcome where I cause no issues of conflict to surface. I know that I fail. I acknowledge my need for conversion to imitate Archbishop Romero and to listen to Bishop Walsh and become a true missioner.

In my room is a poster, which was in the church this past week, which states: "Through the eyes of faith, the starving child, the believer in jail, and the woman without clean water or health care are not issues, but *Jesus in disguise.*" Each day, Jesus comes to me in a different disguise, and I fail to recognize him. Disguised as family members, parishioners, and fellow workers, he enters my life, and I reject him. I am rich and Jesus starves in the poor children. I am free while Jesus is confined to jail in the innocent person, falsely condemned. I don't recognize baby Jesus when I neglect to speak out against abortion. I am oblivious to Jesus on death row and an accomplice to the demeaning of women. My silence reveals that I need a conversion of heart, and I dare not claim to be a missioner. Pray for me, your pastor, that I may recognize Jesus in any disguise and empowered by the Spirit, experience a "Romero" conversion and respond to the call of Jesus, like Bishop Walsh, and dare to be a true missioner.

Father Henry Schmidt, April 1, 2001

My Sandals were disappointed again this year when I was too busy to go out and fly a kite. I love flying kites, sailing in hot air balloons, and watching geese migrate in their beautiful V formation. Those experiences are always so uplifting and freeing of spirit.

But back to flying a kite—we are God's kite. Kite flying is a real challenge. If all the parts are not properly arranged, the kite will not fly at all, or go around in crazy loops, or go up only to suddenly swoop down and crash.

The parts of the kite must be fitted together in proportion, just as the body of Christ, his church must work together. The kite material must be strong, but not too heavy, the cross beams must be correctly placed, the string must be securely attached, and the length of the string determines how high and far it will soar. When all are in correct proportion and in good shape, the kite flyer experiences the thrill of success.

God has carefully constructed our Little Flower Kite. We have given him good material, our faith life, which is strong and durable but not too bulky to hamper our parish from flying high. The cross stave supporting the material of the "kite" is sturdy because its main beam is constructed of the wisdom of our many devoted, self-sacrificing elders, which uphold the cross beam, the vitality of our youth. The tail, which is in proper proportion, keeps the kite in balance because it has ministries which allow everyone to be an active part of the parish life. And the string is unending as we pray, work, love, and share our time, treasure, and talents with the least as well as the greatest, and always for the glory of God and the good of all. What a thrill to behold the Little Flower Kite soars when held firmly in the hands of Jesus, the Kite flyer!

It is hard to construct a good kite. It is difficult to fly a kite. At times the wind is not strong enough, or its velocity is too forceful, and there are times when the rain prevents kite flying. So too, with the Little Flower Kite, there is always need to examine the construction of our kite. The parish, our "kite," must not be overloaded with any one or too many organizations or ministries or it will not soar. The wind of the Spirit, infusing life into a united school and parish raises us up so we can lead others to Jesus. United and guided by the Spirit, we ride the storm winds, the constant attacks of immature divisive people who strive to down our kite. But the greatest hindrance of our "kite" flying results from the rain, the "crepe hangers," who by their apathy void any possibility of it remaining airborne.

Each and every one of us is a vital part of God's kite, and is responsible to do all in our power to make it fly. Our loving Father continues to supply us the materials for a good kite, and Jesus longs to hoist our "kite," Little Flower Parish, to thrill all the community. Placing ourselves in the hands of the Master Kite Maker, Jesus, may he during this season of Lent, repair any damage to his "kite" as we grow in faith and unity, allowing the wind of the Spirit to blow us where he chooses. The length of the string we furnish Jesus to fly our "kite" depends on our trust in his will. The greater our trust in him, the higher our parish will soar, and all who see will thrill in the work of God revealed in our faith lives. Come, let's fly our "kite."

Father Henry Schmidt, April 8, 2001

49

My Sandals encountered many faith experiences this past week, but two of them helped me prepare for Easter.

One day last week, I walked for several hours in the woods. Warmed by the sun returning from its southern vacation, I sat beside the running stream, which played intricate melodies as the water fell on the rocks; I was listening to the spring songs of the birds and watching the delicate little butterflies flit from flower to flower, which were transforming the ugly winter-worn hillsides into a colored patchwork of new life. After some time, I resumed my walk, whereupon I saw my first snake of spring and immediately retraced my steps, leaving the area for safer surroundings.

This inspired me to consider the journey of Lent. Lent began when it was cold and dark, but as the weeks moved along, the days got brighter and the sun warmer. We started Lent with cold, dark, heavy hearts, but as we drew nearer to Jesus, through our grace conversion, they became brighter and the coldness of our hearts warmed with the presence of the Son of God. New views of our families and friends made our lives more peace-filled and as we came to recognize their individual beauty, our lives were transformed from drab divisive days of criticism to glorious days of recognizing their inner beauty and giftedness, for *there was Jesus.*

In the Garden of Eden, evil was depicted as a snake, and when I met the snake in the woods, I turned quickly for a safer path. During Lent, we likewise faced the "snakes" sins of our lives, and have changed our pathway, leaving the "snakes" behind to follow the light of Christ.

As the day ended, I met my nephew working the ground in preparation for planting and as I rode the tractor with him, we saw two to three dozen wild turkeys in the field at some distance from where we were working. The toms were strutting with their tails fanned in glorious array trying to attract the females during the mating season in preparation for new life.

All these signs of new life, manifested in his works of nature, help delineate inner thoughts of how Jesus comes even more in the fullness of our renewed spiritual life.

The second faith experience was at our Small Faith Community sharing when someone read a poem, "The Garment of God." The more I contemplated that reading, the more I realized we are the garment of God, each and every one of us. Each of us adds color, character, purpose, and value. Just as each creature of the woods adds its own individual gift, so do we in this garment of God. Some are the inner garments and are seen only partially or occasionally, some are the outer more visible adornment. Some add class, and some add texture or strength, but all of us have a unique purpose and eternal value. Some garments are worn at certain times, while others are needed all the time. Some parts of God's attire are very practical and some embellish, but all make visible Jesus, risen in glorious splendor and living in everything and everyone around us.

Renewed by our Lenten fasting, prayers, and almsgiving, we celebrate our change of heart and renewed life united as the multicolored garment of the risen Christ. *Happy Easter.*

Father Henry Schmidt, April 15, 2001

The bulb is blooming beautifully on the sanctuary wall of our church, as a result of the many hours Theresa spent each week caring for the growth of this bulb. Each week it continued to grow and bud until it produced beautiful blossoms. Our goal for Lent was to "Cultivate our relationship with Christ." And we spend hours preparing for this deeper, personal relationship.

The fruit of our work was quite evident on Easter when our church was filled with faith renewed parishioners, gathered to sing, pray, and worship Jesus risen from the dead. The cultivating of our relationship with Jesus does not end with Easter, but continues with a greater awareness of what is required to assure we will produce lasting fruit.

We were gifted by Jesus with the "seed of faith," and we pruned away the dead and diseased branches when we gathered for the parish communal penance service and were reconciled to Jesus and those around us. We fertilized that seed by our prayer life and the sacrifices we made to participate in Mass, stations, religious presentations following the soup suppers, and by participating in the Follow Me discussions or Small Faith Communities. We nourished the seed on the bread of life and watered it with the blood of Jesus poured out for salvation. And the warm love of Jesus, revealed in scripture, poured upon each of us so extravagantly gave growth and health to even the weakest and smallest among us. Jesus offers all that we need to grow spiritually, to blossom, and bear lasting fruit. It is up to us to call upon him for these graces, he never forces, nor does he deny us the necessary guidance and help we need.

I have several amarella plants which I care for each year hoping they will bloom, but they do not respond to my TLC (tender loving care). So too we, who have worked hard this Lent to achieve a conversion, may also be faced with the reality that God has a different plan for us. Once we have acknowledged our need to change, we then have to rely on God for the grace to do so, as well as accept his time plan of spiritual growth. Each year my amarellas shoot up beautiful foliage, but they do not bring the gorgeous bloom I long for. In like manner, even though our efforts of conversion during Lent bring forth new hopes and dreams, we may have to wait for the fulfillment of our endeavors.

There is great satisfaction in seeing spiritual accomplishments as we celebrate new life during the Easter season, but we can likewise experience great spiritual growth when we fail to achieve our goal. Then we become more aware of our total dependence on Jesus. Humbled, we are better prepared to acknowledge our imperfections and call on Jesus to reveal his plan. Open to his plan, we trust he will empower and guide our renewed efforts to nurture our relation with him.

Our efforts at nurturing our relationship with Jesus must be ongoing, or else they are futile. As we decorate the church with beautiful multicolored flowers for Easter, we realize that it is a passing beauty, which will soon wilt and die. So too whatever accomplishment made in our spiritual growth will last only for a short time unless we remain focused on Jesus, the risen Lord who offers new life, in his own way and time. Christ is risen, he offers you life, cultivate it.

Father Henry Schmidt, April 22, 2001

When you look at some one, are you more concerned with what you see or who you see? This past Sunday we celebrated the feast of Corpus Christi, the body of Christ. Hopefully we celebrated *our* unity, for Jesus tells us we are the body and he is the head. This beautiful feast honoring the Eucharistic Presence of Jesus in the bread and wine offered at each Mass, emphasizes our oneness in him. Do we see Jesus in everyone around us?

Leonardo da Vinci spent years painting the last supper, carefully searching for the right person to depict Jesus and each of the twelve apostles. His search and painting of the picture took over seven years. After meticulously searching, Leonardo da Vinci found the perfect man he needed to depict Jesus, and then for each of the other apostles, until he came to Judas. He could not find the live model to convey his vision of Judas, until he found a man in prison. When the picture was finally completed, the prisoner asked Leonardo da Vinci, "Do you know who I am?" to which he replied, "No, I had never seen you in my life until you were brought before me out of the dungeon in Rome." The prisoner then said, "I am the same man you painted just seven years ago as the figure of Christ."

The Body of Christ, one and the same, but because of outward appearances he failed to see him. How easily we overlook the Christ within the people we meet, and judge by outward appearances! As we celebrate the feast of Corpus Christi we recall those words of scripture, which remind us that we are created in the image and likeness of Jesus. We need to look beyond the physical and search within to recognize Jesus in whatever disguise he may be using at the moment. We, like the blind man of scripture, need to pray "Lord that I may see" in order to see beyond the externals.

Jesus, in the unacceptable makeup and unusual attire of the young man living next door, in the varying color of people of other races, in the neighbor or coworker who burdens my life, in those who do not qualify as beauty queens or models of the macho man, in the wrinkled body of the lady burdened with Alzheimer, or those who live different lifestyles than we, are all part of the body of Christ, just as much as we. If I am unable to accept this truth, then I may find that I am a withering branch, cut from the vine or dismembered from the living body of Jesus. How often, due to a lack of clear vision or spiritual insight, Jesus becomes Judas, whom we reject simply because we fail to look within.

Every part of our body has value. Each member has its particular function. Some parts are more visible, more appealing and a delight to behold, but all are necessary for wholeness and a healthy body. As we celebrate Corpus Christi, rejoice that you too are a part of this living body of Jesus, and essential in his plan of salvation.

Jesus, infinitely perfect, united us, imperfect members, to his body, by transforming us through his body and blood. Perfected by the grace of this marvelous mystery, let us too appreciate who we are while striving to appreciate every other member of his mystical body. May we be more concerned with "*who*" we see, "Jesus," and less concerned with *what* we see in others.

Father Henry Schmidt, June 24, 2001

Lying on my back on the pier, I looked up and saw the most intricate work of art—the beautiful design of the spiderweb glistening with the morning dew refracting the bright rising sun. The spider was waiting patiently for some insect to become involved in the web. When some vibration of the webbing notified the spider that some insect had been caught, he would prey upon it. It was his mainstay of life. Occasionally the insect was strong enough to break away. How like the plan of Jesus for us!

Jesus has designed a plan for each of us, more beautiful and far more intricate than the most elaborate spiderweb. He places people, events, and multiple spiritual gifts in our lives to make them exciting, beautiful, and reflective of his light. Then Jesus waits for us to become involved in his plan of salvation. The more we get entangled in his marvelous plan, the more life he breathes into us and the stronger we become. When we pray, we are empowered to break away from the manipulating enticements of the world and draw life from the Father of all life.

When the web of the spider is broken or torn, the spider immediately goes to work repairing it and anticipating the next oncoming insect. So too when we ignore or destroy God's plan for us, Jesus immediately goes to work repairing and planning a new way to attract us to his saving grace. No matter how often the web is destroyed, the spider returns to refashion his life-sustaining trap. In like manner, Jesus never ceases to reconstruct our lives, always bent on developing a deepening of our faith and trust along with a personal love response.

If you are truly observant, you will notice that every spiderweb center has its own distinct and unique web formation and that only one spider claims the web. So too with us. No two are exactly the same nor have a like purpose nor are endowed with the same talents etc. Each of us has our own "web" relation with Jesus. Alone, with the empowerment of Jesus, we are to control our "web," to keep it repaired and capable of giving us spiritual life sustenance. We may work close to or share with others, but we are the only one who relates to God via our personal web formation.

The stronger the spider makes its web, the more effective it is in holding those insects, which seek to pass through its network. The more intimately we are connected with Jesus, the more solidly we become rooted in our faith, and the more power we receive to break the "octopus arms" of materialism, secularism, as well as all other "isms," which prey on our spiritual life.

Just as you never hear a spider working and seldom see it idle, so too Jesus works in our lives quietly and continually tantalizing and inviting us to share in his gifts, which guarantee us of lasting life and peace. We all need the safety of a "web"—our pipeline to life, and our security from endangerment. What is the shape of your web, and who do you choose to pattern your web? As we acknowledge the wisdom, beauty, and the need of a web for the spider, how much more do we appreciate our "web system" of grace, the sacramental system solidly attached to Jesus? Guard your "web." Pray that Jesus protect you from all that preys on this life-giving system, your Catholic faith!

Father Henry Schmidt, July 1, 2001

How is the water? If you drop a frog in a pan of boiling water, it will jump out, but if you place it in a pan of cold water and gradually raise the temperature, it will sit and be boiled to death. Sudden changes cause them to react while a slow progression will catch them off guard and lead to disaster. How like us!

If you were told that the parish or school were to close this year, you would react violently, but if over a long period of time, due to failure of response of parishioners, it would slip into oblivion, you would question, how did this happen? Why didn't someone do something?

If our government denied us the freedom to practice our faith, we would cry out in protest but by means of a silent and gradual breakdown of our moral standards and ethical values, we adjust to these destructive changes, unaware that they are slowly draining our faith life, leading to death.

We are concerned by global warming but so apathetical about "faith cooling." We need to heed the words of David Du Plesses "If you will take the great truths of the Gospel out of your theological freezers and get them on the fire of the Holy Spirit, your churches will yet turn the world upside down." *We know the teachings and will of Jesus,* but all too often these truths are kept locked in our "theological freezers." We need to permit the Holy Spirit to enkindle a fire in our hearts *so we will live* deep faith. The world is upside down, and we need to act to turn it right-side-up.

Abortion, death penalty, euthanasia, cohabitation before marriage, addiction to drugs, sex, alcohol, materialism, prejudices, removing God from classroom and public gatherings, insidious undermining of the Catholic Church, and all we stand for, on TV, in the papers, and magazines, etc., have become accepted by our Christian country and the cool water of liberty and justice for all has risen to the boiling point resulting in the spiritual death of many. It is time to hop out of the "heating" water before it is too late.

"I do not challenge you to something easy. I do not challenge you to something that has comforts and luxury. I challenge you to something that involves all you have, but Jesus gave his all for you when he died on Calvary's Cross." (Torrey Johnson)

It is not easy to follow Jesus. It is not easy to give up our comforts and luxuries. It is not easy to leap out of the "waters" of the world and to counteract the growing trend of secularism, but that is what we are all about.

Frogs live amidst the weeds and in the mud and find the pond water to be the safest place in times of danger. But frogs are so attracted to light at night that you can simply pick them up or spear them and so enthralled by flashing silver that they will leap for it and become hooked on a line even when there is no bate on it.

We too live amidst the "mud and weeds" of a material world and are attracted to the flashing lights and amassment of possessions. Let us beware lest we become hooked on a line that gives no life. Remember there is safety in the cleansing water flowing from the heart of Jesus where we share in the fullness of lasting life. How is the water? Cool and life giving or heating and leading to death. Leap, "frog," leap to safety, now!

Father Henry Schmidt, July 8, 2001

One morning this past week as I sat, in the bright sun, outside the office door, I saw a bumblebee, a white butterfly, and a tiny ant moving among the flowers. Each was doing its own thing and leaving its effect on the plants. How like us!

As we make our way on our faith journey, God places people and things in our lives that leave an effect on our lives. The latest person to pass through our lives was Father Carlos. Was his affect comparable to a bumblebee, butterfly, or an ant?

Most likely he touched each of us in a different way. His simple, childlike, easy going manner may have touched some just as a free-flying white butterfly gently brushing your lives, bringing joy, peace, and renewed life. His touch hardly felt but still beautiful and refreshing. Perhaps his deep faith and different cultural lifestyle caused him to enter your life swiftly, with direct purpose, and deeply as a bee penetrates into the depths of a flower. Or, as a bee when abused leaves a stinging impression, did you experience a little sting because of some misunderstanding or cultural differences? Maybe he passed through life like a small ant with little noticeable visible impact. But as an ant leaves a trail for others to follow, he may have opened the way for someone else to finish up what he started in your faith journey.

Mindful of the differences between the butterfly, the bumblebee, and the ant, all which bring good in their own way, so too Father Carlos brought newness and diversity to our parish. Some appreciated his youthful, prayerful, timeless lifestyle, while others found it a bit difficult to adjust to. Not everyone loves or appreciates butterflies, bumblebees, and ants, but Jesus does. Regardless of how he passed through or affected your life, his presence and the affect of his ministry will long be remembered. Our prayer is that he will be welcomed wherever he ministers and that Jesus use him as a butterfly, bee, or an ant to bring life, peace, and love to all.

Aware of the tremendous effect we have on others, we must be careful. While the butterfly, bee, and ant were all doing good, I had it in my power to destroy any one or all three of them. In the overall plan, God places us in the situation and place of the moment hoping that we will work together. If not, we are no longer a beautiful butterfly but a moth destroying the garment of unity, or the bumblebee embittered and injecting poison into the body of Christ, or an ant, which is little by little carrying away the peace of the parish community.

Everyone, regardless of accidental differences, has much to offer for the overall well-being of our parish. No one should wield their power or position to dominate—that only destroys. The humble and simple, the weak and gentle, the compassionate and the caring in the end have the greatest and most lasting effect. "In our dealings with men, however unkind and hurting they are, we must exercise the same patience as God exercises with us. It is the simple truth that such patience is not the sign of weakness but the sign of strength; it is not defeatism, but rather the only way to victory." (Wm. Barclay) We are all necessary in the plan of God. We are all loved passionately by Jesus whether we touch the lives of others as butterflies, bees, or ants.

Father Henry Schmidt, July 15, 2001

One morning early in the week, as I walked from the rectory to the church, the sun was playing peek-a-boo with me through the clouds. The sun was hiding behind and jumping from cloud to cloud, until they ran off to play elsewhere revealing the sun in its full power and glory. We too play peek-a-boo with God and one another.

Cutting open a cantaloupe reveals the vast number of seeds hidden within the melon. No one would ever realize they were there, or the number, until it is cut open. So much beauty and life hidden deep within the melon would simply be wasted unless someone exposes the seeds, plants them, and allows them to grow. So too our many talents and gifts, which produce life, frequently are hidden from others. We need to humbly reveal these blessings from God and use them to give and increase the faith life of family, friends, parishioners, and all we encounter in our daily lives. But instead, we persist in playing peek-a-boo. Why are we afraid to come out from behind the clouds, or open ourselves, so that others may see our faith in action and develop a personal relationship with Jesus? Our witness will plant the seeds of life which, guided and empowered by the Holy Spirit, will reveal the full power and glory of God.

How much brighter and more life giving is the sun when not hidden by the clouds. Imagine all the life which could result from the seeds of one cantaloupe when planted and then from all the seeds resulting from those cantaloupes. So too when we witness to others, they in turn will witness and a loving relationship will spread like fire fanned by the wind through a dry stubble field. Our purpose in life is to help people find a personal relationship with Jesus Christ.

It appears that we are fearful of letting others know about our relationship with Jesus, either because we feel ours is not as good as theirs, or we are hesitant to share with them how real and profound it truly is, lest they view us as "different."

My relationship with Jesus is not perfect or even what I would like for it to be, but we are dear friends and working hard to improve that relationship. Jesus loves me unconditionally, but often I fail to believe and trust in his plan when it is contrary to mine. That is when I try to play peek-a-boo with Jesus, and it does not work. That is when I play peek-a-boo with others, and it is not right. To follow Jesus demands work. Faith grows through sacrifice. Love is a choice freely made. Jesus does not play games with us, he is always faithful.

We are a blessed people, a chosen race, a royal priesthood, and the beloved of God. Jesus loved us so much that he gave his life for us. Jesus wants to share his friendship by his presence in the Eucharist. Believing this to be true, Jesus invites us to reveal the seeds of faith maturing in our lives and producing lasting fruit, so others will long for this personal friendship with him.

"Sick or well, blind or seeing, bound or free, we are here for a purpose, and however we are situated, we please God better with useful deeds than with many prayers of pious resignation." (Helen Keller) So let us stop playing peek-a-boo with God and one another, hiding behind our fear, as we share our faith experiences, because that may be just the seed that Jesus wishes to use to instill new faith life in another.

Father Henry Schmidt, July 22, 2001

Who's going to be crying at your funeral? As my Sandals leave a cloud of dust dashing from meeting to meeting, activity to activity, the admonition of Jesus to Martha in this past Sunday's Gospel flashes before my mental eyes—"only one thing matters" and "Mary has chosen the better part." Amid all the busyness of modern-day life, many of us have stopped living.

So who is going to be crying at your funeral? That will show whether you are preoccupied with trying to get a life, or whether you had the wisdom to live. Will the banker, your boss, your employees, those who have a claim on your life because money is involved, be the only ones to gather? Will your family and those deserving of high priority throughout your life be a part of this picture? What will be the relationship between you and your mourners?

During a discussion with my Promise Keepers Group this past week, these words evoked a deep and lengthy dialog—"The culture we live in values possessions and accomplishments higher than people and relationships. Instead of encouraging and nurturing family and relationship values, our culture suggests professional achievement and financial success are the measure of a man. When was the last time you met a man who described himself in terms of the impact he is having on his children? Our culture has persuaded most men that significance is related more to our balance sheet and our title than to teaching our children and cherishing our wives." (From *The Man in the Mirror* by Patrick Morley) And the same goes for women.

Hopefully, faith is the most significant facet of our lives. Faith built on true love of God, compels and empowers us to value personal relations more than possessions and accomplishments. What does it profit a person to achieve possessions and accomplishments only to suffer broken relationships? No amount of success can compensate for failure at home. If you don't have time for your family, you can be one hundred percent certain you are not following God's will.

It is time we all stop rushing, working, meeting, and being stressed out in our futile efforts to find a life, and take more time for living. Does your spouse and children know you love them as shown in the amount of prime time you share with them? Does Jesus hold the number one place in your life? Living our faith, loving God above all, and our neighbor as ourselves requires wisdom, sacrifice, and perseverance. What are you willing to sacrifice to show your spouse and children how much you love them and to what extent you value your church and school. We pay far too high a price substituting luxuries of life for the love they are really craving and all too often lose everything, family, position, and name.

Who will be crying at your funeral? Hopefully your family and those convinced by your life that "only one thing matters," sharing God's love and not simply those superficial contacts who have or hope to benefit from accomplishments or possessions. Blessed are you if those crying at your funeral have truly benefitted from your sacrifices to preserve and pass on the incredible gift of faith, your committed life of fidelity and love to your spouse and children, and your unique respect of every person, for you have "chosen the better part."

Father Henry Schmidt, July 29, 2001

Looking at the water fountain in front of our beautiful church reminds me each day of our need to live our faith with determination. The water, with endless determination, leaps into the air, striving to rise higher, only to fall back into the pool to try again. Such is the pattern of the faithful Christian, for "We can only reach with determination for the warm hand of God, which we have so rashly and self-confidently pushed away." (Alexander Solzhenistyn)

Racing through life, striving to better ourselves, we are faced with choices, choices which we confront with determination. "We must make the choices that enable us to fulfill the deepest capacities of our real selves." (Thomas Merton) This is where we must imitate the fountain. We often start with our priorities in order, determined to live as Jesus models and invites us to, but then our spiritual pump, shorted out by BONEDA, gradually weakens and stops.

BONEDA is devastating and debilitating. In our society today, *burn out*, causes many to give up their efforts. Unlike the water fountain, regulated in its force to pump the water, they fail to limit themselves and soon are consumed, resulting in burn out. Others suffer from *nervous exhaustion*, taking upon themselves the burdens of all, even those over which they have absolutely no power, failing to trust that God is in complete control. Then we have those growing numbers who are succumbing to *depression* resulting from an overpowering need to control and fail to accept God's plan for them. Still greatest affliction of BONEDA is *apathy*. It is a deadly plague and quite contagious. It quietly undermines the person, home, community, and eventually the church. It destroys the spirit of determination to listen to, heed, and lead others to Jesus by living our faith. The time has come to do some soul searching to determine to what degree, as individuals or as a parish, we are suffering from BONEDA.

Praise God, there are many Little Flower Parishioners who are determined to persevere in living their faith, rising up each day, as our fountain, loving and serving God and one another, falling back from time to time, and aware that we must simply try again.

For those who may be suffering from one or more aspects of BONEDA, and I am among them, I simply compare us to the battery I use in my microphone each weekend Mass. It works well for a time, and then after some use, it weakens and must be recharged. We too, after efforts to love and follow Jesus, weaken and must be recharged by Jesus through our prayerful, careful, and frequent use of the Mass and the sacraments of reconciliation and the Eucharist.

We, like the fountain, must persevere in our efforts to rise up and witness our faith to all who come into our lives, always aware that we may not meet the goal, and even from time to time not rise as high as we could. But Jesus still loves us and empowers us to try again. And when we need a recharge, like the weakened battery, we know where to go, confident that Jesus will forgive us and recommission us to continue our faith journey. And finally, even though BONEDA is contagious and destructive, it is curable. So enjoy the beauty of your "fountain" for you are unique. Keep your battery charged for it is necessary for life. Use BONEDA (Burnt Out, Nervous Exhaustion, Depression, Apathy) as grace moments to salvation.

Father Henry Schmidt, August 5, 2001

Boy, was God busy this past Sunday? He nearly wore me out. If he had that much to do with everybody, then he must have ended the day exhausted. After preparing the church for the Sunday Masses, I helped set up the Quonset for the coffee and doughnut gatherings. Before the first Mass, Jesus came under the guise of needy travelers, and following the second Mass, he came as a needy woman. Next, he led me to celebrate the blessings of a long life, at a family birthday gathering, briefly, before calling me to anoint a lovely faith-filled lady preparing for birth into lasting life. Later, I joined some friends for a meal and lengthy discussion about God, faith and our religion, only to rush from there to meet with my Small Faith Community for further faith sharing and "breaking open the Word" as we allowed Jesus to speak to us his personal message from the Sunday scriptures. Returning home late, hoping to sink into bed, following my night prayers, I was called out to Doctor's Hospital to pray for, anoint, and prepare a lady in the final days of her earthly journey. I ended the day quite late, but happy and rejuvenated by the presence of Jesus leading and using me throughout a most wonderful day. Truly, God must be an all powerful God to be able to be so present and working with everyone in countless ways.

Faith was my energy. Faith to recognize Jesus in the needy, to appreciate the miracle of the Mass when Jesus became alive among us under the appearance in the Eucharist, to thank God for the gift of life celebrated by the family birthday party, and to see their deep love and respect for their grandmother. Words cannot express adequately the peace and healing of the sacrament of anointing and the blessings both I and the lady experienced when Jesus touched her, reaffirming his promise of future life.

The challenging discussion with friends, and my Small Faith Community, certainly impressed me with the value and power of faith and the awareness that everyone on their faith journey is not at the same place or enjoying the same personal relationship with Jesus. Yet he loves each and every one of us regardless of where we are, who we are, and what we are doing. We do not deserve, or merit, his love or our salvation. He is the one who has chosen us, redeemed us, and uses us in marvelous mysterious ways depending on our openness to the movement of the Spirit.

As we reflect on our lives, what do we find? Fear, division, rejection? Faith drives out such maladies for we are convinced that God has planned everything that happens and that Jesus is walking with us and assisting us to use every situation to achieve some greater good. Faith empowers us to live in peace and unity, and accept the diversities of religion, persons, opinions, and situations. We are tested in many ways and tempted frequently to question or abandon our faith. Persevere; it is your lifeline to salvation. Faith fosters unity in diversity, vision amidst division, and uses rejection as the pathway to perfection. Faith frees us from the controlling powers of others and our desire to control. Faith is our foundation for love and love is our building material for hope and hope is the assurance of eternal life.

Today we may be tired. To be tired *in* the Lord is a blessing indeed. To be tired *of* the Lord requires *faith* in your need.

Father Henry Schmidt, August 19, 2001

Where have all the martyrs gone? I don't mean those of the early church who shed their blood for their faith, but those convicted Catholics who truly sacrificed to assure us of a living faith. I will never forget my parents, grandparents, one particular aunt, and all the holy people of my childhood for they were martyrs. They willingly "suffered" for what they believed.

My parents taught us moral and ethical values and the importance of honesty, commitment, and sacrifice, with a special emphasis on living our Catholic faith, not only on Sunday but daily. They stressed the importance of a good name, achieved through honesty and responsibility, for once you have lost your good name, you have lost everything.

Living their faith was the highest priority and making sure that we all were able to get a Catholic education was their focal point. Willingly they did without many things to achieve this goal—never taking a vacation until all seven of us had finished Catholic grade and high school, rarely eating out and always participating in the parish activities.

Most likely they were considered, by some, to be poor because they were not entrapped by the fad or name brands of the day. Most of my clothes were made by my mother, or handed down from older brothers, as was the case with my siblings. My folks dressed simply and neatly and were highly respected by all. Certainly this was not necessary, but to assure our religious education and to model the conviction of their beliefs and values, they were willing to deny and humble themselves to live a simple lifestyle.

How proud they were of their parish! They supported it financially as best as they could, but gave far more by their presence and involvement. Sunday was a day of prayer, worship, and rest. Never did they work on Sunday nor did they neglect to get us to Sunday Mass unless prevented by sickness or impassable country roads, going not out of obligation, but by choice. Together, as a family, we always went early to Mass on Sunday, and not on Saturday night (a privilege granted to those who were unable to participate on Sunday due to work) so they could sleep in on Sunday.

Anyone was welcome at their table. Everyone was invited to share in our family prayer life. All meals were shared together, beginning and ending with prayer. Frequently, there were special prayers of Rosary or devotions depending on the church season. They were extremely generous in sharing their material blessings, and caring and daring enough to share their faith life, out of conviction.

Where have all the martyrs gone? Martyrdom is highly esteemed in the church, but few long to be martyrs. I have great admiration for the many "martyrs" who did not shed their blood, but have had a great impression and effect on my life. It takes a lot of faith and courage to live faith as my parents and a few present day "martyrs." The church is in great need of martyrs today—people willing to endure rejection, criticism, misunderstanding, and belittling; people choosing to make sacrifices to live as faithful followers of Jesus. The church *glows* and our faith *grows* from the lives of martyrs. Are you willing to be a martyr?

Father Henry Schmidt, August 26, 2001

At 3:15 a.m. on Sunday morning, Jesus came to my door asking for help. It was so hard to recognize him, and it was with great difficulty that I responded to his need bolstered by his Word, "as long as you did for the least, you did it to me." The following Tuesday at 8:15 p.m. he came again begging for help, while I was sharing with my Promise Keepers group. I felt like closing the door, but this time I was moved to respond as I recalled our "seven promises." On Thursday, I met Jesus again in a holy, humble, saintly priest preparing for his entry into lasting life and glory, and what a pleasant encounter! What a difference! On Saturday at 4:30 p.m., Jesus came into my life amidst great celebration as our faith community gathered to praise and worship him. How wonderful it was to celebrate with him! And I experienced Jesus in many other encounters throughout the week.

How close do you want Jesus to come to you? How welcome is he? We seldom think of his being present in our daily lives, in the people we meet day after day, but he is truly there. We welcome people who are clean, well dressed, kind, talented, generous, and measure up to all our standards. We are repulsed by others and avoid them at all cost, failing to see Jesus in disguise in both categories. How empty life is when we fail to recognize Jesus!

Have you ever had the opportunity to speak with Jesus, about death or rather the glory to come after death? We are afraid of death. We don't want to think about death, and avoid speaking about it with everyone, especially those who are dying for fear we will disturb them. Truly, we don't understand what death is, or we do not believe what Jesus tells us about his new life.

We are sad when children leave home, when friends move away, or some other change affects our lives, but we accept it, believing we will meet and share again from time to time, but in a different and new way. This sadness is compensated by our hope that in their new life and location, they are experiencing happiness and fulfillment of life and dreams. So too, we are only separated temporarily from loved ones by death, and shall meet again soon. And they are now completely happy in their new life.

As Bishop Lucas presided over our Eucharistic gathering this past week, we experienced the presence of Jesus so much so that we truly celebrated—singing, praying, clapping, dancing, and playing before the Lord. God was glorified, our faith was magnified, and Jesus's living presence was vivified. What a fitting celebration of our redemption! Each Fourth of July we celebrate our freedom and deliverance from bondage with much fanfare, noise, and visible manifestation. Should we not celebrate our redemption and entry into eternal life with as much jubilation?

We need to fill our empty lives with the presence of Jesus. Recognizing Jesus in the least helps us to humbly acknowledge our total dependence on God. Welcoming Jesus when he calls us, in death, encourages others to anticipate his promised glory. Celebrating our redemption each week at the Eucharist allows Jesus to fill the emptiness in our lives. Is Jesus always welcome in your life, or have you laid down certain parameters? Be that as you wish, I assure you he will come knocking at your door this week. Will you open?

Father Henry Schmidt, September 2, 2001

On my desk, there lies a dime minted in 1942. On the front side there are the words, Liberty, and In God We Trust, and on the back we find the words United States of America. Liberty for the United States, and for the whole world, depends on our trust in God. As we pray, we must be open to the guidance of the Spirit who will show us his way to restore peace and unity to our country.

This is a time for faith, not despair. It is a time for justice, not vengeance; It is a time for construction, not destruction. As the smoke slowly lifts, and the debris is removed from the World Trade Plaza, our leaders, and America as a whole, must move forward with a clear focus. Emotionally we are drained, our spirits wilted like plants following the first frost of the fall. Truly, life for all has changed, but not ended. For those called to death, God has granted a new and better life, for those left behind in physical and emotional pain, God offers his healing grace, and to all of us whose lives have been forever changed by a multiplicity of events, Jesus invites to pursue that new plan of life he has in store for us. Trust him; it will be great and exciting.

No word or no act can restore what has been destroyed. Only by living faith can we move on and face the unknown, confident that God is in complete control. We cannot ignore or belittle the devastating loss of countless people nor do we intend to play it down by platitudes, but we look to Jesus who models for us as we pray, "Father, forgive them for they know not what they do." It is in this deep sense of solidarity with Jesus that we beg for the strength to persevere in reforming and reassessing our lives and our country.

To assist us in doing that, we must keep in mind that "Our earth is but a small star in the great universe. Yet of it we can make, if we choose, a planet unvexed by war, untroubled by hunger or fear, undivided by senseless distinctions of race, color, or doctrine." We pray that "God, grant us brotherhood, not only for this day but for all years, a brotherhood not of words, but of acts and deeds. We are all children of earth—grant us that simple knowledge. If our brothers and sisters are oppressed, then we are oppressed. If they hunger, we hunger. If their freedom is taken away, our freedom is not secure." As Catholics, it is our aim that all people shall know justice and righteousness, freedom and security, mercy and love, reconciliation and peace.

Conscious of the implications of the above paragraph, we are plagued by the words "if their freedom is taken away, our freedom is not secure." The more we deprive others of freedom, the more insecure is our freedom. When we reach out to the oppressed, seeking justice for all, then liberty like water flowing through an irrigation ditch rushes in securing freedom for the oppressed and ourselves as well.

May our Lenten hymn become our motto: "We rise again from ashes, from the good we failed to do. We rise again from ashes, to create ourselves anew." May the loss of many lives, the ashes of buildings and all our pains become the seed bed of newness! Carefully examine our failures, let us create ourselves, our nation and world anew, building on a solid foundation that fosters and secures freedom for all. Turn to God, trust in him and let liberty be our law.

Father Henry Schmidt, September 23, 2001

As my Sandals drove along a field of ripening pumpkins, too large to see or appreciate the total extent and value of the farmer's work, I was prompted to compare them with our parish. Hundreds of pumpkins of varying sizes—large, tiny and in between—and each sharing the same basic shape and color and each receiving nourishment and water from the same field, and through the common vine. Every pumpkin appears to be tough on the outside, but in reality is quite soft inside, and each pumpkin seems to be just one individual, yet amidst a maze of networking pulp there is the potential for ongoing life rooted in the many seeds carefully nourished within. Each pumpkin will be used in different ways, some for food, some for Halloween decorations, some will be left and rot in the fields. And some will be broken or hurt in the picking, hauling, or trampled by passing animals, hunters etc. but even then, they are giving much back to the soil for future life.

Each week, our church fills with hundreds of people of varying ages, sizes, talents, and ethnic backgrounds, yet all sharing the humanity and divinity of Jesus—all of equal value regardless of our accidental differences. We gather to receive the needed water of baptism, along with nourishment from the Eucharist and the Word which comes to us through Jesus, the Vine, who has firmly planted us in the field of faith.

How often, we, like the tough pumpkin, attempt to face the future and conquer the world on our own, only to find that we need the help of Jesus and others. Frequently, we are pleasantly surprised to find people as loving and compassionate, after getting to know the real person, and not just judging them from hearsay or from a distance. This knowledge leads to lasting friendships and valuable use of potential heretofore locked deep within, as together they now nourish new seeds to life.

Every parishioner ministers and witnesses in different ways, be they single, married, or serving in religious life. Some have more visible talents and abilities than others, but each is invited to share them in the way that best benefits the whole parish. Some are chosen for special needs, while others appear to be neglected. Remember, God uses each of us in his unique way to carry out his perfect plan of salvation. He frequently uses us to do much without our knowing it. He even uses those broken and hurting times in our lives for his glory and the good of his people if only we allow it, just as our patroness, St. Therese, the Little Flower repeatedly offered the little crosses of her life to "make love loved."

St. Therese did not conquer any nations. She did not live a long life, only twenty-four years, and in a cloistered Carmelite Convent from sixteen till her early death. Yet she did little things well to better the lives of others. Her life of simplicity, humility, and fidelity was enhanced by her endless outpouring of love in little ways. She was a little "pumpkin," often a "broken pumpkin" in a huge patch, and Jesus perfected her through the little ways she shared his love. In endless little ways, may we imitate her, in our daily lives as we continue the work of "making love loved" in our homes and parish! The pumpkins are ripening, just as our love is growing.

Father Henry Schmidt, October 7, 2001

How wonderful it was to stop the clock this past weekend as we changed time and gained an hour! There are times when I wish I could stop the clock to enjoy the moment or to rest or simply catch up. But stop the clock, we can't, so let us appreciate the blessings and love of Jesus in the present moment where he shares life and love with us.

This past weekend was one of those special occasions when I would have loved to stop the clock for it was filled with his presence. Saturday afternoon, I rushed to Carrollton to take part in the annual family gathering to cook apple butter. The clear blue sky with the warm autumn sun was an added blessing as apples were cooked in a huge four-foot kettle over an open fire. With a good imagination, one could visualize a group of "witches" brewing their potion as the crisp apples were stirred with a huge wooden paddle while flames danced around the kettle eerily hidden by the smoke. Slowly they turned into delicious apple butter, which will bring nourishment and delight to many throughout the cold winter months.

How similar to our faith community gathered in worship! Like the many apples we are crisp and separate until Jesus enkindles the fire of the Holy Spirit to warm and soften us as we lose our individual hardness and mesh into his body bringing his life and love to others.

After the apple butter had been canned and the kettle washed and stored for another year, the day came to an end as darkness smothered the sun and cooling temperatures enveloped us like a wet blanket, while family and friends gathered near a huge fire casting light, heat, and ghostly shadows on all who sat on straw bales eating and celebrating the close of another year of hard work and a bountiful harvest. As the sparks skyrocketed into the darkness, they were consumed by the hungry night, long before they could reach the stars, but they persevered. What an inspiration for us as we strive to rise through the darkness of our faith lives in our endless efforts to imitate Jesus! We try and fail, but like the sparks, we don't give up, we try again.

Finally, the time came for a wagon ride over hill and dale enjoying the glory of God under the light of the moon. All that was missing was a witch passing before the moon with a cat on her broom, for the ghosts and goblins scurried through the fields and woods as we alarmed several deer bounding through the wilderness. What a wonderful experience, for the countryside takes on a whole new appearance at night. There is silence and a sense of wonder. The roughness of daylight is not visible, and mystery pervades the atmosphere.

Reality remains the same, but the atmosphere changes the attitude. So too Jesus invites us to see one another in a different light according to the situation. When we see the external roughness of someone or something, then look within the individual or the action to behold the mystery which God has veiled. Seek to behold the unique truth, the secret mystery. Illuminated by the Spirit, may the newly discovered atmosphere change our attitude of the reality!

We cannot stop the clock, but we can adjust our understanding and acceptance of the situation and love the mystery of the moment. Then there is no need to stop the clock, for as love increases, time ceases. Love is eternal.

Father Henry Schmidt, November 4, 2001

It was not written up in the paper, and I'm not sure if it was on TV, but this past week I was shot. It was one of the most painless shootings I have ever experienced. I received my annual flu shot. It is a remedy to help prevent catching the flu. It is not a guarantee that you will not be sick, or encounter some other virus or physical sickness. I appreciate the help it gives, but realize that I still must take proper care of my body to keep from exposing myself to some germ looking for a nesting place.

How like our spiritual life! From time to time throughout our faith life, we come to church and get a shot to avoid some spiritual germ crouched in hiding ready to pounce on the unsuspecting. These booster shots are Jesus's special gifts of faith, the sacraments, Mass, and prayer. They are helps to prevent our falling, but not guarantees that we won't fall because we have a free will and can live carelessly, thereby weakening our spiritual strength and exposing ourselves to the vicious attacks of the world, the flesh and the devil.

Each year many people go for their flu shot, hoping it will be a help. Each year we prepare our little children for their "flu shot," the sacrament of reconciliation knowing it will help. But then all too often we neglect to receive booster shots frequently or even yearly. It seems we have more confidence in human remedies than in the divine medicines—the Sacraments and Mass. We see the visible devastating effects of physical sickness. The results of spiritual neglect are even more destructive—misunderstanding, separation, rejection, hatred, and eternal suffering.

More and more research is being undertaken to control and eliminate physical maladies and at tremendous cost. It is just as important for parents and leaders to make greater sacrifices to control sin and its horrible effects in our lives and that of our children.

This past Sunday, I went to New Salem to enjoy the beautiful fall day. There I am always reminded of the great sacrifices they made just to survive. I am also a bit envious of their slower pace of life which enabled them to reflect on the place of God and others in their lives. Both were essential parts and viewed as a high priority.

The conveniences of the day have captivated our lifestyle and have led many to making fewer sacrifices for those priorities. Sacrifice has been replaced by inconvenience, which is rapidly being trampled underfoot by convenience. In the past, we frequently heard the phrase "offer it up" a prayer seldom used today. Sacrifice is a requirement for some spiritual priorities. When was the last time you chose to or encouraged your family to "offer up" some inconvenience for the glory of God and their spiritual good? These sacrifices are not merely for survival but for salvation.

Unbelievable sacrifices are made for bettering our position or possibilities in life because we have been convinced of the necessity. We need that same conviction if we are to truly live as followers of Jesus.

Pray for the grace to "slow down" and appreciate life. Realize the unconditional love of God who responds to all our spiritual needs. Experience the joy of others who bring fulfillment to life. This happens only when we are "shot" by the love of Jesus. Get your spiritual "flu" shot today.

Father Henry Schmidt, November 11, 2001

This past week I was shocked, on my way to church, when I came upon a totally nude character standing in our schoolyard. What an eye opener to behold the huge tree completely stripped of its leaves and to see that it was not the perfectly formed tree it appeared to be when clothed in its green and recently adorned with colorful leaves! With its outward disguise removed, I could see how misshaped it really was with its gnarled trunk and crooked branches. Now I could see the strength and endurance of years of trials and tribulations caused by nature, animals, and people. It stood proud and sturdy. It had fulfilled its purpose over the years, even though rarely noticed or appreciated, and would respond again in the spring when clothed by God with beautiful leaves.

How like the people around us! We misjudge them because of our biased perception. We evaluate their actions and plans wrongly because we fail to push aside their covering "leaves" and view their motives and inner strength, "their weathered trunk and branches," their intimate connection with Jesus. As we approach the end of this church year and celebrate the glorious feast of Christ the King, may we strive to find the solid foundation on which these people proffer their time, talents, and treasures, namely their deep love of Jesus!

Every tree looks different from the one next to it. The size, shape, color, and the gifts or fruits they offer vary, but they are all necessary and valuable as they satisfy the multiple needs of people and animals in nature. When we begin to destroy carelessly or unnecessarily, we all suffer. If a tree is broken down in the woods by a storm, it damages or destroys others around it. So we must carefully protect our parishioners by acknowledging their gifts and mode of ministry and supporting one another.

Some trees are appreciated more than others, and some have more to give than others. Just as God designed a different plan for every tree, so too he has a unique plan for each of us.

When we find it difficult to accept what others say or do, could it be that we are jealous of their leadership, efforts, and involvement, or that perhaps subconsciously we realize they are beckoning us to change or get involved, and we are hesitant or refusing. In any case, make sure your perception is correct.

Remember the more we are tested, the stronger we can become just like the tree which withstood the forces of nature and man in our schoolyard. It requires that we be willing to bend, or we will break, bringing devastation to all.

On this feast of Christ the King, all who remain proud and sturdy in living their faith, realize that very soon we will stand before Jesus, totally stripped of our "leaves" as the tree in our schoolyard, revealing the causes and motives of our actions. Nothing will be hidden; the truth will reveal the "root" and "trunk" of all our accomplishments. May we not live with biased perceptions lest we be unable to see the forest because of the trees, namely miss the beauty of Jesus's plan for all of us because we are blinded by our inability to accept and appreciate individuals!

Father Henry Schmidt, November 25, 2001

Recently, I took some visitors to New Salem State Park. After walking around the log cabins and stores reminiscent of the time when Lincoln lived and worked there, we went to see the old mill, at a distance from the village on the Sangamon River. What an impressive construction! As I stood there, I was saddened because the song of life was dead—the mill was dead! Its body was decaying, and being carried away by the very stream that so faithfully had worked to nourish the huge giant, by turning the massive gears, now rusted and broken. When life abounded in the mill, it fed the insatiable hunger of the village folks. Now in the silence, the wind echoed the shocking words, "murder—the mill was murdered," and nature was trying to hide the evidence by a camouflage of weeds, briars, and saplings.

When the village was alive, the mill drank from the stream and was nourished with the grain from the fields as happy people worked together to build their community and support the various needs of one another. The song of life was heard from the humming mill preparing the various needs of one another. The song of life was heard from the humming mill preparing the food of life, while flowers and birds added to the beauty and peace of the happy people. Now, the people had all left, the stream was dry, and the fields were barren, the mill was dead, and silence mourned the fatal transition.

As I left this sad scene, I could only think of our parish. In a few weeks, our parishioners will meet to discern our future, as we convene our second parish "Town Meeting." Little Flower, like the mill, has been singing a song of life for over fifty years, as faith-filled parishioners have gathered to support the mission of Jesus in variety of ministries. We need to work together, if the "mill"—our parish is to thrive. When we remain open to God's plans, our faith abounds as we drink of the life-giving waters of the Spirit. If we bring our "grain"—our talents, to the "mill"—the church community, to be shared, we nourish ourselves and the many depending on our support. Truly, the song of life emanates from our Little Flower community, which humming as the "mill" offers the life-giving graces to nourish the happy people who enjoy the beauty and peace of Jesus present in our midst.

If we do not, we will kill the mill. The mill needs repairs from time to time, and needs people capable of making the repairs. The mill is useless unless it has grain to grind, which depends on people bringing their grain to be processed. Then people need to use the grain to sustain their lives. Look around and see how blessed we, at Little Flower are since we have so many dedicated people who offer to work at the mill, repair the mill, and use the gifts offered by the mill.

Aware that Jesus is the "miller" we allow him to choose the texture of the grain. Sometimes he offers us finely milled flour, while there are times he feels that a rougher composition is better for us. We may find the mill is busy and have to wait in line before our gifts can be used, while other times we may be needed immediately. Trusting in the mill and the miller we are willing to accept any challenge required to keep our mill functioning for the good of the whole faith community. Our mill is not dead! The song of life is heard humming from our "mill." Together let us maintain our "mill," careful not to "murder" it.

Father Henry Schmidt, December 9, 2001

This past Sunday night as I waited for my Small Faith Community to gather at the rectory, I extinguished the lights, turned on some soft peaceful music, lit a black candle, and prayed. It was the most wonderful experience, wherein I felt the loving presence of Jesus.

As I sat there, I became aware of many similarities in life. There, amidst the darkness of night, a black candle, totally consumed by a flame brought light, warmth, and comfort.

Living in a world darkened by sin, division, and war, I struggle with confusion and am plagued with questioning of our God. Recalling that sometimes, due to my human weakness, I too am also the cause of darkness; it is difficult to ward off despair. But as I quietly contemplated this sacred moment, I came to realize that out of the almost overwhelming darkness in the world around us and even using weak instruments, like me or other sinners, Jesus can bring light if only we are willing to allow him to use us. It has a cost. Just as the black candle consumed by the flame transformed darkness into light, so Jesus can and will use us, even with our limitations and imperfections, to reflect his Light and bring hope to the world around us.

As the candle abolished the darkness of that room, removing fear and transforming it into a place of peace, glowing with the aura of mystery, encapsulated with calming music, so the presence of Jesus becomes the calming music of peace in our lives when we listen to him and unite with him in removing darkness from our lives and the world.

Recalling the great promises of God to us, and seeing them fulfilled in the coming of Jesus, we resolve to live as a people of hope. Filled with hope, and conscious of a greater life to come, we accept our responsibility to spread the Good News, and reflect the Light of Jesus. This Sunday's Gospel reveals what Jesus expects of us—"go and tell what you see and hear about me."

We no longer wander aimlessly in the darkness for the light has come. Called and commissioned by Jesus to bear this light of life to others, and trusting in his Words, "Be not afraid," we go forth empowered to tell what we see and hear. As our Small Faith Community prayed and shared how and where Jesus acted in our lives, we all grew in faith. It became clear that faith is more than my private relationship with Jesus. We are all part of the mystical body of Jesus, and consequently if the body is to be holy and whole, we necessarily need to communicate the ways that Jesus has touched our lives. Do we ever tell one another how Jesus has acted in our lives, or what we are hearing him reveal to us?

Discussing "go and tell what you see and hear" excited us about the possibilities of helping one another grow in faith by humbly sharing how the Spirit touched our lives. We are all living in a darkened world, enduring our personal weaknesses and hurts, longing to experience Jesus's healing and enlightenment. One little candle brings much light, warmth, and security to a dark room. Revealing our faith story, how Jesus touched our lives in simple or in wondrous ways could offer spiritual light and support to others.

Go and tell what you see and hear about Jesus, for he is the light of your candle removing the darkness, he is the calming music of your life revealing the Good News of salvation.

Father Henry Schmidt, December 16, 2001

In the final weeks before a baby is born, the parents to be are excited and busy making final preparations. Getting ready for the new baby is exhilarating, but the change it brings to their lives is radical. I am getting ready for a new baby. Don't be shocked. The baby is Jesus.

All of us hopefully are readying ourselves for this new arrival. This time of the year is always filled with anticipation, a sense of peace, dreams, and expectations. We all love little babies, and the birth of Jesus is no different.

Parents look forward to their newborn. They are proud to be parents. They smother their baby with love and make a big thing out of the situation. But suddenly reality hits them, that this newcomer rules their lives and a radical change results. Their freedom is gone, their time is so totally consumed by their baby, nights are filled with frequent disturbances, sickness, and a multitude of unexpected and unwanted circumstances governs their once free and peaceful lives.

As years pass, new and more expansive needs enter their lives, as they are responding to the various situations of child and youth. Enthralled and captivated by their child who is a wondrous source of love and happiness, they sacrifice much to fulfill the unending demands.

Yet they are willing and ready to answer these pressing, unending, daily needs, overlooking the great sacrifices of time, energy, and freedom it requires of them. Their goal and aim is to better the life of their child while showing and sharing their love.

As mentioned above, I am getting ready for the new baby, Jesus, and hopefully you are too. If we truly believe this, then we must also realize the radical change that must necessarily result from Jesus entering into our lives.

With the birth of Jesus, his coming into our lives, we are faced with critical decisions. Are we willing and ready to make them? His coming demands more radical changes than the birth of a baby. We are no longer free to do as we please, and he is in control of our times, as he calls us to pray, minister, sacrifice, and love him and others. We will be frequently disturbed and drawn out of our comfort zone, as we respond to his call to reach out to the lonely, needy, sick, and marginalized of our parish and community. Just as a baby forces us to make decisions which are different from our plans, so welcoming Jesus will require us to reassess our original plans and choose responses that are a bit painful and disappointing.

Are we willing and ready to sacrifice time, energy, and freedom to better our lives and relations with Jesus as we share intimately with him and witness our love to others? We dare not say that we welcome the baby Jesus if we are not willing to make that radical change in our lives by putting him before our plans and desires, while prioritizing the illusions of the world.

Celebrate the coming of Jesus in your hearts, homes, and parish this Christmas. Accept the radical change the coming of Jesus demands and allow him to control your lives, and you will experience the true meaning of Christmas. Rejoice and be glad, our Savior has come! He offers a *Christmas* of blessings.

Father Henry Schmidt, December 23, 2001

"Do you see what I see; do you hear what I hear?"—words from a Christmas song pulsate in my ears as that life-giving feast fades into history with memories of 2001.

Did you see the Savior, the son of God, reveal himself in your lives? No angels, no bright star, but I saw him in the sparkling eyes of the children and heard him in the beautiful Christmas program. I saw him in the group of parishioners gathered for the Christmas Novena and heard his message of love and forgiveness. I saw him in the excitement of the season and heard him in the loving words and letters of family, friends, and parishioners.

I saw the Savior last week when God sent us the glorious snow to renew the life of the earth, a visible sign that he comes to refresh all life, both physical and spiritual. I heard God speak in the carols and hymns announcing his arrival and inviting us to welcome, worship, and give thanks.

Christmas day has come and gone; the trees and lights are cast aside or put away. Gifts not appreciated are returned, rejected, or merely neglected, but love lives on. The countdown for the end of this year is rapidly approaching, but life moves on.

As the bells of Christmas fade, we already faintly hear the trumpets of Easter, for "Separate Christmas Day from Good Friday, and Christmas is doomed—doomed to decay into a merely sentimental or superstitious or sensuous "eat-drink-and-be-merry" festivity of December. Bethlehem and Golgotha, the manger and the Cross, the birth and the death, must always be seen together, if the real Christmas is to survive with all its profound inspirations; for the son of man came not to be ministered unto, but to minister; and to give his life as a ransom for many." J. Baxter.

Christmas, the year, and the snow—all quickly pass leaving only memories or hopefully dramatic changes in our lives. Our manger scenes may thrill us, but the cries of baby Jesus, lonely, cold, and unwelcome touch us deeply. His romantic life as a visionary troubadour fascinates us, but the call to follow disturbs us. The Gospel he lives portrays utopia, but his relentless challenge to do the same agitates us to leave our comfort zone. Memories empower us to make the necessary changes to live "Christmas" every day of our lives—Christ within us.

Good and bad memories of the year are etched deeply in our memories, especially the horror of 9/11, but what effect did it have on our lives? We appear to be more patriotic, but are we more Christ filled? We are proud to be an American, and rightly so, but what concern do we show for the rest of the world? We are one body, one family with one loving Father, redeemed by Jesus and guided by the Holy Spirit. Does our belief witness this in our love and compassion for all? Have we simply become American and failed to become Catholic?

The snow was beautiful, and we have wonderful memories of it, especially since it stayed only a short time; but its effects are lasting, for it renewed the earth with its life-giving water.

What we hear and what we see must produce more than memories; they must catapult us into an intimate relationship with Jesus who gives Christmas meaning through Easter. Do you see what I see; do you hear what I hear? Christ is within us—Happy New Year!

Father Henry Schmidt, December 30, 2001

Two leaves were sharing one balmy, sunny afternoon, and this is what I heard. One leaf was complaining because life was so short, times were difficult, and few appreciated them.

"Look at the evergreen tree," the first commented, "it lives for years and not only for a few months." It then went on to relate how wilted it became during the long dry spell, how brutally it was battered by the terrible wind storm, how its beautiful shape had been destroyed by the bird pecking away, and the time the worm decided to satisfy its craving for lunch, and that some of the neighboring leaves had been snatched away by the squirrels to build their nest. The dangling leaf was overcome with grief because so few even noticed his presence and in a short time it would fall to the ground and be trampled underfoot or gathered to be burnt.

The other leaf tried to comfort the first by reminding it of all their blessings. "While the evergreen seems to live, it was not able to offer fruit for others to enjoy. And have you forgotten how much people appreciate the shade and cooling breeze we offer on those hot summer days? I can still hear the people next door bemoaning the loss of the beautiful shade tree in their yard. While the elements of nature and the needs of animals affect our leaves, we are always nurturing and helping others to better their lives. What a blessing to be empowered to help others rather than always seeking self gratification! And besides, after we have supplied the needs of others, we are glorified in our brilliant foliage at the end of our time and work. And even then we do not stop giving for when we fall to the ground we offer new minerals to better the future of plants, animals, and people. Truly we are blessed and how thankful we should be that we can share these blessings from God."

Those leaves are you and me. Do you feel you are being used, or do you rejoice that you can supply the needs of others? There are times we feel we are being used, unappreciated, misunderstood, and bypassed by others. Our perception is often tainted by deception. Then our only hope is prayerful reflection so we can clearly understand who we are, why we are, and how we can share God's gifts and blessings. Our attitude needs to be embellished with gratitude.

We spend too much time and energy complaining and criticizing, which often leads to painful depression. Let us be more positive in our thinking and acting, keeping in mind that what we are complaining about can also be lived as a way to something new. Maybe it is impossible to change what has happened, but we are still free to choose how to live it.

Created special and gifted, we, unlike the first leaf, should not hesitate to share because we compare ourselves to others, feel the competition is too great, or are fearful of what others will say, lest we stifle God's plan. We, like the second leaf, need to freely give ourselves to Jesus who longs to use each of us in his marvelous, mysterious plan of salvation. Open to his will, we too will be glorified in the end and our legacy will have far reaching effects. So when we cannot change what has happened, we change how we accept what has happened. That's God's will!

Father Henry Schmidt, January 20, 2002

FATHER HENRY C. SCHMIDT

Some time before I wore sandals, I wore cowboy boots. Yes, I love to ride horses, and even though I have not done so for many years, I still have an inner desire to mount up and ride the trail. Horseback riding, while exhilarating and a means of bonding with others, can also be difficult and dangerous. Riding a horse is analogous to life.

I loved to ride as long as I was in control, but when the horse took control, riding became difficult and dangerous. When a spirited horse, one out of control, does not like the rider, it will do everything to dismount the person—by walking close to fences or buildings to crush the person, going under low tree branches to brush them off, rearing up or racing uncontrollably seeking to toss the rider. But there are also gentle horses that care for their passenger avoiding danger and protecting them from risky endeavors. Who is in control of your life?

Control is the biggest problem in our lives. We go to extremes to control others; do we do as much to control ourselves? Improper birth control and abortion are the evil means of controlling life for those who fail or refuse to control themselves. When impaired and incapacitated people become a burden and have lost control of their faculties, the trend is to ostracize them in order to have control of our lives. The terminally ill and the elderly, suffering from Alzheimer or dementia, are in grave danger from the proponents of euthanasia, who will not permit anything to hamper their need to be in total control. Like the horse who wishes to control the rider, they have denied that God is in total control and consequently life becomes difficult and dangerous.

This obsessive and overwhelming demand to control is the chief cause of divorce and family problems. One party unable or unwilling to control self, foolishly and with destructive results, tries forcibly to control his/her spouse and or children. What is needed more than anything else in our lives is self-control, that ability to accept and work through difficulties and differences in ways that are beneficial and best for all involved.

Without self-control, we will not stop with trying to manipulate spouse, family, friends, coworkers, everyone else, as well as everything else, we will foolishly try to control God also. Daily we pray "Thy will be done on earth as it is in heaven." This helps us focus on who is truly in charge. God permits all that happens hoping we will use them as grace moments. If Jesus is no stranger, but the one we believe in control, then we will see people and things no longer as a confrontation but a challenge, no longer as oppressor but expressions of God's intricate plan.

Unless God is in control, all is out of control. We, like the uncontrollable horse, seeking to overpower its rider, will destroy. With Jesus at the reigns, we resign ourselves to each situation and peace and harmony prevail. Relinquishing our obsession to dominate, and acknowledging the views of others are essential. "Without this mutuality of giving and receiving, mission and ministry easily become manipulative or violent. When only one gives and the other receives, the giver will soon become an oppressor and the receiver, victim. But when the giver receives and the receiver gives, the circle of love can grow as wide as the world." Henry Nouwen.

Father Henry Schmidt, January 27, 2002

Welcome to the walk is our focus this Lent. How brave are we? You may have taken part in a trust walk, where blind-folded, you trusted totally that another would lead you carefully and safely. Jesus invites us to come aside to an out-of-the-way place to walk with him. Will we trust him totally? He leads us into the desert, but we hesitate. The desert is not an inviting place, but it is a place with few distractions; a place where we can come to appreciate the vastness of God; a time we can become more aware of our total dependence on God; an opportunity to enter into the depths of our souls to determine ways to better imitate and walk with Jesus.

The desert is extremely hot and bitterly cold, awesome in beauty and threatening with dangerous sand storms, filled with life and a constant threat to life, so we are reluctant to accompany Jesus.

Abundantly blessed by God, we have developed an attitude of self-sufficiency, which hampers our willingness to enter into the desert. We are hesitant to leave behind our comforts or to share with others. In order to survive the intense heat or cold of the desert, we need protection. So too when faced with the turmoil of daily problems or the coldness of personal relations, we need the protecting, embracing arms of Jesus. The beauty of others, as the beauty of the desert, is often obscured when in the midst of a sand storm. Again, we turn to Jesus to guard and guide us till the storm passes, and we can clearly see the hidden beauty of those around us. Life is filled with excitement, when we are honest, trusting, and accepting of others, just as the plants and creatures of the desert are exciting and life giving if used carefully. But when not used properly, they become a dangerous threat to our well-being. Let us then walk with Jesus this Lent.

Jesus, in the desert, was tempted in the same way we are with hunger, pride, and the desire for power. In our effort to counteract these temptations we commit ourselves to more fervent prayer, fasting, and almsgiving.

Just as bread will satisfy our present need, and we are well aware that hunger will return; so too our insatiable enslavement to materialism will only momentarily satisfy a need, but our hunger for more will return. So we commit to fasting from food; that we may fast from materialism! Jesus was tempted to prove his father's love, but refused to demand some great sign. We too, must believe and trust that God loves us. Any extraordinary sign demanded of God to prove his love will satisfy for the moment but pride will demand more and more extreme proofs. So we enter into a more committed prayer relation with Jesus where we experience his personal love. In desperation, the devil tempted Jesus with power, but Jesus withstood him. May God give us the wisdom to realize that the world and all its splendor will never satisfy our thirst for power. On our walk with Jesus we commit ourselves to almsgiving, grateful for his blessings and willingly and generously relinquishing our "power" over them.

Jesus *welcomes us to the walk*. Are we willing and ready to go with him into the desert to die and live anew? Enmeshed in prayer, fasting, and almsgiving, and recommitted to our baptismal promises, we walk confidently with Jesus through the desert of Lent.

Father Henry Schmidt, February 17, 2002

What happened to our snow? Did we miss winter? The only signs of winter's snow are the picture on my wall calendar and the little wooden snowman perched on top of my computer. I am most thankful that it has not been a bitter cold winter, but I did miss the beauty of the snow.

It is hard to believe that in the middle of February we have so many signs of spring. Just walk out in the yard, and you will likely see the crocus, star of Bethlehem, and other spring flowers blooming. If not, you may have to remove some of the dead leaves which cover them.

Lent is a time for removing rotting leaves which prevent us from seeing the beauty of God's creation in our lives and in those around us. If you are in the middle of "winter" in your relationship with someone, this is the time to ask Jesus to empower you to put aside those "leaves" preventing you from seeing the "flower" in others. He is willing to help, but we must cooperate by means of prayer, discipline, and sharing with others.

When we are in the midst of the cold and the discomforts of winter, we tend to forget that new and more beautiful life lies hidden right before our eyes and in our midst. The bitter cold temperature, the strong biting wind, and the deep snow cause us to rush past some of God's marvelous creations. When the mild temperatures and the balmy breezes of spring melt the snow, we slow down and appreciate the spectacle around us. Similar effects can be noted in our personal relationships.

Turning to prayer, Jesus empowers us to warm the bitter cold relationships with love; by means of discipline, the biting winds of misunderstanding are changed to balmy breezes of acceptance; and by sharing with others we melt the snow that covers the "dead leaves" which need to be removed if we are to discover and appreciate the unique, buried flower.

How sad that we do not perceive every flower with the same excitement and favor, and worse still that we look upon some as weeds to be disposed of! For, the only difference between a flower and weed is in the eye of the beholder. Jesus sees "flowers" and "weeds" as masterpieces of his creation, and hopefully we can do the same.

During this grace-filled season of Lent, let the light and warmth of Jesus eradicate the coldness of our broken relations, restore life to old friendships, or foster new ones; may our awareness of what he suffered to restore our friendship motivate us to remove any old dead leaves, whatever they may be, so we may see clearly the potential beauty of all who come into our lives!

The killing temperatures, the destructive winds, and the dirty packed snow must all give way if we are to discover and remove the dead leaves, which prevent the appearance of the tender, new spring flowers that excite us with their exotic beauty.

Winter is quickly relinquishing its death grasp on all around us. Spring is anxious to surprise us with newness—longer, brighter, warmer days, and abundant new life. Jesus invites us to a similar spiritual experience. The winter of sin has been conquered by the spring of grace. The coldness of death has been replaced by the warmth of life.

Let Jesus remove your "dead leaves," behold the beautiful people around you, relish the beauty of his work made visible.

Father Henry Schmidt, February 24, 2002

Have you ever played the little BB hand game wherein you are required to manipulate several small BBs, encased in plastic on a small board, until all the BBs are placed in the end position of the star configuration? The least little unplanned tilt of the board will cause each BB to be dislodged. It takes skill and patience. How like the balance and patience required for life!

God has given us three BBs to manipulate in our lives, namely work, play, and worship. Most of us lack the skill or patience to keep them in their proper place. We tend to worship our work, work at our play, and play at our worship. What a tragedy and how frustrating!

How sad that we have become enslaved by our work that it has priority over everything, even family and God! And just as disturbing is the mindset that when we play, we must be champions and consequently we have lost the fun for which play was designed. But the tragedy of life comes when we play with our worship. We pick and choose whatever is convenient and satisfying and rationalize our failures to comply with our self-set boundaries in ways that we play games with God's directives and definitions of sin. We are out of balance!

Jesus said, "You shall worship the Lord your God and serve him only." Do our lives witness this directive? "The entire message of the Gospels is related in this attitude. I think the emphasis can be condensed into a single phrase: *What we worship determines what we become.* If we worship material possessions, we tend to grow more materialistic. If we worship self, we become more selfish still. That is why Christ continually endeavored to direct men's worship." (Harvey Ammerman)

I am certain that if we worked carefully to move all three BBs to their proper place and kept them there, we would experience a tremendous change in our lives for the better. Worship is not a text, but a context; it is not an isolated experience in life, but a series of life experiences. When we worship God only at church, it becomes an isolated experience with little value. Jesus's life was a composite of life experiences wherein he worshiped his Father at all times. So too our lives are to become a series of faith experiences as we truly worship God. Worship is listening to what God might say to us, through music, through words, through fellowship. It is also our response to what he speaks. We worship when we respond with an openness that allows God to change our lives.

The game of life is more difficult than any BB game. Life demands great skill in prioritizing worship, work, and fun and requires unending patience. The unexpected movements from the world, our peers, fellow workers, etc., will jolt our game board and send our BBs scattering.

Let us stop worshiping our work and share with our families. Let us stop working at our play, refrain from excessive competitiveness, and begin to enjoy life. But most importantly we need to resolve to stop playing with our worship and give prime time and priority to God.

Look at your BBs. Are they in order, or has someone or something dislodged them? Remember as you design your dreams and hopes, you determine who you will become. Their fulfillment is based on your worship, and what we worship determines what we become.

Father Henry Schmidt, March 24, 2002

As my Sandals sit before my computer, this first day after Easter, I look up, and I behold a multitude of angels hovering above, as strains of angelic voices fill the room. On my desk there is a rabbit in a rosebush with beautiful white blossoms, and on my computer sits a fluffy yellow chick with bunny ears. No, I have not completely gone off the deep end. All I say is true and are visual reminders of Jesus interacting in our lives.

Thirty-three paper angels swaying in the breeze from the heat vent are a gift from the second-grade students at Christmas. The angelic voices are from a CD "Pie Jesu" playing the mournful melodies of Passion Week. The wooden rabbit in the live rosebush depicts the change which took place in our lives during this Lent, while the baby chick with the bunny ears is symbolic of the glorified change we will experience when we're born into the fullness of life.

What an appropriate connection between Christmas and Easter, for those paper angels who came to me at Christmas to announce the birth of the God man, Jesus, are now proclaiming his tragic death! The wooden rabbit in the budding rose on my desk witnesses to me how hardened hearts were changed as Jesus removed our "Stony" hearts and replaced them with "real" hearts filled with love. And the baby chick with bunny ears, which is not the ordinary image we have, attempts to convey the glorified body, far beyond our imagination, we will experience when we are fully incorporated into the Resurrection we now celebrate and commemorate at Easter. And as I continue to type, the "angels" on the CD have gone from the "Pie Jesu" mourning to "Ave Verum Corpus" with their solemn songs of adoration and praise of the living, risen Jesus. We have completed the cycle—the birth, death, and Resurrection of Jesus.

Frequently I read in my magazine, *Angels among Us*, how God sends his messengers to guide and assist us through "heavenly angels" and "earthly angels" which includes people or animals. I believe in both types of angels, and I have been blessed to experience both. During these weeks of Lent, and in fact, all through the year, we are blessed by the work of his angels. Many are the people who have responded to embellish our liturgies with their multiple talents, be they supplying us with beautiful music and songs, decorating the environment, preparing our people, both young and old, for a fuller entry into and appreciation of our faith, proclaiming the Word, or some of the many other "Martha" tasks, or joining "Mary" in the prayer gatherings, especially the Holy Thursday, Good Friday, and Easter Vigil. These "angels" makes Little Flower Parish special.

The white rose exemplifies our efforts to let Jesus replace our hearts of "stone" with "real" hearts bursting with love, as we warmly welcome the eight new members into our parish and work, pray, and share our lives together, while walking with Jesus who prepares us and leads us to our Resurrection, that entry into glory, which surpasses our wildest imagination.

Hovering choirs of angels may not bless us, wooden rabbits or fluffy chicks may not impress us, blooming roses may not change us, but the loving Jesus, risen from the dead with promises of eternal life, peace, love, and glory does convert us. He has risen and lives and so will we.

Alleluia!

Father Henry Schmidt, April 7, 2002

Spring is here again, and the birds are busy building their nests. Above my front door, some little song sparrows have been trying to build a home. They work tediously but to no avail because as fast as they build, some English sparrows continue to tear it down. Both have a plan, both are uncompromising, consequently no progress is made, and only destruction results.

That can be accepted and partially understood in the animal world, but how do we rationalize such action among mature, reasoning people? How can we justify it in a country/world relation, a parish/school situation, or family/parish formation?

How sad to see rich and powerful countries selfishly allowing, or even causing poor and weaker countries to endure incredible suffering and lack of basic needs! How distressing to see parishioners divided because of personal plans even to the point of working against and tearing down the efforts of one another! Bitter is the pain between families when parish formation differs from their expectations. That's for the birds!

When God revealed his plans to the birds of how they were to build their nests, some failed to listen and thought they knew how to do it on their own, while others listened to the whole story of nest building. The robin listened. The barn swallow did not. As a result the robin heard the full message and was able to build a complete nest and place it in any bush or tree that it chose. The barn swallow, hearing only half the explanation of nest building, decided to begin on its own. Consequently it builds half a nest which must be attached to a building and is deprived of the freedom of the robin. Which are we?

The song sparrow, the English sparrow, the robin and the barn swallow are all living out the lifestyles that God fashioned. But they are birds and know no better. We do! We are all one family, one body, and united, we build up the living, loving body of Jesus. Divided, we, like the sparrows, destroy one another and the work entrusted to us by God. When we fail or refuse to listen to God's total plan for family, parish, country, or world we limit the freedom and blessings of all, and become dependent on things other than God.

Jesus died, rose from the dead, and after returning to his Father, sent the Holy Spirit upon us, his Church, calling us to believe the Good News, to share it with family, parishioners, friends, and with all the places in our lives. God is inviting us to appreciate and witness our faith in a variety of ways, among them the drive to revive our Parish Church/School, the Harvest of Thanks, Springtime of Hope Campaign, the universal participation in the weekend liturgies, the sharing of your time, talents, and treasures, as we enter a stewardship way of life, the sharing of faith in Small Faith Communities or organizational gatherings. We are to be a people of prayer, both private and in communion with others, especially with our families.

We can listen carefully like the robin and respond generously, or like the barn swallow, which will limit and deprive us of potential freedom and glory. We can work enthusiastically as the song sparrow, or imitate the English sparrow and respond negatively. We are not birds. We are followers of Jesus. Let us profess our faith enthusiastically together.

Father Henry Schmidt, April 21, 2002

My Sandal path has been long and varied over the past forty-five years, since I, with seven other men lay prostrate on the floor of the Cathedral and heard the words of Bishop O'Connor, "believe what you read, teach what you believe, and practice what you teach."

How varied was that path! I ministered in four parishes as an assistant—three had schools and one had two missions. After that I was pastor of four parishes—three had schools and one had two missions. Some were small and others were quite large, but all were exciting and most enjoyable. The church structure has been in constant change ever since I was ordained. I was ordained into a Latin Church, before the great outpouring of the Spirit during Vatican II, when things appeared "black and white" and the churches were full of people. Some parishes were more open to the wishes of the Spirit while others were more hesitant to welcome the renewal.

My priesthood has experienced suffering, pain, frustration, and disappointment which are to be expected, because it is a part of everyone's life. But my years shared intimately with Jesus have been blessed with incredible blessings of peace, joy, health, and love. I have seen blind faith of the former church blossom into living faith centered on love. I have worked with people who were Catholic, out of fear of punishment, become active followers of Jesus when they entered into a deep personal relationship with him. On my walk with Jesus I have seen marvelous miracles. I have experienced "the miracle" at Mass, as well as miracles in administering his sacraments, miracles of spiritual and physical healing, the miracle of human life and the miracle of a peaceful entry into eternal life. And the list goes on . . .

When my Sandals began the path that led from home and family, priesthood was looked upon as something very special. Then parents considered it to be the ultimate blessing, families held them in high esteem, and parishes encouraged, supported, and celebrated this call from God. What has happened to our understanding or appreciation of the priesthood?

It was difficult to leave my family, our farm life, and the idea of my own family, but the sacrifice was well worth it, and God has been working overtime to fill my life with blessings. There is no comparison between the value of priestly work and any other. The work of medical people, great as it is, can never preserve life or restore it, while a priest, as the instrument of God, restores the life of grace and assures us of eternal life. The latest development of modern technology may for a time better our lives, but never give lasting satisfaction and peace. The satisfaction and reward of the priesthood far surpasses even the greatest monetary benefits of all entertainers, sports or otherwise, for you cannot buy the joy and excitement of contemplating Jesus for all eternity, which alone is supplied by a priest. What vocation will ever offer the variety of life, or the blessings experienced in the life of a priest? No other vocation is as essential as the priesthood, for only a priest can celebrate Mass and give us the Eucharist, forgive sins or prepare a dying person for the entry into the new and lasting life. I thank God daily for his call to serve as a priest. I pray that he will continue to use me as an instrument of peace, love, and life. Pray for me, all priests, and for more vocations to the priesthood.

Father Henry Schmidt, May 5, 2002

Since I am unable to walk on water, I am looking for pontoon sandals so I can walk in my basement which is under water. Every fifteen seconds, the sump pump in my basement hums its happy tune as it continues to faithfully remove the water gushing into my "unwanted" pool. Due to weakness, the walls no longer prevent the water from flooding my basement, but thanks to the genius who designed the pump, I and countless others, are spared from disaster.

This welcome hum of my sump pump reminds me of my own weakness and the compassion of Jesus who faithfully graces me as he continually saves me from the disaster of sin. Due to weakness, sin seeps into my life, frustrating Jesus's plan for me. By his death and Resurrection, he developed a means of helping me and all repentant sinners, as he offers us the "sump pump" of the sacrament of reconciliation to head off disaster.

As we celebrate the feast of Pentecost, the birthday of our Church, with the powerful outpouring of the Spirit, it may be well to take an inventory of our spiritual life. First we must consider the very building itself, our soul. Our soul is made in the image and likeness of God, destined to live forever. Sin damages and destroys our personal relationship with Jesus. What is the condition of our soul right now? If God would call us home, are we ready, and would he welcome us with open arms? Is there a need for some repair? Do we find the seeping of imperfection and sin growing into a steady stream needing a "sump pump" to ward off disaster?

By means of baptism, Jesus firms up the faith foundation of our soul and with the help of parents, the church, and others, we maintain and build on this foundation. Is there evidence that we are building wisely, and maturely seeking to repair any damage from our sinful mistakes through the prayerful reception of the sacrament of reconciliation? How often do we use it?

Damage from excess surface water left untended can destroy our possessions, or it can lead to growth and bettering the situation. The careless person ignoring the problem, will undergo repeated destruction, but the wise person will learn from the experience and repair the walls, get a sump pump, arrange things so the water can no longer destroy or develop some ingenious way to protect and save their treasured possessions.

The same is true with our spiritual life. Sin unattended can cause continued and greater damage, ending in disaster, or we can learn from our mistakes and plan ways to avoid them, seek forgiveness when we fail, and work to eliminate them all together. Sin in itself is wrong, be it slight or serious, but cooperating with the grace of God we can use the experience as a spring board transforming our lives when directed by Jesus.

The unwanted water in my basement is not totally wasted, but carefully directed out into my yard, to give life to the grass and flowers. In like manner, unwelcome imperfections and failures can be used to encourage spiritual growth if we are open to the direction of Jesus who uses all experiences for our good and his glory. We cannot walk on water, nor eliminate all sin, but we can direct both water and sin in ways that promote new life. Keep those pumps humming!

Father Henry Schmidt, May 19, 2002

Rejoice for the Lord is near. Dismiss all anxiety from your minds . . . (Phil. 4) This past Sunday we celebrated Pentecost, that day when the Spirit of God drew near to us, the Church, the people of God, to be our guide and protector until the end of time.

After many dark and cold days, filled with torrential rains, the sun burst forth with its brilliant light and warmth on Pentecost. For many tired of the rain and nearing nervous exhaustion from fighting the flood waters, it was a welcome sight. It was truly a day to rejoice.

As the apostles, weary from the traumatic experiences of the suffering, death, and ascension of their beloved friend, Jesus, welcomed the outpouring of the Holy Spirit on Pentecost, so we, distraught from the physical and spiritual terrors plaguing us, gladly welcome the Holy Spirit into our lives. We rejoice for the Lord is near.

Our churches were alive with songs of praise and adorned with colorful banners and streamers depicting the presence of the Spirit's outpouring of gifts upon the church, and symbolizing the tongues of fire cleansing our souls and removing all anxieties from our minds.

As the Holy Spirit descended on the Apostles on that first Pentecost, he empowered them to go forth, without fear, with divine guidance to proclaim the Gospel News and witness by their lives their faith and trust in God's plan. That same Spirit waits to be welcomed into our lives. He offers incredible gifts and graces to each of us. The Lord is near, dismiss all anxiety.

The Apostles, ordinary, uneducated, fearful men, questioning the plan of Jesus were transformed by the Spirit into men of faith, open to the wisdom of the Spirit, ready to live the Gospel despite the cost and empowered to do the ordinary in extraordinary ways. Like the apostles, we often try to excuse ourselves from proclaiming and witnessing the Gospel, but because of Pentecost, we can no longer refuse because the Lord is near to dismiss all anxiety.

Following Jesus necessarily requires that the Spirit burn away our imperfections and fears. We, like gold in a furnace, are being refined and perfected. At the final session for those welcomed into our parish family at the Easter Vigil, our discussion revealed that everyone is gifted by the Spirit who calls us to use our gifts for the good of the Church. Hesitant at first, we eventually see the working of the Spirit in our lives when given the freedom to act through us.

Amazement filled the hearts of all that first Pentecost when the Spirit spoke in varied tongues. The Spirit, our Church, still speaks the message of salvation and in all languages. It is even more amazing that the Church could have survived the attacks of heresies, schisms, human errors, and divisions, while protecting the truth as revealed by Jesus. It has been guided by the Spirit.

Just as we adorn our churches with bright colors, so God embellishes our souls with the gifts and fruits of the Holy Spirit. It takes time and effort to adorn the church, and it takes prayer and sacrifice to acknowledge the presence and plan of the Spirit in our lives. This being true, may we be Pentecost to all we meet. Rejoice, the Lord is near! Dismiss all anxiety. We are guided, guarded, and empowered by the Holy Spirit. Let us begin.

Father Henry Schmidt, May 26, 2002

This past week the path of my sandals was suddenly changed by a phone call. The bishop asked if I would agree to become pastor of a parish with a school and two missions, and the only priest in the entire county. Recalling the promise I made to Bishop O'Connor forty-five years ago, on the day of my ordination, "Do you promise to me and my successors, obedience and fidelity?" I humbly and sadly responded, "Yes." How difficult and life-changing a yes can be!

When the angel asked Mary to be the Mother of God, her yes brought great joy to the world, but much pain and hardship to her peaceful, humble, and faith-filled life, as she left her family and friends to do the will of God, questioning and trusting in God's judgment for her in his plan of salvation. When God asked Jesus to become man, his "yes" brought redemption to the world, as he left the glory of heaven to carry out the mysterious plan of his all loving Father which resulted in incredible suffering and death. So too, my yes to the bishop brings much joy and hope to the three parishes, awaiting a pastor, but much sadness to me as I leave this outstanding parish, where I have spent one-fourth of my priesthood, some of the happiest years of my life and grown immensely as I have shared in your faith lives. Leaving some of my most treasured friends and the special support groups will be the most difficult and painful part of my "cross" of moving, since there are no words or ways that I can fully express or show my heartfelt love for you.

I sincerely thank you for your kindness and support, your many prayers, and your patience and willingness to forgive me, even when you did not understand me.

I humbly ask forgiveness from anyone whom I may have hurt. I assure you it was never intentional and without my realizing that I did at times.

I know that in obeying the directives of the Church regarding Liturgical ceremonies, some were annoyed, and sad to say some may even have let the parish. My hope was to pray and celebrate in ways that would deepen the faith life of us all. Please forgive me.

I am deeply edified by the sacrifices you make for the faith life of your parish, to those who have participated in the Koinonia and Gift weekends, the Small Faith Communities, the Promise Keeper groups, those who gather for daily Mass and for the First Friday adoration. That is why this parish is so special and growing in faith so visibly and rapidly.

Vatican II called you to become involved in ministering to the needs of your parish faith life, and you have made a remarkable response. And the increasing number living a stewardship way of life is most satisfying.

Your new pastor will be different, so give him a chance. Warmly welcome him. Try to work together in discerning what is best for *all*, especially for your *faith life*. When you truly live your faith, all else falls in place and becomes quite insignificant.

Again, I love you, will pray for you, and miss you much. We may be separated by miles, but I will remember you. I leave with this prayer: "Jesus lead me to where I am needed, but not wanted, and give me the faith and courage to leave where I am wanted, but no longer needed."

Father Henry Schmidt, June 9, 2002

As the water has receded and solid ground reappears, my Sandals continue on the pathway of faith filled with a spirit of hope. Difficulties burden our lives because we are people of limited optimism or unlimited pessimism, which all too frequently lead to despair. As followers of Jesus, we are called to be a people of hope. We tolerate the world in chaos, struggling with pain and violence because we trust the church would be there to give us joy, peace, and hope. But today we hear people, lacking in hope, saying, "I cannot deal with the fact that in the church people are fighting, divided, and struggling with each other." Despairing, they are no longer willing to stay within the church; they walk away. But in leaving this broken and divided church, they are lonelier and find themselves walking without Jesus.

Our most painful suffering which leads us to despair seems to come from within, from people we least expect. "We cannot go around despair to hope. We have to go right through despair. We will never know what hope is until we have tasted real despair." (Henri Nouwen) Jesus experienced that too, but being neither an optimist nor a pessimist he speaks to us about hope—a hope built upon the promise that, whatever happens, God will be with us.

We are being tested globally and locally by slanders and attacks from various sources, and at times we also have our internal differences, but we stand firmly founded on the hope of Jesus's promise. Whether life goes well or proffers disturbing situations, we use the occasion to benefit.

Examining the damage from the flooding, we search for the hidden blessings. Flooding destroys crops, but leaves new and rich soil in the fields. New and better crops result. Often, the "valuables" destroyed in our basements had not been used for some time, and most likely were not working, so now, we have a legitimate reason to toss them out. Basements are repaired and new appliances make them better than before. Difficult opportunities for growth girded on hope.

The damaging "flood waters" of division and misunderstanding continue to rise and recede with the passing of time. With each invasion, there is some damage to persons and parish, but hopefully as we work through our differences, filled with hope, we grow in faith, love, and solidarity. Tempted to despair, we pause, work through the "flood" and build anew while tossing out the old stylized, long unused and limited ways of interrelating. Just as every flood combines good and bad, destruction and construction, so too, as we face the onslaught of damaging floods, we are called to be a people of hope.

With each new problem, let us start the pump and drain off all anger, and clean up and repair broken relations with the framework of forgiveness and the fresh paint of love, so Jesus can refurnish our spirits with peace and newness. We are not optimists wearing rose-colored glasses, nor are we pessimists failing to note any possible chance of a unifying solution; we are hopeful, trusting that Jesus will lead us and draw good from every situation.

Together, empowered by the Spirit, we can face our despairs—personal, global, or ecclesiastic. May we allow Jesus to use each "flood" to destroy the useless and restore newness in us! We are not pessimistic, nor optimistic; we are hopeful!

Father Henry Schmidt, June 16, 2002

While on retreat, Father John Canary, our director spoke each day of the beauty, the challenges, and the pain in the life of a priest. The love of parishioners living in deep faith is a great motivation for the sacrifices required in living out the call of a priest. The attacks and enticements of the secular and material world present tremendous challenges, which can be endured only with the love and prayerful support of dedicated parishioners. And the call to move on to serve the needs of God's people is among the greatest causes of pain and "darkness." Faith in God and sharing an intimate friendship with Jesus empowers me to cope with such transitions.

These words of Archbishop Camara partially express who I am and what I feel . . . "For me, being a priest isn't a choice, it's a way of life. It's what water is for a fish, the sky for a bird. I really believe in Christ; Christ to me is not an abstract idea. Being a priest has never disappointed me; he's a personal friend. Celibacy, chastity, the absence of a family, in the way you laymen understand it—all this has never been a burden to me. If I've missed certain joys I've had, and I have others so much more sublime. If you only knew what I feel when I say Mass, how I become one with it! The Mass for me is truly Calvary and the Resurrection; it's a mad joy! Look, there are those who are born to sing, those who are born to write, those who are born to play soccer, and those who are born to be priests. I was born to be a priest."

My priestly ministry is awesome. No words can express the powerful presence and action of the Spirit while celebrating the Mass or administering the sacraments. Words fail to express my heartfelt gratitude for the joy you have brought into my life during my years ministering to you and being ministered by you. I have been the greater beneficiary.

Saddened and reflecting on the plan of Jesus, while sitting on a bench in the warm sun at the King's House Retreat Center, I beheld a tiny blade of grass swaying in the gentle breeze and a beautiful silver butterfly, no larger than a dime, flitting at my feet. Contemplating this sight, I became aware of the magnitude of our God. That blade of grass, that tiny butterfly not seen by anyone else, God created just for me, his glory, and my pleasure. God was acting in my life at that moment, transforming that dark night of my soul into an occasion of hope and light, empowering me to persevere in doing little things well.

Clearly did I see in that experience the importance of each of you. If God uses grass and butterflies to bring hope and light to those in darkness, how much more can he use you? God reveals his promise of a brighter future in surprising little ways, and you have been one of them. For just as the preschool children's imprinted hands, in a rainbow of colors, on a posterboard hanging on my office door promises life and hope for a brighter future, so the many ways you have woven your lives of faith into the fabric of my Sandal path assures me our working together will bear lasting fruit. In many little ways you have been instruments of God's grace to me. Realize your special, unique value.

Butterflies, grass, hand prints, treasured friends, one and all God uses to restore light and hope to the dark spots of my life.

Father Henry Schmidt, June 23, 2002

87

After one week, my Sandals are slowly forming a routine and adjusting to the new faces and reestablishing the various committees in the three parishes, which are to help guide the faith life and financial stability of our wonderful parishes. Remember, everyone is a part of this overall plan, and your input and assistance is essential. Parish unity and community requires a solid family faith life founded on love and compassion for all, especially for the least. No one is too small to make some difference.

Reading an article in the *Maryknoll* magazine, I came across an African proverb which brought out that point so clearly. "If you think you are too small to make a difference, try sleeping in a closed room with a mosquito." God uses even the littlest things to make a difference. Now, he is waiting to use you, if only you will let him. When each of us gives what we have and can, then God can do great things.

Driving through the country these past weeks has brought this home so clearly. Looking at the newly harvested wheat fields reminded me of God's plan for each of us. A farmer plants a single grain of wheat, and it grows and produces abundantly. Then the wheat is harvested, and the straw is bailed so that it may be used for bedding or other purposes. Consider the process of the wheat—after bearing grain, it is cut, compressed into a rectangular bale, bound by wire, and stored until needed. The wire is very important to keep the bale intact and the straw manageable. If the wire breaks, the bale loses its value and is left in the field, unless the farmer tries again to mold it into another bale. What a difference one small grain of wheat has made!

As each of us lives our faith life, producing lasting fruit like the straw, we are cut and formed into the person Jesus created us to be. This forming requires the compressing pains of sacrifice, self-denial, forgiveness, and humility. This is possible only if we are open to his grace plan. Just as each bale is formed from many individual straws held together by the wire, so we, many, are united and held together by the love of Jesus, the "wire," which gives us value. Then in time, Jesus will use us in his plan of salvation, in the manner and at the place he deems best. No one is too small to make a difference, not even you.

If a tiny mosquito can have such a great affect, and a tiny grain of wheat can make such a great difference, then, certainly we should have a greater appreciation of who we are and the unique difference we can make in God's plan of salvation.

Jesus has called me here to work, share, and pray with you as we grow in and cherish that marvelous gift of our faith. Nothing is more precious and essential, not even life itself. Physical life will end, but for those who have experienced a living faith, death is only the doorway to the fullness of life—complete and lasting union with Jesus.

The question facing each of us, in this world of material possessions, is how much am I willing to sacrifice to show my love of Jesus and my gratitude for his gift of faith? The answer lies in my conviction that "no one is too small to make a difference." Are you willing and ready to make that difference?

July 14, 2002

As I sat at my table, I saw a container of popcorn, and it reminded me of what it means to be a follower of Jesus. The gallon jug of corn was hard, cold, and of little use as long as it remained idle and safe in the container. Only when it is removed from the jug and placed over the heat, will it become soft, warm, and of use. But that requires a great sacrifice.

How similar to us! We love to remain in the safety of our lifestyles, our "jug," and ignore those around us. When we do, we are cold and impersonal, failing to allow Jesus to use us. Only if we are willing to move out of the security of our life choice, and face the "heat" of the mission of Jesus, can Jesus soften our hearts, warm us with his love, and use us as instruments of peace and life. That too requires great sacrifice.

During these few weeks that my Sandals have been walking amongst you, I have seen many people who have freely chosen to sacrifice themselves for the good of their parish and community. As a result, we all benefit, and I see hope of great things to come. Just as each grain of corn sacrificing itself fills the whole bowl with nourishment, so when each of us gives of ourselves, the whole bowl, our parish family is filled with blessings resulting from the efforts of others.

We are all entrusted by God to be good stewards and to use the things he has given us in ways that are for his glory and the good of his people. All that we have, we have received, and all that we have received, we are to give away! We live in a society that has duped us into believing that the more we possess, the greater we are and that our possessions guarantee us security. We are slowly being consumed with the devastating cancer of selfishness. Our only hope of cure, our salvation, depends on living a stewardship way of life.

Jesus proclaims a teaching which is contrary to the culture of death so prevalent in modern society. Jesus came to give life and to give it more abundantly. All too frequently, we see a lack of respect for God's creation as we pollute earth, sea, and sky. Selfish people seek what they want regardless of the cost to others, even if it means destroying the precious gift of life. As good stewards, we are called to respect all creation, and especially God, the creator of all life.

We are not hard grains of corn; we are ministers of God's graces. We have far more to give than popped corn, which satisfies a temporary need; we are empowered to give life—both physical, which is temporary and divine, which is eternal. We are the chosen people of God called to be good stewards. Our use of material gifts will determine how we appreciate our spiritual blessings. Our appreciation of our spiritual blessings will determine how we will use our material gifts. Faith is the foundation for both!

Is your faith alive enough to empower you to be "popped" for Jesus, that is, are you willing to live and sacrifice that his message of salvation be available for others, or has the spiritual cancer of selfishness weakened your efforts to be good stewards?

July 21, 2002

89

As my Sandals made their way across the yard, I noticed how dry and hard the grass was becoming due to lack of rain and the exceptionally hot sun the past weeks. How like many followers of Jesus, who failing to receive the nourishing Eucharist and overextended with the busyness of their world, are becoming dry and hard. Just as the grass needs rain and cool temperature to revive, so too we need to welcome Jesus into our daily lives in order to revive our faith.

We all believe in God, love Jesus, and want to follow him, but at times we take him for granted when we allow nonessential things to become more important than those truly required for salvation. How is your "grass"—your relationship with Jesus—hard, dry, and dying or soft, green, and alive?

Jesus, our Lord and Savior, loves each of you personally, and I, as your pastor, come among you with the same love. All I can do is reveal to you his unconditional love; I cannot make you love him or those around you; your response of love must be personal and freely given. And now is the time.

During the past two weeks, I have celebrated the Mass of Resurrection for two parishioners and for a priest of our diocese. Last November I mourned with a priest friend when his father died, two weeks ago we buried his mother, and this week we celebrated the Mass of Resurrection for his brother. Thanks be to God, all were ready for their call, their "grass" was alive.

The dry grass reminds us of death, but also of the Resurrection. Even though the grass seems to be dead, it has deep roots, which sprout forth new life following a rain or when it is watered. Likewise when we neglect to live our faith and walk close to Jesus, we begin to weaken and die, but our deep-rooted faith when nourished by Jesus will likewise manifest new life.

The compassion of Jesus compels us to reach out to family or parish members who are in need of reconciliation or nourishment and encourage and support them in whatever way we can to bring them back to the fullness of his grace. Our young people face the philosophy of convenience and immediate gratification and tend to seek the easy way. Those who have been disenchanted with and abandoned in marriage feel unwanted. The elderly and unskilled feel useless along with a multitude of others who experience insecurity for various reasons. These are the ones we need to bring back to Jesus so he can renew their faith. We cannot neglect or abandon anyone. They are the grass which needs special watering and nourishment, which only Jesus can supply.

If there are times that our "grass"—our faith seems to be hard and dry, be not anxious, we need only to turn to Jesus, who will restore newness to our faith lives. We spend much time, energy, and money beautifying our yards, which are here today and will be gone tomorrow; let us do even more in beautifying our spiritual lives, which are eternal. Let us do it now, together!

July 28, 2002

As my Sandals made their way around a quiet pond on a bright spring day, I saw frogs, toads, tadpoles, and fish. The water was still and the chorus of croaking frogs resounded with their praise of God. When I came near, they jumped to safety in the water. The toads were silent and tried to hide and disguise themselves amidst the grass and weeds. The little tadpoles darted swiftly about in the water seemingly fearless of my presence, feeling safe in the warm embrace of the pond, while the fish glided with grace and ease through the deep glittering spring-fed waters. Such was life at the ole country pond. Let us note the parallel with our faith life.

Are you a frog, a toad, a tadpole, or a fish? A frog is one fully relying on God. A toad is one tuned on another deity. A tadpole is one of those about developing peaceful or loving encounters. And a fish is one fashioned in spiritual holiness. When Jesus examines the life flowing from his baptismal water, what does he find?

Gathering at meetings and celebrating the Eucharist with the people of the three parishes during this past month, I have seen many *"frogs."* Their faith life is most inspiring and exciting. Like the frogs, their praise of God resounds, and when danger or difficulties threaten, they plunge into the "water," the open arms of Jesus who protects them. They rely on God to help them endure the difficulties of life and celebrate his presence and blessings when things go well. Peace and confidence fills their lives because they are convinced that God has a plan for them and is in complete control.

Occasionally I will see a *"toad,"* someone confused about their priorities and having a need of a better relationship with Jesus. They try to hide from him as they wander from his Church and rationalize their lack of involvement in parish activities. Some believe their disguise is working, but no one can hide from Jesus who continues to search for them. He beckons them to jump into the safety of the "water," and be renewed with the cleansing water of his life-giving sacraments.

But it is so exciting to see the many *"tadpoles,"* the vast number of people who are developing a deeper and more intimate relationship with Jesus, while growing in faith, working for peace and justice and striving to love one another. We have a grave responsibility to live our faith as we carefully guide and assure their proper development, into a *"frog,"* who will praise and glorify Jesus now and forever.

How blessed we are to also have an abundance of *"fish,"* who with ease and grace live in the security of Jesus's love, longing for the time when the waters flowing from the baptismal pool will empty into the kingdom of eternal life and love.

Warmed by the light of the son of God, bathed in the cleansing waters of baptism, nourished on the food of life, and secure in the protective grace of the sacraments, we find life as a follower of Jesus patterned closely after life at the ole country pond. Let us then together praise God as we develop into the person he created us to be. Enjoy your "swim" with Jesus in the pool of life.

Father Henry Schmidt, August 4, 2002

My Sandals enjoyed a wonderful week up in the hills of Marquette State Park with over one hundred people ranging in age from a few weeks to some in their seventies. Each day, we gathered to pray; to discuss true love and unity between couples and in family life; to celebrate the Eucharist, and to discern how couples and families could grow in faith and share it more fully in our home parishes. It was an awesome experience and Jesus was powerfully present.

We shared meals and fun times around camp fires and the pool, and were playing games while bonding with our families and forming lasting friendships. Everyone came to know Jesus more personally and intimately and benefited from this quiet time away. Hopefully, we all left with a new appreciation of our individual value, the need for commitment to our spouses, and the blessings of family life.

The days we are camping in the woods are difficult days for the little "critters." The small children are continually on the prowl searching for and catching the little lizards and other crawling creatures. God made these little creatures for the woods, but they are an attraction to the children who want to catch the most, the largest, or the fastest for the race on the final day of camp.

These defenseless creatures, of the woods, remind me of the many people who face the enticements of life. It seems that we human beings, made in the image and likeness of God and created to dwell in his loving embrace, find ourselves in the same situation as the creatures of the woods. Trying to live Jesus's plan, we all too frequently find ourselves bothered and overcome by attractions, which capture us, be it possessions, power, position, or pleasures. For a time we try to run and avoid captivity, like the little lizards fleeing from the children, but eventually many are caught. The littler children have a hard time catching their prey, but the older ones manage because of their speed and capability. We too manage to avoid succumbing to the littler pleasures, but the greater and more enticing seem to overwhelm us.

The creatures of the woods have a difficult time surviving when displaced from their natural habitat. Fortunately, thanks to wise parents, most are released at the end of the week to return to the woods where they were meant to dwell. However some are not so fortunate. A few die in captivity during the week at camp and others when taken home by the children. We too are created to live in the loving graces of Jesus. At times we are snatched out of our grace zone, but thanks to the loving concern of others and the mercy of Jesus we too can be released from whatever has captivated us and return to the safety of the church, the natural habitat for followers of Jesus.

On the final day of camp, when the "critter race" takes place, many are disappointed and are crying because their critter did not win the race. Hopefully, we will not experience the same disappointment and remorse because we, failing to follow Jesus, entered the wrong race in foolish imitation or competition with our peers. As long as we are held captive by the "creature comforts" of possessions, power, position, or pleasures, like the creatures of the woods, our spiritual survival is in jeopardy. We need to break away from our captors and return to the safety of

Jesus's plan. This can be done when we appreciate our unique relationship with Jesus, live our marriage commitment faithfully, and witness deep faith with our families, guided by the Holy Spirit. We are not critters captured by creatures, but children freed and cared for by our Creator.

August 18, 2002

The wise ole owl, sitting quietly in the barn loft, looked out at the gurgling brook running through the pasture. For years the horses, cows, pigs, chickens, ducks, and geese, both wild and tame, along with the farmer and his family had enjoyed life on the farm and then this pastoral scene experienced a change.

Late one fall, the owl noted the arrival of a new comer, "Mr. Beaver" along with his wife. They worked hard and were fast damming up the stream to make a "beaver pond" to catch the winter snow and early spring rain. They did great work, but it caused some problems until the pond was full and the overflowing stream continued to refresh those deprived of its cooling water.

Then one late spring afternoon, the owl spotted another new family as "Mr. and Mrs. Badger" decided to take up residence at the "beaver pond." Soon trouble developed as the Beaver family who worked each day to repair the dam to keep it from leaking, noticed the Badgers were continually digging into the dam to make their home, which weakened the dam and caused leakage. And so they were continually engaged in a never ending combat—one building, the other tearing down. But still the quiet, peaceful life of the other animals and the farmer's family went undisturbed, as they drank the refreshing waters and swam in the cooling stream.

As the pond developed, it collected fish of all types; among them was a blowfish, which was quite different from the ordinary fish in this beaver pond. Unlike the majority of the other fish, he began to feel superior and exaggerate. He had the unique ability to blow himself up to become many times larger than normal in order to scare off other fish who sought to attack and destroy him. But he also began to take claim for the beautiful pond, which the "Beaver" family had worked so hard to build, in order to intimidate and control the other fish in the pond. He even threatened to get the "Badger" family to destroy the pond if they would not accept him and his demands. His continual blowing things out of proportion brought great chaos to all who sought to live in peace and enjoy the blessings of the beaver pond. Meanwhile the farmer and his family enjoyed the beauty of the summer, as the ducks and geese swam in the pond, the cows and horses drank from its clear waters and the pigs wallowed in the cool mud of its banks.

Quietly and patiently, the wise ole owl watched life change on the farm. Jesus too watches patiently as we choose to be a "beaver," working hard for the good of our parish, a "badger," constantly criticizing or tearing down and destroying what others have labored to accomplish, or a "blowfish," bragging or bullying to control, while contributing little to develop the faith life of our parish.

Our parish (i.e., the church and school) is like the pasture, and we are like the animals, each having something to offer, open to accepting others and what they bring, and living in harmony, while Christ offers us the refreshing waters of the sacraments and the Mass.

When a new "beaver" brings an idea, good for the all the parish, let us accept it, and not become a "badger" undermining their efforts, nor a "blowfish" destroying them. If we love and accept each other, for who we are, as Jesus sees us, we will welcome beavers, badgers, and blowfish in his "Pond," and all the "animals" in the pasture, the whole parish will benefit and our faith life will prosper. What do you choose to be: "a beaver, badger, or blowfish?"

August 25, 2002

Sitting at the ball game with the sun blazing down, the dark cloud forming in the Northwest was a most welcome sight. Gradually the sun disappeared and the temperature dropped. Seeing the clouds renewed our hope that we would receive some much needed rain. But our hopes ended in disappointment. We saw the clouds, but we did not experience the fulfillment of the promised rain.

Adam saw the clouds, but not the rain. Noah saw the clouds and enjoyed the rain. Pharaoh saw the clouds, but never experienced the blessings of the rain. John the Baptist beheld the cloud and anxiously awaited the rain. Time and again God sent clouds of hope via Old Testament leaders, the prophets, Mary, the apostles, and especially his son, Jesus, but only a few were open to the rain. Are we cloud gazers, or are we truly open to the rain?

Throughout salvation history, God has sent his "clouds" of revelation, but worldliness and wickedness like strong winds have blown the clouds away so that people of every age, including the present, miss the "rain" of his grace.

This past week, people gathered to commemorate the tragic event of September 11, which affected countless lives. Did we learn from that day of terror or did we simply see the cloud and miss the rain?

The days following 9/11 brought about a remarkable witness of patriotism along with some momentary return to God. Many noted these "clouds" with hope, both that we would make greater efforts to abolish terrorism by assuring peace and justice for all, and that we would experience a continued increase of more turning to God. The clouds dissipated, and the rains never came.

Like Adam, whom God blessed abundantly, many crave for more even if it means ignoring God's plan and so we suffer. Like Pharaoh, who had power and riches in abundance, some enslave others and out of greed fail to heed Jesus's plea of compassion by refusing to share with those devastated by poverty.

Jesus spoke to us on September 11 just as clearly as he did to any of the Old Testament leaders or the people of his time about the evils of sin and the need to turn back to him. All saw the clouds, but only a few experienced the rain, for most were soon caught up by the "winds," the enticements of today's society. Now, one year later, life has returned to routine. Patriotism continues to ignore equality and justice for the entire world, and once again, God has been confined to church.

We continue to deny the right to life of the unborn; and allow the removal of prayer from school. We have taken his commandments from our halls of justice and are trying to remove him from our currency. Living by a personal interpretation of his moral and ethical guidelines, we neglect to pray and readily excuse ourselves from Sunday worship.

The demand for the "sunny days" of worldly materialism have prevented the "clouds" of faith from bringing the fulfillment of needed "rain," grace, and intimate union with Jesus.

All life suffers when there is no rain. Our social, emotional, and spiritual life suffers when there is no grace. Welcome the clouds of grace that you may experience the fulfillment of the rain, the presence of Jesus in your life.

September 15, 2002

A few months ago, driving along the highway, I was pleasantly surprised to see a beautiful field of sunflowers. They were young and glowing with color. They were tall and able to move about freely as they swayed in the breezes and followed the sun. The countryside was enhanced by this youthful glory.

This past week as I passed the same field, its glorious, golden glow gone, the stalks were bent and hardened and consequently the flowers were no longer able to follow the routine path of the sun. Aging had transformed the beauty of youth into apparent, useless waste. To the foolish, it may appear that way, but the wise could appreciate the fulfillment and the blessing of the life cycle of the plant.

While passing, I heard two aging sunflowers discussing the situation. One was bemoaning the fact that due to aging, they had lost their beauty. With their bent backs, they were becoming restricted in their movements and furthermore, they could no longer remember to perform their routine action of following the sun. The other sunflower quietly and gently comforted the sad flower. Remember, the sunflower is beautiful, and pleasing to the eye in its youth, but its value comes only when it matures, loses its sensual beauty and produces its many valuable seeds.

How like the schema of our life! Frequently, I hear elderly people discussing their inability to function as they did when they were younger, or how useless they imagine themselves, or how forgetful they are. Oh! that they would listen to the wise, accepting sunflower, who realized that our value is not what we do in those young developing days, but that we bear lasting fruit. The world lusts for the beauty of youth, Jesus values the seeds of sanctity, the result of mature faith.

We generally place too great a value on the beauty, vitality, and accomplishments of young people, and ignore the inner, hidden value of our elders simply because they have lost some of their external beauty and mobility through aging. In the eyes of the foolish, they have little, if any value, but to the wise, they possess a wealth of valuable seeds.

The true value of life is not our external physical beauty, which so quickly passes, no matter how we try to attain it, and there is no way we can sustain it, for aging is inevitable. We value all life, the unborn, the young, and the old, for God alone knows what age or stage of life is most valuable for each of us. But certainly our value does not come with what is visible to the eye. Our value comes from our inner being.

In the young sunflower, we may see beauty, but let us consciously realize the value contained in the maturing sunflower, whose seeds produce oil and food. While youthful beauty may be the envy of the worldly, it is wisdom and sanctity, which accompanies mature faith that assures lasting life.

May our young people realize the true value of our faith as witnessed by the elders of our parish, and may our elders never underestimate their importance in God's plan of salvation. Beauty is in the eyes of the beholder, value is in the mind of God.

September 22, 2002

As I walked past the air conditioner next to the church, I noticed there were weeds all around and in the midst of them I saw one lonely dandelion blooming. A little further on, I came across a bed of blooming flowers no longer in their prime beauty due to the lack of rain and the approach of fall. What a visible example of life!

The weeds were alive and not affected by the elements of summer or fall, and the lone dandelion was showing forth its God-given beauty; yet these plants are branded and condemned as weeds and are of no value and consequently should be removed solely on the grounds that they are not flowers.

Why are we unable to see the beauty of God's creation in the weeds, while we protect the dying flowers next to them, which have lost their beauty, simply because they are classified as flowers? Is this not the way we all too often perceive those around us?

When a child exceeds academically, displays excellent physical or mental talents, has a beautiful appearance, they become the "flowers" which attract our attention. When a person is blessed with some mental or physical disability, or does not measure up to the world's standards for acceptable appearance, they are branded as our "weeds".

Weeds and flowers are all created by God. The book of Genesis tells us, "God created the heavens and the earth and all things therein, and God saw that it was good." Who are we to condemn or reject God's work?

Certainly the talented, gifted, and the beautiful are to be treasured, but so are those others who we tend to ignore, overlook, or even reject. There are no human "weeds" because all are made in the image and likeness of God. All possess a soul to live and praise Jesus now and forever, regardless of their external appearance.

I know some beautiful and loving people who are "blessed" with mental and physical disabilities. I recall John, a young man, born with Down's Syndrome, who is one of the most loving and caring people I have ever met. He lives with childlike trust and loves, cares for and shares with everyone, and is the epitome of compassion and forgiveness. He works, and he prays with incredible faith. He is a special "flower." Then there is little Trevor, a small child, who can do nothing, but love. To many he appears to be a burden, but to his family, he is the center of attention and a growth opportunity in faith. Are we to presume he is praising and glorifying to God less than his healthy brother and sister or other children? The mystery of suffering is the doorway to salvation. Mental and physical giftedness is indeed a blessing, but Jesus uses everyone in his own unique way to glorify his Father.

Many people have influenced my faith life, especially my parents and family, but I am most thankful for Kathryn, a sweet elderly lady, who deepened my faith simply by the way she genuflected and made the sign of the cross. The "seeds" of that "flower" hampered by failing health are deeply rooted in my faith life.

God made the weeds as well as the flowers. God has created each of us with our differences and blessed each of us in his unique way. No one is a "weed" in Jesus's plan.

September 29, 2002

Listening to the news, I heard about the investigation at some air force base where a number of defective parachutes had been discovered. Certainly, we have reason for alarm because it could lead to serious injury or even death. We are very careful when it comes to caring for our physical life because we know the consequences if we don't.

No parent would allow their child to jump from a plane aware that they had a defective parachute, or worse still, without one. They will do everything in their power to help them attain a safe landing. All to preserve a life we know will soon end.

While our children are at home what are we doing to prepare them spiritually for that day they will "jump from the safety of the plane"—that is leave home? As parents and leaders, we have a grave responsibility to prepare them for this "jump" and a safe landing, that is, save their souls. Jesus has given us a "parachute," the sacrament of baptism, and the safe "ropes" of the sacraments, the Mass, prayer, and sacred scriptures for living our faith. When these ropes are in good condition and securely attached to the parachute, we are ready to "jump." The jump may be difficult and dangerous due to the storm winds of temptation and the attacks of the devil, but there is nothing to fear for Jesus assures us of a safe landing if we do our best and trust in him. We must do all we can to preserve our lives, not this passing one, but the one that will be everlasting.

Beginning a new school year, we are preparing our children for the sacraments of Reconciliation, Eucharist, and Confirmation—three powerful lines attached to our parachute. Frequently the powerful "rope" of reconciliation is detached once we have made our first confession and never to be used again until we prepare for confirmation or later in life. Such neglect makes for great danger.

The thrill and excitement of our little children preparing for first Eucharist is a moving experience, but what are we doing to help them maintain their appreciation of this unique sacrament? It appears that with the passing of time, this "rope" becomes somewhat frayed. We do not detach it, but use it too routinely. We lose our appreciation for the Eucharist, when we fail to believe that Jesus is truly present and alive, and then our attachment to Jesus is in peril.

As we continue our faith journey, Jesus offers us another powerful "rope," the indwelling of his Spirit through his special gift of confirmation. We prepare long and hard for the day of confirmation. We profess our faith before God, our bishop, and our parish family. We resolve to actively live our faith in a visible manner.

This is one of the most powerful "ropes" of our parachute. It guarantees us safety through the most difficult and dangerous challenges of our faith life. Jesus guarantees that the Holy Spirit will guide, strengthen, and protect us in every situation of our faith life, if only we will call upon him. Yet, in many cases, this "rope" has been tampered with or totally detached. Many people no longer participate in Mass, fail to regularly use these sacraments in a meaningful manner, and no longer profess their faith.

It is time we check our parachutes. We do this through prayer and reading his sacred scripture. It may need to be repaired. It's worth it. It will save your life.

October 6, 2002

As the pears were picked from the tree at harvest time, they were carefully placed in the basket by the packers preparing them for the market. Following the long trip over the rough and winding road, he was pleased to see that most of them made the trip in good condition. What a wonderful analogy of our life!

The pressure of the large pears had little effect upon those in the bottom of the basket and most remained firm and in good condition. However, a few of them, being over ripe or poorly handled were ruined under the pressure. They became mushy and so lost their value. Pears, like all fruit, must be harvested at the right time and handled with care if they are to survive the pressure when placed in groups with others. Pear pressure is much like peer pressure.

Our young people, growing up in our modern technological society, are faced with the extreme pressure as they go through life. As parents and leaders, we have a great responsibility to watch over them so that they are protected and allowed to develop firmly in order to be ready to endure the pressures placed upon them when they enter into the world. The TV, the video, and the computer, along with the accessibility of drink and drugs, plus the "free thinking" regarding sex, have placed enormous pressures on our youth. Those who are not carefully prepared, will, like the overripe pear or mishandled one, become soft, mushy, and be crushed under the pressure confronting them. Peer pressure is more destructive than pear pressure.

It affects children, youth, and adults. It destroys those not properly prepared, and crushes those not firmly disciplined in their faith. Even our little children, so far advanced today, are affected by the fads and media around them. Our teenagers have a difficult battle on their hands choosing between moral and ethical values while warding off the tempting pleasures proffered by peer pressure. Great is the need for parents, teachers, and leaders to guarantee their proper handling and preparation at the various stages of life. It is difficult, and we will meet with much resistance because discipline and limitation is not readily welcome. Early and careful spiritual formation or pressure will strengthen them, make them firm in their faith, and prevent them from succumbing to peer pressure. Jesus challenges the youth, firmly founded in faith, to reach out and help those who have become "mushy" or being destroyed by peer pressure.

Adults also crumble under peer pressure. The constant dissatisfaction with their status quo and that destructive compulsion to keep up with the Joneses have ruined many a marriage and destroyed the peace and unity of the family. Bigger houses, newer cars, unneeded and seldom used RVs, fancier boats and an ever increasing list has crushed too many who were unable to stand up and resist peer pressure. Jesus warns us of this when he says, "What does it profit a person to gain the whole world and lose their soul?"

We are not pears, but we become mushy and are easily destroyed unless we remain close to Jesus, listen to him, and let him carefully handle our lives. Pear pressure poses problems. Peer pressure postpones perfection.

October 13, 2002

While driving this past week with friends and enjoying the beauty of the colorful leaves, we stopped at an orchard stand to purchase some apples. While standing there, I noticed some honey in a comb which reminded me of various bees and their parallel to the Church members.

There is the sweat bee, the bumblebee, the wood bee, and the honeybee. The sweat bee, tiny and most aggravating, loves to take advantage of a person's physical labors, relishing the salty perspiration and offering nothing in return, except to sting you if you accidentally squeeze it. The bumblebee, large and a threat to all who get too near, with its painful sting, flies about making noise and changing from flower to flower. It takes all the nectar back to its hive deep in the ground, selfishly storing it for later consumption.

The wood bee is busy drilling holes into wooden beams of barns and sheds, making a comfortable place to dwell, thereby weakening the structure of the building. And the honey bee is busy producing honey and even making the comb in which to store the fruit of its hard labor, which is a tasty delight to those who eat it.

I do not fully understand the lifestyles of the various bees, nor do I fathom the lifestyle of some Catholics. We have some who, like the sweat bee, refuse to get involved in the work or activity of the church, but continually enter the picture to relish the fruit of other people's labors. And if they don't get what they want, or find themselves being squeezed into action against their will, they strike out and sting or hurt those around imposing some obligation or responsibility upon them. They seek "favor without labor."

There are those who, like the bumble bee, make a lot of noise and threaten the peace and unity of the faith community in order to get their way. They are continually changing ideas and plans, thus confusing others, while selfishly reaping the blessings of the parish efforts hoarding all for their personal pleasure. They appear to be big, showy, troublesome, busy bodies. These "crow without show."

The wood bee parishioners continually attack or oppose whatever active parishioners propose or undertake to better the school or faith life of the parish. Their continuous complaints or criticism, like the wood bee drilling into the wood, gradually weakens the enthusiasm and destroys the motivation of active parishioners until their plan collapses and all ends in frustration. These are the "drillers, not the thrillers."

What empower a parish are active members like the honey bee. The honeybee spends its time working for others by pollinating fruit trees and plants so they will produce abundantly. Then it returns to its hive to produce honey, which assures their livelihood throughout the winter months as well as that which is enjoyed by people. Here we have "workers, not shirkers."

Honeybees work together for the total well-being of the hive. In a healthy beehive, there are different types of bees, each with their own designated work. So too, in an active, faith-filled parish, members with various capabilities work together sharing the fruits of their labors. God creates sweat bees, bumblebees, wood bees, and honeybees, so we must accept them all, although we prefer honeybees.

We are not sweat bees, bumblebees, wood bees, or even honeybees, but we can all be "busy bees" working together to preserve and renew the faith life of the entire parish.

October 20, 2002

How is your roof? Does it need repair? Daily I see roofs being replaced and hear the pounding of the nailing guns as churches, houses, and building of all sizes and shapes in the surrounding communities are being repaired due to hail damage. This is being done by conscientious people desiring to protect their property and the contents within. My question or concern is not for material roofs but for our spiritual dwelling. Isn't it time for us to repair the spiritual roofs of our souls damaged by the attacks of sin?

When we fail to repair the roof of a building, the entire structure suffers and gradually deteriorates, as well as the contents it houses. God created each of us and placed us on the solid foundation of Jesus, enclosed us within the walls of faith, and placed a roof of grace over us. At times, we experience damage from the world, the flesh, or the devil, and are in need of roof repair or a total replacement. We appear to be more concerned about the condition of the roof of our house than we are of our soul.

When we replace them, even if only slightly damaged, we are quite careful in choosing the company or person to work on our buildings. We require a guarantee of their work and are greatly concerned about how other people will react to the appearance of the work. The company, the worker, and the appearance of their work are all so conditional, yet we trust them.

When we suffer from spiritual damage, Jesus is always ready to repair. He guarantees his work of forgiveness and empowers us to return to the faith community with a whole new appearance, renewed in the life of grace. We have nothing to fear when we ask his forgiveness and help to repair our damaged lives. Yet many neglect to use the sacrament of reconciliation, claiming forgiveness directly from God in other ways.

When was the last time you admitted damage to your spiritual dwelling and received the sacrament of reconciliation? It is not a sacrament for those who have severe damage to their "spiritual roof"—the life of grace, but one most helpful for those who have only minor damage. We replace a roof with minor damage to prevent greater destruction. Should we not use the sacrament of reconciliation as a means of forgiveness for venial sins in order to prevent the greater destruction of serious sin?

Some buildings are also getting their siding replaced due to the hail damage. We too need to look at the condition of spiritual siding, the walls of faith, which along with the roof of grace, protects the contents, our soul. Perhaps it is time for us to undertake a more prayerful use of the sacraments and Mass in order to restore our faith life and allow Jesus to cover us with his grace.

Try as we will, it is impossible to build a house with permanent walls and indestructible roof in this world, but Jesus expects us to live in a way that guarantees a lasting place in heaven. Hopefully, we will come to a better understanding of the value and need of the sacrament of reconciliation and call upon Jesus to reconstruct our damaged spiritual roofs as only he can do. We all need to check our spiritual roofs regularly for damage. Jesus offers the best repair—reconciliation.

October 27, 2002

On my office desk is a large red candle which has not been used properly. It has been lit frequently, but never allowed to burn very long and so it has burnt unevenly and only in the center, thus resembling a red chimney. All too often Catholics tend to live their faith in the same way.

We are challenged to keep our "candle" of faith life burning properly. We, for the most part, go to Mass each weekend, and so our "candle" is lit and burns for that short time. When we leave the church, we blow out our candle and live in darkness. Repeating this process week after week, results in a faith life that is uneven and forms a "chimney like" relationship with Jesus.

In order for our faith life to burn evenly, we need to live it every day. We are to bring Jesus and our beliefs with us into our daily routine, family, and business life. Failing to do so will result in burning only the center of one's life where we try to keep and relate with Jesus while ignoring other people and opportunities where Jesus invites us to witness our faith. Tunnel faith is selfish and risky.

True, your candle will burn, but only a little of the center and most of it will be wasted.

Such a candle does not give much light to others. My big red candle no longer reflects a warm, welcoming glow in the room; it merely pursues its goal of burning till the entire wick is consumed. Is that all our faith means to us? Certainly, Jesus had more in mind. He gifted us with faith, to know, love, and serve him everyday, in every way we can. He longs to share his love and friendship with each of us, individually and communally. Our love for Jesus is limited and stifled when we share with him on Sunday only or just privately in the depths of our hearts and are incapable of recognizing him in every person and event of each day.

When we do, then our "candle" is glowing and attracting others to Jesus, our Savior. Seeing his plan in every aspect of our lives and not only at Sunday Mass, our "candle" is burning evenly and totally. We are being consumed by the flaming embrace of Jesus's love and not merely pursuing a "hoped" for goal of life after death.

The church celebrates the feast of All Saints to keep before us those beloved family members and friends who met the challenge of living their faith in ways that kept their "candles" burning evenly, while sharing the love of Jesus. These are the people who lived their faith in simple, ordinary ways at church, home, and at work. They are the ones who reached out and touched the lives of others around them. Their example and sacrifices made it possible for us to share and live our faith today.

Believing the Words of Jesus, "You are the light of the world," we must keep our "candle" burning evenly as we reflect the light of Christ daily. Now is the time to check your candle!

November 3, 2002

Driving home from Greenfield this past Saturday afternoon, I was thrilled to see a flock of geese flying over the highway. But there was something wrong, they were not flying in the usual V shape, they were all in one line. It was quite evident that they would not go very far due to their flight pattern. How similar to our faith life!

God has created us for a specific flight pattern just like the geese and if we try to change it, we will fail and not go very far in our pursuit to holiness. When geese are migrating, they instinctively choose a leader and form their V to save energy and encourage one another to persevere in their efforts to achieve their destination. The lead goose knows the way and guides those following who support one another by their honking. In order to live our faith we must do the same.

We are tempted to live our faith in a one-sided way as we foolishly neglect or overlook the essential side of the "V"—the spiritual. We become too involved in the physical and material part and at times even refuse to follow the leader, Jesus.

We make attempts to live without our required leader, but soon realize we are not going very far. It is essential that we recognize Jesus as that leader and trust he knows the way.

Once we have accepted him as the leader, then we can form a balanced V. On the left we have birth and on the right we have baptism, next we have childhood with its partner reconciliation followed by youth on the left and the Eucharist on the right. As the V expands, we see adolescence and its spiritual partner, confirmation, and close behind comes adulthood with its corresponding partner of marriage, ordination, or the call to a religious or single walk of life. Each "goose" on the right calls out to those on the left encouraging them to persevere in their spiritual migration from earthly values to spiritual, and to eternal goals.

Following Jesus, the Leader, their flight will be swift, straight, and sanctifying, as they transform the ordinary and secular into the extraordinary and spiritual. We have much to learn from the partnering of the geese.

What a shame to see some trying to live only the "left" side of their "V" for they won't go very far, and are likely to die along the way! How unfortunate, for without the encouragement of their partners on the right side of the "V" to live a faith life, they weaken and gradually drop out of the formation. Lacking a leader and support, they are doomed.

Geese fly by instinct, a gift from God. It is a thrill to see and hear them flying safely to a new location and life. We are guided by our free will, a unique gift from God. Making the proper choices is far more thrilling and rewarding, for it leads to eternal life.

As autumn rapidly changes into winter, so life rushes us into eternity. Let us not live our lives in a "beeline" rushing to and fro but faithfully live it in a "V" line.

November 10, 2002

With temperatures dropping and the sun going south for the winter, we rarely see any mosquitoes. Yet they are still lurking in the woods and stagnant ponds awaiting the return of the sun, and the hotter it gets, the more they will prosper. But who misses them, since they are a bother? Many people look on Catholics with the same reaction.

God created the mosquitoes even though we see no good reason, and we are tired of their bothering and biting us. God created Catholics, and some people do not want them around any more than mosquitoes because they consider them bothersome. Due to misinformation and misunderstanding, they feel their "freedom" limited. "Mosquito" Catholics reveal the boundaries for followers of Jesus, witness the safeguards of his guidelines, and share his love with everyone, especially those trying to eliminate them. Mosquito Catholics are the "white martyrs" of today.

Some Catholics, having drifted from the "Sun," Jesus, and feeling the cooling of their faith no longer live in a way that pricks the conscience or bothers people around them. Still many, who open their hearts to the warmth of the "Sun," Jesus's love, proclaim his Word in ways that are most effective.

It may be that the only reason God created mosquitoes was to bite and bother us, but I find that quite unlikely. Their purpose, like that of many other creatures of God, is a marvelous mystery. However, God did create Catholics to actively live their faith, even if it bothers and disturbs others. Warmed by the grace of Jesus, we are empowered to reflect his light and proclaim his truth as he uses us to show others his way.

Mosquitoes abound and we never seem to be able to eliminate them. The same is true of Catholics, for the more they are persecuted, the more they flourish. Throughout all of salvation history, the church has survived and Catholics have abounded, whether the faith of some at the time dwindled or persecution increased, because Jesus guarantees that it will last forever and the "gates of hell will not prevail against it."

Catholic "mosquitoes" have survived the "spray" of heresies, schisms, scandals, and severe persecutions and will survive till the end of time. The Church, tested in every age with new and different means of affliction continues to prosper due to "mosquito" Catholics responding to the call of Jesus to witness.

We do not appreciate mosquitoes nor understand why God created them. We do not appreciate our marvelous gift of life, but we do know why God created us—to know, love, and serve him in this life and to be happy with him forever in the next. That automatically requires that we take up our cross as "unwanted mosquitoes" daily and follow him.

If we truly know Jesus, our love for him is unlimited. Such love leads to an uncontrollable willingness to serve him. To serve him is to be a "mosquito Catholic." Who do people say you are a "mosquito crusher" or a "mosquito Catholic"? Your faith life will reveal the answer!

November 17, 2002

The heavens were opened and the glory of the Lord burst forth! A few days ago as I was driving, I beheld a most spectacular sunset. The clouds, like molten gold, poured down from heaven, formed polished stairs leading up to a brilliant throne on which rested the blinding sun. A limited vision of the infinite glory of God! Beauty beyond words! God's glory revealed in nature!

God teaches much through nature. Beauty, power, harmony, interrelationships, and the need to share, as well as the destruction that results when the elements of nature are out of balance. When examined prayerfully, we can see the negative of our lives.

Once upon a time, many aeons ago, the various elements of nature were summoned by God to a conflict resolution seminar. The sun, moon, and stars were quarrelling about the amount of light each was allotted. The wind and breeze were dissatisfied because of the difference in power. The lightning, thunder, and storms were under criticism by the other elements of nature because their rowdiness and noise were frightening and dangerous. The rain and snow were vying for first position in supplying the most water, and it had gone to the point of endangering life. And the seasons were totally out of balance. Fear, frustration, criticism, and misjudgment were now destroying God's plan of life. Consequently, God saw a need to put an end to this turmoil by reminding them that he was in control and he expected them to obey his plan. Is it possible that we need to be reminded of the same truth?

At this seminar, God reminded the sun, moon, and stars that each had different responsibilities, for if all three were hot as the sun or as cool as the moon or divided as the stars, we would certainly perish from the heat or lack of it and the need of light.

Then he took the breeze and wind to task. The gentle spring breeze was to call forth new life, while the wind was to carry the needed moisture to sustain all life.

When hearing the complaints that lightning, thunder, and storms were too noisy and at times can be dangerous, God spoke in their defense because when properly used they supply humans electricity. Their benefits far outweigh their damages.

As for the rain, snow, and seasons, God reminded them of his mysterious, marvelous plan. He called them to achieve unity in diversity. The seasons would necessarily be a part of the yearly cycle, but each year it would be different for the sake of newness and to slowly reveal his mystique.

When this negative of nature is developed under the light of the Holy Spirit does it not clearly reveal a picture of us? We, like the elements of nature possess beauty, power, and a variety of marvelous talents with the potential to bring unity amidst diversity if we are truly guided by the Holy Spirit and are doing the work of Jesus.

Criticism kills enthusiasm and motivation. Mentoring builds relationships which lead to friendships. Harsh words hurt, while gentle suggestions heal and bring peace. Keep in mind then, to handle yourself, use your head, but to handle others, use your heart. Then the glory of the Lord will burst forth for all to see.

November 24, 2002

In years gone by, one of the prizes often given at the county fair booths of chance was the replica of the three monkeys. One covering its eyes depicting the idea of seeing no evil, the second covering its ears signifying that it heard no evil and the third covering its mouth so as to speak no evil. These three monkeys remind me of the three types of faith life that have been prevalent in the church in the last fifty years. There were those who did not see, those who did not hear, and those who did not speak.

Let us consider the first monkey, those who did not see, but continued to live their faith.

When I was first ordained, a huge number of Catholics lived a "blind faith." They did not understand the church teachings, and maybe did not even believe them, but practiced out of fear of hell, with a minimal trust in God's Word. Some did not have the opportunity to delve more deeply into the church's teachings, while others were leery of doing so for fear it would require changes in their way of living. They were for the most part blind to the love of Jesus.

The second monkey models those Catholics, following Vatican II, who covered their spiritual ears so as not to hear what Jesus was saying. They did not want to accept the life-giving changes revealed to the Church by the Holy Spirit. Nostalgically they clung to the past. They liked a church where everyone was required to do everything exactly the same, and "good and bad" was very "cut and dry." Some depended on a God of force and punishment to coerce others to obey and submit to their will. Hell was that tool. Others felt cheated when things formerly sinful were no longer considered sins, and so closed their minds to the mercy and wisdom of God. It's not fair! Consequently, some, misunderstanding the changes in the church, chose to accept only the teachings and beliefs appealing to them. They no longer listened to the truth. Because of their deafness, many lost their faith.

The third monkey represents modern day Catholics. Only a few speak of the beauty and value of our faith or realize its need. Faith life for many is dead. While Vatican II removed the blindness of those open to the movement of the Spirit to a deeper appreciation of the newness of our faith, some wandered off in their blindness and got lost. They refused to follow the light of Christ leading to the life-giving Mass and sacraments, and suddenly discovered their faith was dead.

Our churches are much emptier today than they were fifty years ago because many no longer acknowledge Jesus as their needed Savior. We have denied God's teaching regarding sin, we see no evil. We no longer believe in or fear hell; we refuse to hear of the accountability of our lives of evil. We neglect to speak against evil or encourage everyone to live lives of deep faith.

Faithful Catholics see Jesus as a loving Savior lighting our way; hear his life-giving Words and live them faithfully; and speak of his promised glory to all who believe.

Which monkey models you? Hopefully none!

March 23, 2003

THE PASTOR'S SANDAL PATH

One night at a RCIA gathering, someone passed around a paper with a couple of paragraphs. We were asked to read it and tell how many times we found the letter "f" on the page. It was amazing to see how many were unable to find the correct number. Most everyone found the letter in the big words but failed to note it in the small words, especially at the end of the word.

Not being a psychiatrist, psychologist, or psychoanalyst, I really cannot explain this unusual result. All I know is that it happened. With this in mind, I would like to draw a comparison to the way we frequently see things in life.

We recognize the great things people do. We record accomplishments and events which bring notoriety to famous people, but regularly fail to see the wonderful thing done around us simply because they are being done by ordinary people.

Everyone knew about Mother Teresa of Calcutta and the marvelous works of mercy she performed for the poor and needy around the world. Pope John Paul II is frequently in the news because of what he says or does. His effort to lead the Catholic Church along the path established by Jesus is well known. We see those in prominent positions of leadership like the "f" in the big words in the reading, but we fail to see as equal those humbly ministering to God and his people quietly without fanfare or spotlight.

We have a wonderful parish and quality school where we see the workings of the principal, teachers, and staff who give so much to achieve and maintain our standards. They certainly deserve recognition, but what about the dedicated cafeteria cooks, the maintenance ladies, the minute men, and the many people who volunteer in a variety of ways, assisting those receiving the accolades, yet are seldom seen or rarely heard? We notice the work of the "role" people and those who are involved in the "big" action, just as we find the "hunted letter f" in the big words, but are at fault in not acknowledging those, quietly working behind the scene, who persevere until the end, long after all the "hurrah" has become silent.

As members of the body of Christ, we realize that we are all equal in his sight. He has a special work for each of us. Mindful of the Words of Jesus, "Whoever wishes to be first, must be last, and the servant of all," along with the words "Whoever humbles himself will be exalted, and whoever exalts himself will be humbled," we strive to see the beauty, value, and uniqueness of everyone, not just the great.

We are not seeking to find how often "f" appears on a page. We are seeking to love and affirm the unrecognized. We may fail because we are unaware of their accomplishments. Sometimes we deliberately overlook them because we seek the praise and recognition.

Careful attention while reading the page was required to see the "f" in the little words and at the end of words. Lent is the time for us to make greater effort to see God using *all* people in his plan of salvation. We can't all be first. We won't all be great in the eyes of the world. But if we find the hidden "f" on each page of life, that is see Jesus in the least, we will be great in the eyes of God.

March 30, 2003

Rain, sleet, snow, and sunshine made up the weather collage this past week during the brief committal service at the cemetery. This was due to the rapid atmospheric alterations, accompanied by gusty winds, resulting in the camellia changes of Mother Nature. Can we not visualize a parallel relationship with God?

Sometimes "rain" abounds as we weep over the wrongs of our infidelity, only to be followed immediately by "sleet" as we give the cold shoulder to someone or neglect to listen to Jesus who tells us he is present in the least and marginalized around us. Being aware of this new situation, we revert to "snow" as we try to cover over and excuse ourselves forgetting that God knows what lies in our heart, but the snow will soon melt revealing whether or not we are drawing near to the forgiving Jesus who longs to fill our soul with the warm "sunshine" of his love. We are as changeable and uncertain as the weather. How can this happen so quickly?

It results from situations in which we interact with people around us. We are greatly affected by the people we encounter. Some move us to "rain," to repentance, as we try to make progress in our spiritual life, while others cause "sleet" on our faith journey and we abandon the pathway of grace and refuse to listen to Jesus's call to "love your neighbor as yourself." At times we give people the "snow" job, ignoring our wrong doings or acting as though they were not even present in our lives. Suddenly we encounter people and bring light, happiness, and warmth into their lives, like "sunshine," sharing true love, living our faith, imitating the life of Jesus.

We frequently hear people complain about the uncertainty of the weather and their inability to dress accordingly. What must be the reaction of Jesus or those around us, when we are so unstable in living our faith? How do we cope with our fluctuating changes, or those who are a part of our life?

Regardless of how weak our faith may be, or how quickly our faith "weather" may change, Jesus still loves us and wants to share more intimately. His reaction is patient forgiveness and encouragement to be more steadfast in living deep faith. We cannot regulate how people around us live their faith, but we can witness to them by how we live. Living a deep faith, we can cope with our weaknesses. Strengthened by the graces of reconciliation, nourished on the Eucharist, supported by our prayer life, and guided by the Holy Spirit we gradually allow Jesus to become the stabilizing force of our lives through the warmth of his love. Mindful of all that Jesus endured because of our sins; we more readily accept the differences of others and forgive.

The sun always remains even when it rains, sleets, or snows. Jesus is that "sun," the son of God, who is always present even in those inclement days empowering us to live our faith. Lent is a time to check your faith "weather" and welcome the son who melts the snow and sleet and ends the rain that blocks our clear view of Jesus.

April 6, 2003

In God's mysterious plan, he took me to the "land of Oz" this past Sunday to teach me an important spiritual lesson. The story, "The Wizard of Oz," unfolds as a result of a tornado. Dorothy is privileged to meet three enlightening teachers, the scarecrow, the tin man, and the lion. On the journey, the very things her friends desired were the things lacking in her life; a brain to think clearly, a heart to love purely, and the courage to face life. How cleverly God reveals his message!

Only after the laughter and thrill of the outstanding presentation by these wonderful young people had faded into history, and I returned to the "land of reality" did God begin to reveal the parity with our faith life.

Analyzing my faith life, I could see times when I, like the scarecrow, longed for the ability to know how to make the right choices needed to help people find, not a "wizard" but Jesus. There were times I needed a "loving" heart to welcome Jesus, not in the bad "witches" of life but in the least. Certainly there were times when I, like the lion, lacked courage to stand up against evil and abandoned the plan Jesus had designed. But the marvel of it all is that we have more than a "good witch"; we have the Church which comes to our rescue; straighten things out and shows us the way home.

That night shortly after the play, I attended two youth gatherings where young people, unlike Dorothy's friends, were busy using their brain planning for summer bible school, opening their hearts in loving care of God's little ones and courageous enough to live their faith openly. Another group was experiencing the need for the light of Jesus in their lives, and their responsibility to become disciples of Jesus and go out to lead their families and friends from darkness to light.

These young people had found "the wizard," Jesus, and he had granted their wish. He had given them a brain to think clearly, a heart to love purely, and the courage to live faithfully. They experienced what Dorothy eventually came to see—the blessings of family and friends to share and walk with when facing the unknown mysteries of life.

A tornado is synonymous with a whirlwind. There are many of our young people, along with some of us, who are caught up in the "tornado," the whirlwind of life and are floundering about like the scarecrow, the tin man, and the cowardly lion, confused, anxious, and searching for the "way." Looking for the "wizard" Jesus, we are confronted by the "wicked witch" of the world. We are in need of help from the "good witch," the Church to encourage and guide us along the way to Jesus.

Thanks to the wonderful people of "Oz," those dedicated youth leaders and faith-filled parents, more of our youth are finding their way to the "wizard," Jesus, who gives them courage to think correctly and love properly, aided by a strong support system of faith.

The play was very entertaining, but there is a valuable message therein. We, like the scarecrow, the tin man, or the lion, at times need to heed the "good witch," the Church, and follow the "yellow brick road," Jesus's message and the sacraments if we are to find "the wizard," Jesus who alone can get us home.

April 13, 2003

Christmas trees, jack-o'-lanterns, fireworks, and Easter eggs are the customary symbols of the four seasons. In three of the four seasons, the object is destroyed for our pleasure, the tree is cut and dies, the pumpkin is carved and rots, the fireworks are ignited and exploded, while the egg becomes part of us and gives us life. The egg is a perfect sign of the meaning of Easter. The tomb which contained Jesus is empty. He has risen. He longs to nourish us, especially in the Eucharist. The shell is empty as the egg nurtures life in those who partake. Jesus died to give us new life, and the egg must be destroyed before it can give life.

While walking one afternoon, I found an abandoned bird's nest. In the nest were two eggs; one was broken open and empty. It had given life. The other was whole, it was lifeless, and it had failed to die to self in order to give new life and now was dead.

Many tombs in the garden where Jesus was buried were full; the stones were not rolled back, and the bodies were dead. Jesus's tomb was broken open, it was empty, like the egg, and he was alive and life giving. He was willing to die to conquer sin. He rose from death fulfilling the promise of a greater life to come. His example empowers us to die to self, so we can break open the "tomb" of sin and rise with him to fullness of eternal life.

This past week, coming home from the store, I dropped a dozen eggs. Two were badly broken, so I ate them immediately. Four were slightly cracked, and I boiled them so they would keep until I could use them. The rest remained in good condition for later needs.

This reminded me of the Easter mystery. Jesus was "badly broken," killed, and his life-giving powers made available immediately. The apostles and early Christians were slightly "broken" by harassment and persecution. Jesus used them to give life, at a later date, when they suffered martyrdom. Countless followers of Jesus were not "broken or cracked," neither persecuted nor martyred, but have imitated him and died to self and sin and allowed him to use them. These sacrificed their lives over the years that others, including ourselves, might hear and accept the Good News. Are we "broken, cracked, or whole"? Is Jesus using us to give life immediately, in the near future or later?

This past holy week, we recalled our salvation history beginning with the creation of the world down to the present time. The long line of prophets and holy men and women of the Old Testament lived in anticipation of the coming of Jesus, our Savior. Jesus made the ultimate sacrifice, forgiving our sins, conquering death, and restoring life as he rose from the dead. Now the time has come for us to make our choice.

We can live and be cut down as the Christmas tree, enjoying passing worldly pleasures, ending in death, or be carved as the jack-o'-lantern, into bizarre expressions, only to rot in our death-dealing sexual experiences, or live showy, explosive lives, like fireworks, blown to pieces, when we foolishly allow the devil to control our lives. What a waste!

We now have a choice, like the "two eggs," either to let Jesus "crack" our sinful shell and free us to live a new life or to remain lifeless within our "shell" of sinful, selfish satisfaction. Christ has risen and is alive, are we?

April 27, 2003

The curtain of the Carrollton High School play opens, and "Footloose" unfolds with an evening of entertainment and deep lessons. The new student finds himself in the middle of a huge "storm," a moral battle, and he is pummeled by all the self-righteous officials of the small town. Well-meaning and caring people, leaders of the community, have refashioned the guide rails of life into a suppressing chain of enslavement. The "freedom train" no longer has straight, solid, guidelines upon which to run; it has been chained to the emotional fears of one who has forced others to conform. The life of the community has been stilted. The talented high school students marvelously portrayed how imprisoned one can become when not open to God. The capable cast also witnessed an even greater message, namely, those who persevere and those who turn back to Jesus will achieve peace and harmony, and right will triumph. The efforts of the new student motivated the others who gradually led the embittered minister to a change of heart allowing the Spirit of God to restore proper directives to their community living.

The Spirit acts in the events of our daily lives in powerful and exciting ways too. Everyone needs the guidance of Jesus both in spiritual and secular decisions. We need to be careful lest we, like the minister in the play, become emotionally imbalanced as a result of some tragedy in our lives and then closed-mindedly try to dominate others according to our rigorous, overprotective restrictions.

When we are confronted with people who seem to misuse their powers of leadership, we, like the new student, must patiently encourage them to rethink their decision and help them to prayerfully discern the will of God. We certainly need the secular and spiritual guide rails on which every life must travel, but we are to avoid forming overburdening chains of enslavement which destroy life. No community, parish, or school should be harshly stilted because an individual or group refuses to be open to the will of Jesus.

We may not feel "footloose," but we are chosen by Jesus, empowered by the Holy Spirit, and sent to live the Good News. Truly, the Spirit is acting in our parishes. Last Saturday and Sunday, two babies received baptism; on Sunday, the Spirit blessed our parish picnic with a beautiful day, moved large numbers of parishioners to work together, and protected everyone from accidents. On Tuesday, the Holy Spirit changed forever the lives of those who received the sacrament of confirmation, empowering and challenging them to more fully witness their faith. On Wednesday, the Spirit of God hovered over our parish as we celebrated a loved one's entry into eternal life. This Sunday, our children will experience the presence of Jesus in a new and special way as they receive their first Eucharist. The Spirit longs to direct all our secular and spiritual decisions.

We, like the young people in the play "Footloose" can change our lives, our community, and better the world, when empowered by the Spirit and guided by Jesus. We Catholics are certainly "Footloose" for we are chosen by Jesus, empowered by the Holy Spirit, and sent to live the Good News. We hear the Good News, believe it, and live it. Truly, the Spirit is present among us and acting in every phase of our lives.

May 4, 2003

In my office there is a clock which runs, but its hands do not move. There is one in my bed room whose hands move, but it does not run correctly. Another old clock in a spare bedroom is not running at all because it needs to be wound. This morning, when I went into the secretary's office, her clock was blinking and showing incorrect time due to a brief electric break. My wrist watch has been confined to my pocket for convenience. In the front hall, a grandfather clock proudly and clearly chimes the passing of time, and in the kitchen a wall clock notes the hours by a variety of birds' calls. These clocks with their differences present a good analogy of God and us. All clocks need someone to care for them if they are to run correctly. We all need God if we are to live correctly.

Some people are nominal Catholics, but do not practice their faith. They are like the clock, which runs but whose hands do not move. Others practice parts of our faith, but do not live their faith correctly. Like the clock whose hands move but runs improperly, there are some Catholics who live their faith, but are suffering from "burnout" and are "wound down." They are no longer involved in the activities of the faith community; they need to allow Jesus to enkindle his love within their lives again. Then you may see Catholics floundering about "blinking" due to power shortage, because they have briefly lost contact with Jesus. From time to time, you will find Catholics who have been "put in a pocket" because they did not fit in with or measure up to "the group" and so were put aside. We need to welcome and value everyone with all their differences. Jesus longs for unity amidst our diversity in order that he may be proclaimed and worshipped by all.

According to his plan, Jesus uses some of his people to witness and proclaim the Good News loudly like a grandfather clock. He also uses people to make known his plan of salvation in a variety of ways like the song birds on my kitchen clock. Jesus invites each one of us to be a part of his master plan. Occasionally we may need God, the "clock repairman," to make adjustments or replacements so we will function properly and correctly to witness the true time: time to love him and one another.

The size, shape, sound, and the make up of every clock is unique and beautiful in its own way. All have the same purpose; telling the correct time. The people of God vary in their physical, mental, and spiritual make up, making us special and unique, but all have been created to glorify God now and share lasting life and love.

Some clocks are expensive, some cheap; some ornate and fancy, others plain and very practical; some are antiques while others are new; a few are collectables although most are disposable. So it is with material things, but we are not clocks. No one is cheap or plain or disposable for Jesus. We are extremely valuable, so much so, that he sacrificed his life to ransom us. More than fancy and ornate, we are unique and greater than any collectable, destined to share his friendship for all eternity. Convinced of Jesus's love, may we allow him to make any necessary "clock" adjustments in our lives! No one is disposable. Jesus treasures and loves each of us.

May 11, 2003

Global warming is the "hot" topic of our day. It is the result of unjust lifestyles and our failure to live as good stewards. All the talk and warnings, sad to say, for the most part falls on deaf ears. We and future generations will pay a heavy price.

Global warming is truly a threat to our natural resources and to our very life, but it is far less threatening than "faith cooling," which is rapidly eroding our social, ethical, moral, and spiritual standards. We are presently paying a profound price, and unless a change comes soon, future generations will pay the ultimate price, loss of eternal life.

Along with global warming, our natural resources are being depleted and abused by our polluting the air, land, and water. In like manner, our "faith cooling" has led to the depletion of religious vocations, polluted the sanctity of family life, perverted our social life, malformed our ethical code and rationalized society's immorality.

Recently, I went to the high school prom. It was exhilarating to see beautiful couples promenading into the hall, but it was extremely devastating to hear the great number of names who were from broken marriages. I mention this not in judgment or to condemn, but to exemplify the heavy price of faith cooling.

Materialism has handcuffed religion and brainwashed our young people into believing that things bring happiness and not people. Possessions have wrestled with self-denial, power, and prestige has tackled simplicity and humility, and self-gain has overpowered service, thus diminishing religious vocations drastically. Only one with a living faith can detect this deception and discern the beauty, joy, excitement, and reward of religious life.

The sanctity of marriage and family was established in the Garden of Eden when God said, "Be fertile and multiply; fill the earth, and subdue it." This commission proves that God saw a greater value in people than in things. We were to subdue the world and not let the world subdue us. Where have our large families gone—families that fostered religious vocations? Why so many broken homes? How do we account for couples living together before marriage? Faith cooling has allowed secularism and materialism to pollute the sacredness of sex and the sanctity of the family.

The media has destroyed the social standards established by the church along with its code of ethics, while morality is based on a malformed hypothesis: it's OK if you don't get caught and do it if it feels good. Sin has been eradicated from our modern thinking. The confessionals have been abandoned. Sinners have become professional rationalizers. This has not resulted from global warming, but from faith cooling.

Global warming inflicts disastrous results on society, but faith cooling corrupts our spirit, pollutes our love of others, and destroys our intimate relation with God. Intelligent people will put a halt to global warming before it destroys the world, but "Spirit-filled" people will seriously combat faith cooling before it destroys our soul. We are that "Spirit-filled" people, so let us begin!

May 17, 2003

This past Sunday my Sandals found themselves in a situation of indecision. Had the time turned back, were they in the present or was it a taste of the future? Enjoying the Booster Club Variety Show, I saw the potential future in the entertaining acts of the very young, the talented performance of some senior members of our community, and the vitality of the in-between ages reliving the past, enjoying the present, and dreaming of the future. As the show progressed, I became aware of the predicament of time we all face.

Most people fail to live the moment; they are bothered by age, find it difficult to handle the dilemma of imperfection, and consequently are unhappy.

Living in a rocket-pace age, we are too busy to live. We strain to stay alive, pay exorbitant prices to appear young, and are destroyed by extravagant competition. So what do we gain by our speed and modern resources to look young, if we are shattered by peer pressure and misuse of time?

When I was young, life was more difficult. We had less money and sacrifice was a routine part of life. But we used our time more judiciously; we took time to live and to love. We had a greater appreciation of God's place in our lives; we valued self-esteem and respect. The majority of people lived lives of commitment—to God, family, church, country. One's good name was the key to happiness as opposed to possessions.

Families were the core of life, love, and happiness. Little children were considered an asset; parents were the stable foundation of the home, and grandparents were a treasured source of wisdom. Families were not perfect, but family members accepted each other and worked to help one another. We needed God and each other and spent prime time with both.

I was reminded of this truth during the variety show when the cute little dancers were welcome, even though they were out of step. We were deeply moved when a "senior" fiddler who, judged by modern society would have little to offer excited our spirits by his exceptional playing. Along with both ends of the age spectrum and a person with disabilities, a great diversity of talent was offered by varying ages in between, including rock, funny, spiritual, and inspirational. The "Booster Club Variety Show" proved that "variety" when properly used can truly booster our spirits.

The spiritually mature are not bothered by age, the passing of years, and are capable of accepting people with physical disabilities because they realize that God uses both in his plan of salvation. Time is a limited gift from God. The young, the old, and the "special" are blessed with talents and abilities to share in all categories of life. The young should not be ignored because they add newness to life, nor should they shun their elders whose experience embellishes their lives and offers examples to imitate.

It was fun to recall the "oldies," both the music and the personalities, but they are gone, and we cannot go back. Learn from the past. Dream of the future, but live the present. God uses each of us, right where we are, just as we are if only we allow him. May our lives become the best "variety show" giving praise, thanks, and glory to God! Now is the time for "our show" to begin!

May 25, 2003

I've never spent much time with a giraffe, but I have spent many hours with ants in the woods watching them as they worked tunneling into the ground, carrying in food supplies, or going about their daily pattern of life. If you had the choice, which would you prefer to be—a giraffe or an ant?

Perhaps an examination of the factors of each will aid our decision. The giraffe is big and tall; it can see over a greater area and is extremely visible. It has great potential for carrying heavy objects. The ant, on the other hand, is small and so short that its vision and visibility is extremely limited. Its ability to move heavy objects offers no competition to a giraffe. But is that a plus or a minus? The giraffe is limited as to where it may go due to its size; it needs huge doors, large spaces, and can never live in obscurity. The ant can go almost anywhere—under the door, over the wall, in extremely small spaces, as well as large. Contrary to the inability of the giraffe, the ant can build its own dwelling above or below the ground and more readily achieve security and safety. So it seems both have their good qualifications as well as their limitations. So what's your choice?

There is an immense difference in the lifestyles of these two creatures of God, but they visualize our lifestyle choices. Jesus could have used the giraffe and ant as his imagery when telling the story of the Pharisee and the tax collector. Can you see the similarity?

The Pharisee, like the giraffe which always look down on others with head held high, looked down on the tax collector. He wanted everyone to see him and praise him for all that he was doing. Inflated with pride at his accomplishment, there was no room for God. He had the wherewithal to do great things for others, but his power was thwarted because he was blinded to the needs of others due to his excessive egotism.

The tax collector, lowly, like the ant, thanked God for all he had done for him and through him. Aware of his limitations, he welcomed God into his life. He did not seek glory or recognition, but humbly prayed for forgiveness and reconciliation with anyone he may have hurt. God used his weakness as the source of grace, power, and life.

We are not giraffes; we are not ants. We are the chosen of God, made in his image and likeness and destined for eternal life and love. We need to imitate the giraffe at times and the ant at other times. We hold our head high as we live our faith, but not in a sense of superiority. We are lowly, like the ant, as we love and accept all people, convinced that we are all equal in God's eyes. We appreciate our power, the indwelling of the Holy Spirit, when we face temptation and evil, yet we are too gentle and meek when ministering to the needy and outcast. Jesus urges us to act quietly and out of sight, like the ant when we pray and perform works of mercy, so as not to be seen while glorifying God, but he commands us to be strong and visible like the giraffe when defending our faith, or fighting the world, flesh, or devil.

The moral of this analogy is to use your gifts and talents with humility and gratitude glorifying God. Regardless of our position, power, or influence, we are all accountable to Jesus for we are stewards, not owners, of everything we have, even our lives. Giraffes can crush ants; ants can destroy giraffes, and people will do the same unless we live the mysterious plan of God, accepting our differences and loving one another. So which will you be—a giraffe, an ant, or a special you?

June 1, 2003

Grass!—Have you ever taken time to lie in a pasture of soft spring grass? It feels good; it smells great and embraces you as you rest in the warm sun. It is a beautiful sight and even more appealing when near a pond of sparkling water and dotted with golden dandelions. What a unique signage of Jesus!

People are continually working to improve their yard paying exorbitant prices to get it to grow. When it is hot and dry, they water it to make it grow. When their yard appears spotty or uneven, they fertilize it. And then when it grows, they mow it off. This appears a bit foolish and wasteful, but not as ridiculous as the way many live.

Too many waste their lives trying to achieve a phantom goal. Peer pressure and the world have manipulated our lives so much we are unable to just "be." We must continue to improve ourselves. We spend incredible fortunes on irrelevant degrees, on climbing the status ladder, on impressing our neighbors, and when we achieve "their" standard, they mow us down by proposing a new goal; consequently we are rarely happy and never experience satisfaction in who we are and what we are doing.

The grass keeps growing, and the mower keeps mowing both in our yards and in our lives. We need to stop and realize that the grass in our yards will continue to grow; it looks dead during the winter, but springs forth in new life; it may be spotty or ragged or in need of weeding during the hot, dry summer, but it still has life in its roots and will slowly spread with a minimal assistance from us. It does not have to be "picture perfect."

God has created each of us unique and special. He has a plan for us: not to be destroyed by the world, but to be a faithful follower and friend of his son, Jesus. We may look less than perfect in the estimation of the world, but fear not because Jesus knows we are not "picture perfect" and offers us all the assistance we need to live—his incredible loving presence.

Jesus is like the soft spring grass, gentle, refreshing, and always ready to embrace us in his strong, protective, loving arms. Like grass, he continually endeavors to enter more fully into our lives, regardless of how often we cut him down and look to other flippant goals that fail to satisfy. There are times when our relationship with Jesus wanes and our faith life seems to wither because we have wandered far from Jesus, but he is still waiting to spring up anew in our hearts. There are days when our friendship appears spotty, blotched, or even weedy due to our careless use of, or worse still, our failure to use his sacraments, Mass, and prayer, but Jesus assures us that the Father will prune, graft, and nurture us so we can produce more abundantly, if we are willing.

Thus the love and presence of Jesus, like grass, continue to grow and flourish even when we continue to cut it down; it has deep roots and always springs up again after we turn away in the coldness of our hearts; and when we try to remove it from our lives, he patiently waits for another grace moment to burst forth anew. Never will we be able to destroy the love and presence of Jesus in our lives. We may cut him out and leave him, but he never abandons us.

Grass is green as a sign of hope—new life. We can trust in the compassion, mercy, and unconditional love of Jesus regardless of what we do. He is our only hope of salvation; he is like fresh, soft, green grass besides restful waters. Come, rest in The Grass!

June 8, 2003

Watch your step, it's poison! How often I heard someone say that to me during my week of retreat! Frequently, the foot paths were bordered with lovely, healthy poison ivy. It had grown up among the flowers and amidst the beautiful honeysuckle vines which grew profusely in the woods. Woe to the one who did not recognize the evil lurking there. The result would be much pain and suffering. It's hard to believe that good and evil can exist so close together, or that sin can disguise itself as good. We are confronted with such conditions both in nature and on our faith journey.

The person who does not know the danger of the "three-leafed" culprit, tramples freely and carelessly among the emerald green vines, only to experience the painful results for days to come. Likewise, those who do not walk close to Jesus along the pathway of his truths will suddenly find themselves in the midst of "poison." God offers us many beautiful flowers or gifts along the way of life, but we must be careful that we do not foolishly trample through "poison" (sin) in trying to get them.

God enables some to achieve positions of leadership, but then we must be careful that we do not let the "poison vine" of power entangle us and lead us astray, resulting in our using and abusing people. Blessed with abundance, we must imitate the detachment of Jesus lest the poison of greed destroy the beauty of his generous gifts. God fills our lives with pleasures, but all too frequently we fail to distinguish the poison intertwined amidst the pleasures. Our foolishness will result in much pain and suffering, like poison ivy.

Poison ivy, left uncontrolled, can climb trees and become so intense and powerful that it destroys the tree. Sin ignored in our lives has the same result. Faith-filled followers of Jesus walk with confidence and trust because Jesus says, "I am the way." Aware that along the way there will be temptations, difficulties, and failures, we cling to Jesus who protects and guides us; forgives and restores us. Poison ivy vines are very strong and deadly, but we are attached to a greater and more powerful vine, Jesus, who tells us, "I am the vine, and you are the branches, whoever remains in me, shall live forever."

With this confidence we walk carefully amid the poison, enticing though it may be, always keeping our eyes on the gifts and blessings of God, the true "honeysuckle" and special "flowers" along the path of life.

Once we have come to appreciate the friendship of Jesus, everything around us takes on a new meaning; our priorities are attuned to the spiritual and eternal, and the attractions of the world, flesh, and devil are greatly minimized. In the darkness, we are attracted to the light of a small candle, but when the sun shines, it is hard to even notice the small candle burning. Away from Jesus, even little sinful pleasures appeal, but when the glorious light of Jesus fills our lives, he satisfies all our needs, and we become oblivious to passing sinful pleasures.

So watch your step for "poison," and choose Jesus the way, the truth, and the light; the sweet smelling "honeysuckle" of your life.

June 15, 2003

I have little love for spiders. Yet they are remarkable creatures of God and give us a marvelous analogy of Jesus.

One morning this past week, someone called my attention to an intricate spiderweb hanging from the awning covering the front steps of our church. It is amazing to see how delicately and precisely the spider forms its web; it is beautiful!

The spider, having established its web with "runways" going in every direction for quick movement along with many connecting "crossroads" to trap flying insects, then moves to the center to await further action. When some insect flies into this net and becomes entangled, it causes the web to shake and sends a message to the spider, which then swiftly attacks the prey before it manages to break loose either spinning webs around it to secure it or injecting toxic poison to kill its victim.

This geometrically designed art piece, looks very delicate, but is quite strong and is also a class A sonar system. Regardless of where the insect crashes into the web, it becomes trapped and the spider, which is situated in the center, is immediately aware of the intruder and rushes to kill.

Aware that the spider uses its web to kill and destroy, while Jesus never does anything to kill or destroy us, I can still visualize a similar system whereby Jesus affects our lives.

Jesus, cognizant of the dangers of the world, flesh, and the devil, has established a safety system, which far surpasses that of the spider.

Jesus, like the spider, has founded an intricate and powerful "web," his Church; it encompasses the whole world. He has formed this web with channels of grace flowing through the sacraments, the liturgy, and prayer, with "cross" webbing of the corporal and spiritual works of mercy, the beatitudes, and the gifts of the Holy Spirit. These delicate, intricate webs are strengthened by the power of the Bible. Having completed his work, Jesus now sits in the middle of his kingdom overseeing our every encounter with temptation or sin and waits for a call to action.

Anytime one of his followers is attacked, he rushes to their rescue. The least disturbance in our lives, alerts Jesus who is watching over us and he supplies whatever is needed to deliver us immediately before we become too weakened or poisoned by our attacker. Never will he allow us to be overpowered, if only we will welcome him who shelters us under the "web" of his Church.

Regardless of our feeling toward spiders, our admiration of their capabilities of genius is so insignificant when compared to the "infinity" of Jesus. The spider has a very limited web, while Jesus's "web," the Church, is universal; the spider builds to destroy, while Jesus destroys, evil and sin, to build a lasting kingdom. Still the spiderweb, which reaches out in all directions helps me to visualize the incredible "web" of Christ Church through which his life flows into the world for all people. So shake the "web" when under attack, and Jesus who longs to be the center of our lives will instantly rescue, guide, and give you life.

June 22, 2003

Buzz, Buzz, Buzz. That was the sound of a swarm of bees in search of a new hive as they hung from one of our trees. There were hundreds and hundreds of bees adhering to one another and surrounding the "queen bee" protecting her, while others were out scouting. What an unusual sight, and a wonderful example of how a species protects itself; as well as a good analogy of a parish!

Be careful so you don't get stung. Bees do not attack us and will not sting us unless we provoke or hurt them. For the person who knows how to handle bees, they can be gently encouraged to enter a container and be escorted to a new location where they will hive.

The bees will go with the queen, but they will fight to protect her, so if the beekeeper is able to move the queen, the swarm will follow and settle in their new hive and produce honey abundantly. In order to move the swarm, the beekeeper has to gently move the bees to avoid crushing or killing any lest he infuriate the swarm to attack and sting.

Our parish is like an active beehive and our "King bee" is Jesus. It is our responsibility to protect our "King" and follow wherever he leads us. Faithful Catholics depend totally on him, and like a swarm of bees, will fight to defend and protect our king.

Each swarm of bees is unique; it differs in size, and choice of place for their hive, but faithful to their "queen bee" which unifies and directs the life of the hive. Regardless of the size or location of a parish, Jesus must remain the center and focus of the parish, and we must remain faithful to him and his mission. If we believe that his message is our guideline, there is peace, harmony, and unity and no one gets crushed or destroyed and "honey," (grace,) flows bountifully. His Gospel message alone brings unity and offers the direction necessary to assure the safety and life of the parish.

The purpose of the beehive is to foster the life of the bees. They work tirelessly from early spring and well into the fall to produce enough honey for the hive to live. A good and wise beekeeper knows that he must not take all the honey from the hive, but assure that enough is left for the bees to survive the winter. The purpose of the parish is to evangelize—to proclaim the Good News, the life and teachings of Jesus, so its members will live. This is a difficult task. The world continues to entice the "bees," followers of Jesus, to slack off in their work of proclaiming the Good News; while at the same time, along with flesh and devil it consumes too much of the "honey," which Jesus offers, thus causing a shortage of food during the winter attacks of sin; or to foolishly seek their nourishment outside the church, which ultimately leads to death.

This being the case, we are challenged to protect our parish Catholic school, our "spiritual beehive," which our "King bee," Jesus, uses as his main source and guide of life, unity, and spiritual nourishment. Jesus sent his apostle and disciples to evangelize, to teach; that is the reason of our parish, the purpose of our school. A parish without a school is like a beehive whose beekeeper has carelessly taken too much honey, thus endangering the very life of the hive. As responsible "bees," let us swarm around our spiritual beehive, our Catholic school and protect his message of salvation, assuring future generations of their needed "honey" for eternal life, a Catholic education.

Be careful lest you get stung by failing to follow our "King bee," or crushed and destroyed by the pleasures of the world, or die from lack of spiritual food due to the deception of the flesh and the devil. Our Catholic school is a "beehive" of eternal life!

June 29, 2003

From miles around, and even out of state, people gathered to see the launching of the latest space shuttle. There is always a spirit of excitement and accomplishment when the shuttle speeds off into space as planned without problems, delays, or difficulties. There is likewise a sense of great concern during the countdown—those final moments of launching, as well as apprehension that the mission will go well and the return will be safe. Great is the pain, sadness, and disappointment when it fails.

Thousands of people gathered to share in a special launching; not of an ordinary space shuttle, but of an extraordinary "spiritual shuttle." With great excitement and joy, Catholics, from all parts of our diocese and distant dioceses, gathered to share in the Jubilee proclamation of our Catholic faith.

The day was beautiful, and the crowds were overwhelming; the hope for the future faith life of our diocese and the church reached a high peak and the celebration of the Liturgy was awesome. The launching of our faith shuttle was truly a tremendous success; now our church must fervently and faithfully carry out the important mission of evangelization.

Down through the centuries, the spirit of the church—the grace-life of Jesus, has put forth innovative ideas to foster living faith. It has been successful, and it has had some unsuccessful experiences, for which we seek forgiveness of God, and reconciliation with those around us, within and outside the Catholic Church.

It is easy to sit back, look over history, and criticize and condemn the failures of those previous "spiritual shuttles," resulting in the hurt and death of many. Some "launchings" were done carelessly, while others, well planned, resulted in disaster due to proud, vain, and jealous opposition. We are not accountable for the disasters of past "spiritual shuttles." We are to assure the safety of all involved in the "spiritual shuttle" of 2003.

The insatiable craving for material possessions, the rationalization of the corrupt use of sex, and the devastating evil of drugs are sabotaging our present efforts. Freedom of choice, freedom of speech, freedom to do what is personally gratifying is presenting unbelievable danger to the success of our latest "spiritual" launching. Truly, we are being brainwashed and drugged. We are in desperate need of a successful spiritual renewal, a return to the use of good "drugs." There was a time when young people were "drug" to church for Sunday Mass, "drug" to catechism class, "drug" to vacation Bible school, and "drug" to the family table to pray. They were also "drug" to the woodshed when they disobeyed their parents, told a lie, brought home a bad report card, or did not speak with respect. Those "drugs" are still in my veins, and they affect my behavior in nearly everything I do and say and think. They are stronger than cocaine, crack, or heroin. If more children had this "drug" problem, our faith "shuttle" would be right on course.

As we celebrate 150 years of faith in the Springfield Diocese, we have enthusiastically and successfully launched our "spiritual shuttle." Some may criticize our efforts and the cost, but remember the cost of our "faith shuttle" is far less than any space shuttle launched by the United States of America, and the effects are far more lasting. We question the value of the space shuttle program, but a true follower of Jesus realizes that no sacrifice is too great as we develop our "spiritual shuttle," which proclaims the truth, showing the way to life.

July 6, 2003

Faith, fireworks, or formation? This past week, throughout our nation, we celebrated our freedom with extravagant displays of fireworks. How strange that we use explosives to celebrate our deliverance from slavery, war, and suppression! What beauty, thrill, and danger in this annual event recalling and reminding us of the sacrifices and efforts of so many to achieve and maintain our freedom! Is it just for one day?

Placing our faith and our freedom side by side, I see a parallel. All too frequently, we live our faith like we celebrate the Fourth of July, forgetting that our faith journey is not just celebrating momentous events, but a time of formation.

The mere celebration of the Fourth of July with fireworks, marching bands, and eloquent speeches does little to preserve our freedom. It must not become merely a time of recalling the past, but a time of calling us to work, speak, and sacrifice together as we discern and empower our leaders to maintain the rights and privileges for all as declared in our constitution. It is our responsibility along with local, state, and federal leaders, to assure the formation of a government, which upholds the peace and justice of all, lest it become merely fireworks.

Is it possible, that the busyness of our "instant" gratification society has also forgotten the importance of our faith? Have those special moments in our faith life become mere "fireworks"—beautiful, thrilling, and exciting just for the day? The birth of a child, a marvelous creation of God, is something very special and deserving of "fireworks," great celebration, annually, but the work of formation continues each and every day. The baptism of a child is likewise a day of celebration, "fireworks," for the child is born spiritually and begins a faith journey. But the "fireworks" are wasted if daily spiritual formation is neglected. The mismanagement of faith formation ends in disaster.

Many people celebrate the Fourth of July annually but do little throughout the year to foster and preserve our freedom. Parents are conscientious about their children receiving the sacraments of baptism, first reconciliation, first Eucharist, and confirmation, amidst extravagant "fireworks" but some neglect the ongoing formation, which is equally important.

Fireworks are beautiful, but once ignited they are destroyed. Their beauty excites and thrills us, but after the glitter and glare fades, empty casings are all that is left, along with fading memories. Fireworks properly displayed renew our spirit and can encourage a deeper appreciation of our liberty; contrariwise their careless use becomes a source of great danger, even life threatening.

In like manner, the careful use of God's gifts encourages us to live our faith; motivates us to forgive and to love others; but if the grace moments of our faith life are only passing experiences like "fireworks," and not forming us to become Christlike, then our lives are empty and tormented by fond memories of a failed love relationship. The misuse of these special gifts of Jesus becomes a source of danger leading to possible death.

Enjoy the fireworks but work for freedom. Appreciate those special sacramental moments, but live your faith fully. Our faith is not fireworks, but daily formation.

July 13, 2003

Slowly as the sun dropped behind the parched lifeless hills of San Lucas, Mexico, my Sandals approached a group of two—to three-year-old toddlers gathered in what appeared to be a "little men's" business meeting. When the six little "merchants" saw us coming, they swarmed around us, like vultures attacking a tasty "road kill" hoping to make a sale. How sad to see these wee ones forced to beg in order to survive!

Aside from the feeling of pity, I was truly inspired by their tenacity and perseverance and the foresight of their parents. Further along the dirty street, their parents sat watching making sure that they were safe and noting how well they performed the task assigned to them; they were in training. Those little ones while experiencing rejection or success were being taught how to handle these little trials; how to peddle little things in preparation to assume the responsibility of selling more valuable merchandize. Those parents realized the essential need of early training for those "miniature" businessmen to assure survival of the family, as well as preparing them for their future. Could this not be or should this not be a model for Catholic parents, in fact, for all Catholics who truly value our religion and see how essential it is for our faith survival?

Each of us has the grave responsibility to live our faith. Most of us were blessed by God with this gift of faith at birth; although others received it later in life. My faith, from birth on, was solidly rooted by the example of my parents. They sacrificed much, not only things they wanted, but also things they needed in order that we might have the privilege of a Catholic education. They carefully watched to assure that nothing took precedence over living our Catholic faith. From little on they encouraged us to love, to accept, to forgive others when experiencing rejection or success, and to sacrifice our time, talents, and treasures in appreciation of our faith. They set our priorities early on to realize the value and need of deep faith if we were to survive spiritually.

Those six little toddlers, as well as multitudes of others in the area, certainly did not appreciate all the rejection and the long, hot, tiring hours they had to undergo to help their families survive. The parents undoubtedly were pained that they had to beg and engage their children in this difficult embarrassing endeavor, in order to subsist.

Catholics in the early centuries experienced rejection, suffering, and even death while living their faith. They believed the sacrifice was worth it. Do we?

Some Catholics today, still experience similar persecution, but most of us will not. We are faced with a more covert undermining of our faith; we are not persecuted, but we are pressured by the attractions and promises of modern day living and buckle under peer pressure to pursue what is not essential, in fact, often detrimental to our emotional, physical, and spiritual well-being. Such harassment kills not only our body, but our soul.

We are extremely concerned and demanding when preparing for the "work" world; we pay exorbitant prices to achieve that goal. We motivate our children, almost forcibly, to walks of life promising high income. Should not our concern for their spiritual preparation, their Catholic education, their faith formation, and their salvation be as great?

The parents of the "six toddler businessmen" knew the importance of careful, early training for physical survival. Their example can help us prioritize our lives as we focus on what truly is essential for our survival, our eternal survival. Will we?

July 20, 2003

Have you ever been bitten by a grasshopper? I know you are not a plant, but they do not limit their menu to plants only. It encompasses plants, a variety of other materials, and even people. Several months ago, as I sat in the woods enjoying the quiet and beauty of nature, one bit me. It was quite painful. I know that God had a good reason for creating them, but I have some difficulty in finding that reason and consequently in welcoming them. They really can be very destructive as can be seen in my backyard where my hibiscus plants look like a war zone with so many leaves riddled with holes; the work of unfriendly grasshoppers.

What a contrast to the butterfly which adds beauty to the flower beds, helps to pollinate them, and does no harm as it flitters so airily and gracefully from plant to plant! They are most welcome and uplifting as they silently go about their work improving plant life.

We can learn an important lesson from these two quite different creatures that God has placed in our lives. One hurts and destroys while the other unites and builds. In everything around us, God can teach us lessons to help us improve. Let us take a few minutes to look at our lives. What do we find? Am I a grasshopper or a butterfly? If we are honest, we will likely see times when we have been a grasshopper, and times when we were a butterfly. But generally speaking, how do people see us?

"Grasshopper people" are those who never seem to be satisfied with the situation, be it a decision made by the church, school, or organization, or with the people who try to carry out the group decisions. They are always eating away or tearing down the decision or the people assigned to carry off the task, thereby causing much pain and hampering the planned outcome. Dissention and confusion result; pain and injury devastate the group and the worthwhile project, like the flowers in my backyard showing the scars of repeated attacks, is blemished. Without pest control, the whole plant will soon die. In like manner, so will the faith life of a parish. Only prayer control will save it.

"Butterfly people" bring freshness and joy to the group. With endless effort, they offer support and affirmation, always careful not to hurt or destroy while consciously working to renew and better life. When something is misunderstood, they make every effort to peacefully clarify the situation. If someone is experiencing hurt or pain as a result of "grasshopper people," they gently work to heal and restore. "Butterfly people," like butterflies, are a blessing; they are truly life giving.

From time to time God allows "grasshopper people" to test the metal of our faith—to see how much we trust in his plan. Guided by the Holy Spirit, we do all we can to avert their damage. When it is beyond our control, hopefully more "butterfly people" will spread the love of Jesus. With their help, this suffering may become a grace moment bringing a change to the "grasshopper" and a blessing to the entire group.

We all love colorful butterflies and so does Jesus, but he also created and loves grasshoppers. We are not butterflies, nor grasshoppers, but children of God. God loves us even with our differences, weaknesses, imperfections. Let us do the same. God can change ugly caterpillars into beautiful butterflies, and he can change "grasshopper people" into loving "butterfly people." Want to help him?

July 27, 2003

I love windmills; the kind you could see driving through the country in years gone by as well as those nostalgic windmills scattered throughout the countryside, which I saw when traveling through Holland. I have always wanted to have a place with a windmill, for windmills remind me of our faith relationship with Jesus.

As one drives through the countryside today, windmills are a rare sight. To see one that is in good condition and still functioning is a great thrill and a cause of excitement. It is most disheartening to see a broken, neglected, and an abandoned windmill.

A good windmill is a compilation of a fan, a wind-catcher, a tie rod, a pump, and a deep well with an abundance of water. A broken fan or missing wind-catcher destroys the effectivity of the windmill. A disconnected tie rod or a malfunctioning pump prevents the windmill from pumping water and a dry well is useless.

Few farmers have windmills today as a result of the changing times. Horses are a rare sight as they are no longer used for work, with only a few for pleasure riding, few raise dairy cows or beef cattle because these have become specialized industries, and hogs are no longer a part of every farm but are now raised in huge confinements, so the need for the windmill is all but obsolete. Still the modern electric pump was the most devastating factor in the death of the windmill. How like our faith lives!

We are like windmills. God has fashioned each of us like a carefully made windmill. His gift of life is our fan, our faith is the wind-catcher, the sacraments is our tie-rod, Jesus is the pump, grace is the deep well giving life, and the Holy Spirit is the wind empowering our "windmills." What a blessing and thrill when our windmills are properly cared for and functioning! How tragic when they are broken or neglected!

The modernization of the family farm has brought improvements for the farmer as well as problems. Modern-day society has done the same for the church, and our faith life. Our secular materialistic society has little concern for God's "windmill." We live as though our life is ours to use or abuse as we choose. Our "fan" is bent and broken by the misuse of drugs, alcohol, and sex as well as by the various "isms" of today. Many people have completely detached their "wind-catcher" and no longer practice their faith; their "tie-rod," their use of the sacraments, has been replaced by passing glittery substitutes of money, media, medicine, and modernization. Consequently, separated from Jesus, the "pump"—their very source of water, "grace," is disrupted and the "wind"—the Holy Spirit blows in vain. Windmills on the farm may no longer be essential for the well-being of the farm since electric pumps have replaced that need but our spiritual "windmill" is vital for salvation. If your "windmill" is malfunctioning, now is the time to repair it. Pray that God, our Father and Creator, repairs your "fan" by helping you straighten out your life and your "wind-catcher" by deepening your faith. Ask him to reconnect you to the pump "Jesus" by means of a new "tie rod," the sacraments so you can enjoy the abundance of water, his grace, and live. Remember the wind, the Holy Spirit is always blowing; the well, God's grace, is always abounding, and God waits to repair your "windmill." Isn't it time?

August 3, 2003

130

Frogs, frogs, and more frogs all throughout the church. We all know that there are bats in the belfry and cuddly church mice in the attic, but now we have frogs too. What next? Maybe we could start a petting zoo. Since most people do not relish bats swooping around the church, we will have to count them out. There is not enough room for everyone to stand on the pews should a mouse dart across the sanctuary. Consequently, they would be unwelcome; but what about the frogs?

This past Sunday, there were over three dozen "frogs" in the church. They really had things hopping and were truly croaking up a storm. They were warmly welcomed and hopefully they will come each week to add to our celebration and offer praise to God.

This lovely group of "frogs" were the youth of our parishes who had just completed a weekend of sharing, praying, singing, and getting to know Jesus more intimately and personally. These young people, *fully relying on God*, were a great inspiration to all who gathered to celebrate Mass. This group of "frogs" outdid any group of frogs around a pond with their "croaking" for their singing, praying, and active participation brought the church to life. God acts in marvelous, mysterious ways, and he showed that in the faith response of these young people who were open to his message and guidance as a result of those dedicated adults who sacrificed much time and effort allowing Jesus to use them as his instruments for renewing faith. The "pond" is full of wise and faith-filled "frogs" who are guiding and guarding our "tadpoles" in their faith development. Truly, our church is alive.

Earlier in the week, while at Christian Family Camp in the woods at Marquette Park near Grafton, I saw a great variety of life in a multitude of critters, in families, and in the church. The little folks were catching grasshoppers, granddaddy longlegs, lizards, frogs, and baby snakes for the critter race on the Olympics day; family life abounded with babies a few weeks old, infants, children, teenagers, college students, parents, and grandparents; and the church was visibly alive as families and groups shared their faith experiences, celebrated beautiful liturgies, and discussed the doctrines and teachings of our faith.

Both experiences were grace moments where Jesus was acting powerfully. At family camp, as in the "frog pond," people were helping and loving one another and trusting fully on God to bless, guide, and protect them. Little children played freely and wandered about the camp while parents enjoyed themselves in various ways trusting that their families were safe. People volunteered readily and regularly when needs arose. I am deeply impressed by the high school and college students who return year after year to share this family-based and faith-founded week at Christian Family Camp.

"Frogs" and family campers have much to "croak" or sing about for Jesus is the solid foundation of our faith; our families are hungering and searching for Jesus at all ages and there is an increase of Catholics, now in the tadpole stage, who are developing into "frogs" as they *fully rely on God*.

We are afraid of bats; we run from a mouse, but we welcome "frogs." So if you feel like a tadpole swimming in the vast lake of mystery, continue to fully rely on God as you develop into a *frog*. The world, the church needs more "frogs." Are you one?

August 10, 2003

Occasionally, you will see a funeral floral arrangement shaped like a wheel with one or more spokes broken depicting the death of family members. Wheels with all spokes intact run smoothly; broken or missing spokes present difficulties as you well know from a bicycle mishap. Let us now check one of our four spiritual wheels; the commandments, the Mass, the precepts of the church, and the sacraments. We begin by examining the condition of the fourth wheel, the sacraments. This wheel requires seven spokes to function properly.

When Jesus formed this wheel, he saw a need for each of the seven spokes, but over the years, people have foolishly ignored, broken, or removed certain spokes. They are hampered and are making little or no progress in their spiritual journey. What it the condition of the spokes in your spiritual wheel?

Most people have maintained the major spoke baptism, although some for the wrong reason; they look on it as something "magically" guaranteeing salvation, while failing to understand it is birth into a faith life that must be nurtured and lived daily. The next spoke reconciliation is less fortunate; it is rarely used by a vast majority who do not see its need or spiritual value. Many are trying to function without this special spoke, which Jesus frequently used during his life, and now offers to us. Pride, vanity, and ignorance have almost destroyed this spoke. Great is the need for its rejuvenation. Catholics as a whole have kept intact the third spoke through habitual reception of the Eucharist. But the burning question remains, do they really believe that Jesus is present under the appearance of the bread and wine? If so, then why is it such a burden to participate in Mass, to visit Jesus present in the blessed sacrament at times other than coming to Mass, and to change our pattern of life? The fourth spoke of this wheel, confirmation, certainly is bent or disconnected by many who receive this powerful sacrament and then quickly ignore it due to the busyness of the world.

Jesus placed two spokes in this wheel to assure proper service of his people; matrimony for the procreation and education of families, and holy orders for the spiritual care of his followers. What has gone wrong? Couples cohabitating or engaging in premarital sex has resulted in the horrors of abortion and the very foundation of solid, Catholic families is being undermined. Holy orders, formerly looked upon as a special vocation, now is being devastated by the news reporters who seem to thrive on destroying the church by magnifying the tragic actions of a few. Along with that, the enticements of materialism have nearly emptied our seminaries. The damage to these two vital spokes has caused much havoc to Catholics as they suffer a spiritual drought.

Then there is the spoke that many fear, holy anointing, believing that to receive it they must be dying. Jesus meant it to be a powerful healing sacrament for body and spirit.

What is the condition of your spiritual wheel? We all need to check our spokes. We are not concerned about the broken spokes in a funeral arrangement or on our bicycle, but the condition of our soul which thrives or falters depending on the shape of our sacramental spokes. Jesus alone can repair your spiritual wheel! Will you let him?

August 17, 2003

This is the month to own stock in tissue products as the tears flow and tissues blow. Mothers will cry as their first child or maybe the last child will begin their first day of school; students who enter their first year of college will cry along with mothers and maybe even some fathers will draw hard on the tissue supply. Big changes are altering routine lives and tears of joy, sadness, concern, and loneliness are silently and visibly flowing.

Parents love their children and want the best for them. There are tears of joy and a sense of pride when they see their children mature and accomplish great feats, but there are also tears of sadness as they watch them enter into different phases of life, causing concern and separation. Aware of the temptations and evil lurking in the world, some tissues will mark the parents' great concern about the well-being, both physically and spiritually, of their children as they leave home. Many tears will flow on the part of both parents and students due to loneliness resulting from that first time lengthy separation. Oh, for some stock in Kleenex or other tissue company!

Tears are normal; trust is required. Trust in God and in your children is reasonable for those who have lived a deep faith life built on the solid foundation of Jesus's teaching. Much of what you are feeling is analogous to what God experiences when he creates us and places us in this world.

God rejoices in his creation for it is perfect. He frees his children to live in this world; to be separated from him. He celebrates our accomplishments as we mature physically, emotionally, mentally, and spiritually. Great is his concern for us journeying in this land of "exile" for he is aware of the destructive temptations we face, which, when succumbed to, can temporarily or even permanently separate us from him. He realizes our extreme loneliness while wandering on earth, but he permits this to prove our love and fidelity. Yet Jesus has given us the means to face these temptations and remain faithful. He trusts us to make the proper choices. If you have prepared your children to live their faith in a Catholic home environment, now, like God, you must trust them.

As your children move through the various stages of life, each phase will be showered with tears and tissues as you encourage and support their choice of vocation and rejoice in their accomplishments. These are welcome tears, but there will be bitter tears if they are unfaithful to their God, reject your guidelines, or fail your dreams of success.

Success is not to be measured by the number of degrees behind their name or the number of digits on their pay check but rather the degree to which they love God and care for others, especially the less fortunate and the outcast. Success in God's plan is not contingent on amassing material possessions but on the developing of an intimate friendship with his son Jesus, who offers us the ultimate success, salvation.

May your tears be a nourishing shower watering the fertile soil of each new aspect of their life! Since the value of stock, including tissue products, is going down, invest in prayer and forget the stock market for prayer and lived faith are more productive and profitable.

August 24, 2003

This past week when my sandal strap came loose, it became useless. Therein I saw a comparison to our faith. Sandals are made of some solid material under foot, two straps crossed over your foot, and a strap behind the heel along with one around the ankle to hold it firmly to you foot. When all components are in place and in good condition then sandals are useful and enable a person to walk safely.

How like our spiritual sandals! Our faith is the solid material or foundation required for our spiritual journey. The two crossed straps over our feet are love of God and love of neighbor. The strap behind our heel is the Gospel Good News and the strap around our ankle is Jesus present in our daily lives.

Sandals are necessary and valuable for the overall well-being of our body and without them we are hampered or unable to get about to carry out our daily tasks; so too our spiritual sandals. What is the condition of your sandals?

As we examine our "love of God" strap, we notice it is frayed because we find it hard to choose our god. We profess our belief in the true God of our fathers who ransomed us from the slavery of sin and saved us from spiritual death, but at times we weaken and choose false gods that promise to fulfill our passing pleasures. Our worship of God demands the highest priority in our lives; if not our sandal strap becomes weakened or so loose that we are no longer capable of living our faith fully.

What about the cross strap of our spiritual sandal—love of neighbor? Most of us need to have this strap repaired because of our racial, gender, nationality, and religious prejudices.

Living in a world which is slowly losing its appreciation of and respect for life has resulted in severe damage to this sandal strap. Emphasizing equality of women has lowered our respect for them; we now fail to appreciate their feminine characteristics. Accepting the misconstrued concept of "choice" has inflicted irreparable damage to both women and babies. The backlash of terrorism has widened the rift of racism and closed our minds to the fascination of national cultures. Love of neighbor is possible only when we believe that we are all equally loved by God regardless of accidental differences.

The strength of the strap behind our heel is measured by our love of and living of the Gospel Good News. Do we read it on our own? We hear it on Sunday. Reading and hearing the Gospel Good News may deepen our love, but it has value only when we live it in our daily lives. Otherwise it is like having a good sandal strap but not putting the strap around our heel. Such carelessness endangers our spiritual lives.

The true test of one's sandal is how snugly it adheres to your foot. The most essential strap of your spiritual sandal is the one around your ankle, the friendship of Jesus. The faith we live, and the love of God and neighbor, resulting from the acceptance of the Good News is all pulled together by the ankle strap; the presence of Jesus in our daily lives. If Jesus is not real in our lives, it's like wearing a pair of sandals but not buckling them around our feet; they will fall off or cause us to stumble and fall. Our personal love of Jesus and the depths of our friendship help us to adhere to the sole of our spiritual sandals, our faith.

I had my loose sandal strap repaired. Now I can walk safely. We need to repair our spiritual sandals in order to securely walk our faith journey.

August 31, 2003

Have you ever heard the corn grow? You can if you stand in a field on a quiet, warm, muggy night in the spring. Have you ever heard the corn talk? If you listen carefully, you can hear their long leafy tongues whispering in the gentle breeze.

With a little imagination, you can hear them reading from "the diary of a grain of corn" the following story: For many months, I along with my family and extended family were happily enjoying life in the security of a big, new silver bin. I was so thankful to the farmer for the blessings of life, the security of the bin, and the opportunity to share time with loved ones. Enjoying the present situation, we gave little thought to the future.

Suddenly one bright, warm spring morning, there was disturbance in the bin as one by one members of the family were taken away. Finally, I too was taken and buried in the cool dark ground where we remained for a long time fearful of what lay ahead; afraid that we were going to die. Slowly, I felt changes taking place—I was not dying, but beginning to grow; up and up I grew enjoying the warm sun and the gentle rain, and so happy to be really alive. It was then I saw all my loved ones sharing in this new life. The little body I had treasured was now transformed into a beautiful, tall stalk which began to produce new life grains. No longer confined to a bin, I was free to live a new life.

Time quickly passed—the days became very hot, the winds were strong, the rains were few, and we began to lose our vim and vigor, but we stood tall and strong against all the elements of nature satisfied with the life we had lived and the grain we had produced.

As the days shortened and the temperature dropped, concern for our future plagued our minds. But nothing had prepared us for what lay ahead. Early one cold morning, we were alarmed when word spread that the farmer was cutting our stalks and taking our grain away. Gradually, words of assurance came from our elders reminding us that our life work had been completed; we had produced new seed life and though the life we knew and treasured was ending, new life continues on.

Listening to the diary of the grain of corn, we see the close parallel to our life. We, who are conceived in the eternal plan of God, in a moment of time, are transferred from his loving arms to begin earthly life, come forth from the darkness of the womb into the light of the world to share in his divine life through the waters of baptism and the nourishment of the Eucharist. We grow and grow enjoying the health of youth and the ever-present graces of God. Thankful to God for the blessings of life, the love of family and friends, we treasure the friendship of Jesus.

Years quickly pass as we cultivate new life, both physical and spiritual. Gradually we notice loved ones being taken away from us. We realize that our lives are slowly deteriorating as a result of age and disease. Like the grain of corn, we are concerned about our future, but not in fear, for we know that when God calls us through death, it is not the end, but truly the beginning of a new and eternal life of peace, love, and happiness. So we persevere in living our faith, humbly satisfied with our life work, trusting in God's promise of a new and greater life. Finally, the day comes when we too pass through the darkness of death into a new and glorious life where we see all our loved ones. Now we are free and living the fullness of life.

You may be unable to hear the corn as it reads its diary of life, but you can clearly hear Jesus read his diary of life, the Bible.

September 7, 2003

In our parish office we have an impressive copy machine; massive and threatening. It was capable of effectively reproducing with remarkable speed and accuracy. Yet for several months it had been malfunctioning and over a month ago it crashed totally. We have lamented this loss, for it played a very important and central part of our work life. We have searched companies and models and consulted experts trying to resolve this situation. Now, it is time to replace the broken machine with one capable of reproducing clear images of the original.

Rarely do I watch TV, but during the war in Iraq, I saw the toppling of the huge statue of Saddam Hussein. It was a sad, solemn, hopeful moment. But the toppling of his statue did not destroy him. Ironically he had produced several "look-alikes." He chose to be a "copy machine" reproducing his image as his safety precaution rather than that of Jesus for the good of the country. Isn't it time to check the condition of our "copy machine," namely our lives?

God created each of us in his image and likeness; everything we do is to reproduce that image clearly and correctly. Sometimes however, our "copy machine" misfeeds and our image of God is like a wrinkled page. This results from refusing to accept the will of God in its totality; we water down certain parts and so the true image of Jesus is distorted. If we fail to keep our lives centered on Jesus, our "copy machine" pulls the paper through improperly and the impression is lopsided. At times we focus too much on the worldly and our copies are blotched with ink smudges. Occasionally, our lives do not reproduce any of God's images, so our "copy machine" will send forth a totally blank page. There are times in our lives when we choose false gods, so it causes a paper jam and stops the entire machine. As you live your life, do people see a clear and correct image of Jesus?

Each one of us is a "copy machine." Hopefully we are not becoming an empty, huge statue waiting to be toppled; nor a copy machine reproducing the wrong or distorted image of Jesus, nor a totally useless machine taking up space like the one in our office. If our lives do not clearly reflect the image of Jesus, we need to be repaired so we once again reproduce the image of Jesus.

Every day, we are to "copy" Jesus. Our reproduction of Jesus will be the pattern that our children, family, and friends will use on their "copy machine." It is vital that we show them the true Jesus—one who loves us unconditionally.

God patiently waits for us to allow him to fix our distorted lives. Jesus never topples us like the hated statue of Sodom; he never disposes of us like a broken, useless copy machine. Sometimes it may be necessary for us to allow him to make drastic changes in our lives so that we will function properly, but Jesus is the master mechanic and has specific designs for each of us.

So check your "copy machine,"—your life. We are concerned about more than replacing a broken copy machine in an office, more than the freedom of a persecuted country; it is the very salvation of our souls.

September 14, 2003

Gathering with about two dozen parishioners in a local vineyard, we played hide-and-seek with the grapes. The vines did everything they could to keep the clusters of delicious grapes hidden amidst their large green leaves; when we found them, we had to fight to free them. Sometimes the vines had sent forth little security ties to support the weight of the grapes. At other times, as the grapes matured, vines or wires became imbedded in the clusters, making it difficult for us to harvest them. But the fruit of our labors was worth the effort.

The words of scripture, "The harvest is plentiful, but the harvesters are few," took on a personal and very realistic meaning this week as my Sandals sloshed around in the mud picking grapes. The fact that I worked in the drizzling rain certainly emphasized the immediate need for action. Never would I have believed that grapes grew so bountifully. This beautiful, small vineyard heavily loaded with juicy, ripe grapes urgently in need of harvesting, conveyed in a small way the greater need for a multitude to harvest the many vineyards clinging to the hillsides where Jesus walked and taught. Without harvesters, all the fruit would be lost, for time was of utmost importance.

Jesus uses the analogy in making a comparison regarding the salvation of souls. He knew his time was short. He saw the need of followers who could prepare and care for those open to his Word. Knowing that his vineyard would rapidly multiply and produce abundant fruit, he called for harvesters.

Beginning with the twelve, then the seventy-two, he expanded his call. His calls for harvesters continue to the present time. For too long we have thought that priests and maybe sisters are those harvesters; they are, but no one is excluded. Jesus calls young and old, married, single, religious, and those who are parents and those who are not.

As we gather in the vineyard of our church, around the vine of Christ, "abundant fruit," countless souls needing to develop an intimate relationship with Jesus evoke an urgency of harvesters. The "mud" of weak faith and the "drizzle" of apathy deter our enthusiasm. Jesus protects us under his "leaves" grace. The devil tries to draw us for the safety of his leaves by means of materialism, secularism, and atheism.

Jesus clings to us the "fruit of the vine" by tying us securely to himself by his sacraments; as we mature, we become imbedded in him by means of the Mass and prayers. The devil tries to cut us away from the vine by offering us the fruit of popularity, power, and possessions.

Thus we must carefully prepare and protect our children, family, and parishioners by living our faith with enthusiasm and encouraging them to cling to the vine, Jesus, as we bring them to God; that is our work as harvesters in the vineyard of God.

What a joy it was to harvest grapes while sharing with parishioners in the vineyard! It is a greater joy to share with parishioners harvesting lasting fruit from the Vine, Jesus, for the glory of God and the good of the kingdom.

September 21, 2003

One glorious warm fall day, I escaped from my office for a few short hours and drove out into the country to enjoy the beauty of autumn. As I walked across the field, the gluttonous corn picker repeatedly gorged itself with the new grain, pausing briefly from time to time to spew out what it had too rapidly consumed, only to greedily repeat its apparent insatiable appetite for more.

Watching this pattern reminded me of how often we crave for more, nearly destroy ourselves in order to satisfy our wants, and then sadly realize our disappointment, and so resume the charge to get more. Most of us are addicted. Like the corn picker, we seem unable to control our appetites. People frequently speak of sexual, drug, or alcoholic addictions, but there are many others addicted to compulsive eating, sleeping, using the Internet, gambling, sports, and the list goes on. Whatever causes an imbalance in our lives, even when it is good, is tantamount to an addiction and needs to be carefully corrected.

We cannot excuse ourselves as many try by blaming our difficulty or addiction on our parents or someone else. Certainly, others may have a great affect on us, but each of us has a free will to make the right choices. The corn picker has no choice but to consume whatever gets in front of it, but the driver of the machine can and does make decisions. The machine can blame the driver for careful or careless harvesting of the crop and the upkeep of the machine, but the driver cannot blame the machine for his decisions.

We are not machines. We are special children of God made in his image and likeness and blessed with intelligence and a free will. However, at times we act like machines and succumb to our addictions.

Standing before our "spiritual mirror," Jesus, what do you see, a responsible Catholic or a "machine"? A "machine" sleeps in on Sunday morning while a responsible follower participates actively in Mass. A "machine" equates sports, boating, or pleasure on a par with Mass, while a responsible Catholic chooses to prioritize his values. A "machine" is driven by our cultural society, slavishly and foolishly pursuing vocations and lifestyles that tantalize us with monetary rewards, while a devoted Catholic esteems a catholic education and their faith as treasured gifts of God. They freely choose to be responsible stewards of God's gifts, using them only in ways that deepen their friendship with Jesus and give glory to God. A machine does not care what it consumes, but is compelled by the driver to devour whatever he places in its way.

Today's society, so tainted by the culture of death and no longer driven by God, has relegated us to the status of a machine. It expects us to accept and devour the weeds of a secular and material world. But we are not machines; we are responsible Catholics who freely choose to let Jesus drive us as we harvest the wholesome grain of the Gospel.

The harvest is plentiful. There is an abundance of good grain and a plentitude of weeds. We, as responsible Catholics, need to carefully select our driver, control our addictions, and avoid becoming "machines."

September 28, 2003

God gives every bird its food, but he does not throw it into its nest. All throughout the spring and summer months God has cared for all the birds in his own mysterious way. Now, many of them will be leaving us, while others will remain continuing to trust in God's providence. Those migrating and those electing to remain instinctively pursue God's preordained plan of survival. Do you need to migrate or do you experience God's presence where you are?

I am always amazed by the different types of birds. As winter stealthily approaches, one can frequently see hundreds or maybe even thousands of black birds flocking for miles each morning searching for food and returning at the close of the day to the same resting place. What is even more spectacular is how they can fly so close together, diving or turning in unison seemingly spontaneously, neither colliding nor touching another bird in formation. Their ability and agility to maneuver their flight is enviable. Their capability to locate food miles distant from their gathering place and return each day has the accuracy of radar. Their collectiveness and perseverance is their life-stay as they prepare for their migration to distant areas in winter.

We have much to learn from the birds about how to live in unity and harmony; how to trust in God, and to recognize our incredible value. Jesus proclaims this truth when he says, "Are not two sparrows sold for next to nothing? Yet not a single sparrow falls to the ground without the Father's consent. You are worth more than an entire flock of sparrows." Why do we hesitate to trust God's plan for us?

God gives every bird its food; but he does not throw it into its nest. It must go in search. God supplies our every need but we must do our part and work with him. The total dependence and trust of birds, their willingness to migrate to better themselves when things are bad, and their perseverance to achieve their goal are qualities often missing in our lives. Unlike the birds, we set a course different from God's, while flaunting our independence, which ends in disaster. We refuse to "migrate," to change from our selfish close-minded ways in order to grow in faith and draw closer to Jesus.

When the church offers a new means of faith development, many lack the ability to maturely adjust and flounder around hurting themselves and others close to them who are willing to "reform" guided by the Holy Spirit. Unable to make the necessary "faith maneuver," they experience a crisis of faith. Each time we go forth on a faith venture, we need to keep focused on our source of "food," the Eucharist. No matter how far we journey, Jesus, our Light, guides us with absolute accuracy attracting us like a powerful magnet preventing us from becoming lost. Endowed with a faculty, greater than animal instinct, we possess an intellect and free will to discern what is essential for salvation. Truly, we are worth more than an entire flock of sparrows; more than all the birds of the air.

Birds of a feather flock together. We are not birds; we have no feathers, but as faithful Catholics, followers of Jesus may we, like the birds, work collectively in unity and harmony trusting in God to supply our "food" as we "migrate" from sin to salvation!

October 5, 2003

A cloud was my companion this past Sunday afternoon as my Sandals wandered off the beaten path, across the harvested fields, amidst the turning leaves, and under the toasty sun.

It was a most unusual experience. The sky was sapphire blue and the air was crystal clean; and there was just one cloud, fluffy, white, and about the size of a dolphin. It lingered, hovering above me as I meandered through the fields, wasteland, and over the hills; it was my companion all afternoon as I enjoyed God's nature. It remained faithful as I drove home. Later that evening, when I went to the youth gathering, I was amazed to see it still suspended in the east slowly disappearing as darkness enveloped it. Where did it come from? Why only one, when usually there are many clouds bunched together? How come it was not blown apart or away like passing clouds on ordinary days?

As I watched that unique cloud's tranquil journey, I envisioned Christ who is present in every moment of our lives hovering over us, never rushing nor abandoning us, gifting us with life, journeying with us throughout our years, and remaining with us even as death silently wraps its unrelenting arms around us, pulling us from our physical state into that longed-for spiritual state of unending life.

There are storm clouds passing through our "sky" of life, dark, destructive clouds confusing and blinding our view. There are groups of clouds of varying sizes and shapes that dazzle us with their fleeting beauty while blurring our vision of the truth. But there is one "cloud" that lingers and remains faithful through the failures and enticements of life and that is Jesus.

Very few people likely noticed that "lone" cloud because they were too distracted and busy enjoying the day. One needs to be more attentive if they are to really see. That same night, I saw the end of the movie, *Our Town*, on TV. It showed a young mother who died in childbirth. She was buried, and united with all her ancestors in the new life. When given the chance to come back on earth to see the people of her home town, she was distraught and greatly disappointed; her family and friends were too busy and attentive in achieving their personal desires to see and appreciate one another, so she chose to return to "death." How sad, but true; often we are too preoccupied with personal wants to really "see," that is, appreciate one another, or notice the "Cloud," Jesus, longing for us to welcome him into our lives and to follow him. Oh, we see people and things around us, but we do not perceive the inner person—God's unique creation, nor acknowledge God's presence in the marvelous, intricate things of nature.

All the things we chase after in life quickly evaporate like the wind-blown clouds. Only by a disciplined, self-controlled life of faith are we willing to slow down, to set our priorities in order, and elect to follow the ever present "Cloud," Jesus. We are to trust his presence even when the dark of night, "sin," prevents us from seeing him. He is the indestructible "Cloud" in our "sky" of life.

October 12, 2003

Is God a hawk or a tiger fan? Do you have any idea how difficult it must be to be God? Try to put yourself in his place: both groups are praying for their team to win and for their opponent to lose. Now, multiply this anomaly countless times over every minute, and you see what confronts God perpetually.

At the homecoming football game this past Friday night, I experienced a little of the difficulty confronting God. Players from two of my parishes were competing. People from both towns were asking me, "Who are you praying for?"

I was praying for both teams: praying that they play fair, that no one would be injured, that there would be good sports, and that players and spectators would conduct themselves in a manner that would glorify God.

Both teams won; true, one had a higher score, but both teams won God's favor by playing well and fair. Both teams won his blessing as he protected them from serious injuries. They are to be admired, for they witnessed good sportsmanship both during and after the game and the spectators behaved in a Christian manner.

Football is a good analogy of Christian life. We Catholics have a goal and must fight hard to gain yardage, being knocked down by the opposition, rising and trying again, gaining sometimes, being pushed back at others, but we persevere. Sometimes we fumble and lose the ball, at other times we are penalized for our mistakes, and occasionally we are injured and must have time out to recover.

Each game confronts us with difficult teams: sex, drugs, alcohol, greed, and peers. We have good coaches, referees, and many cheering us on to victory. Regardless of which "team" we are battling, we have parents, teachers, and leaders coaching and preparing us to face up to our opposition by following the guidelines of the church. Jesus is the referee; he judges our efforts and enforces the penalties resulting from our infraction of his rules. Such penalties affect the whole team, our individual family, and parish as a whole. When we are injured and temporarily unable to "play" the church ministers the healing care needed to get us back in the "game." Our support or cheering squad is the best, for we have the church universally praying for us: the church triumphant in heaven and the church militant on earth encouraging and supporting us.

We have much to learn from a football game. Only a united team can hope to win; any split or division of the team weakens the possibility of success. One person calls the plays and as a team, they do their best to carry it out. Likewise, the church determines the moral and ethical "plays" or directives and together we strive to follow.

As a player on Jesus's "team" we must expect blocks, fumbles, injuries, gains, and some losses as we face those extreme opposing "teams" of addictions, a death-culture society, keeping up with the Joneses, deterioration of the family, and "no need" for God. These we can conquer, but what is damaging our "team" is lack of faith, trust, commitment, apathy, and irresponsibility on the part of many "players." We have the best "rules" for the game of life—the scriptures, the life of Jesus, and the teachings of the Catholic Church. Jesus is a superior "ref" and our equipment is top notch: the sacraments, Mass, and prayer.

There is more to the "game" than knowing the rules. Playing responsibly, sacrificing on the part of the whole team, and good sportsmanship are likewise essential. When we do that, then we can all pray to God to win, and we will!

October 19, 2003

God loves to play hide-and-seek. Each day he disguises himself in unusual objects and unsuspecting people and waits to see if we are capable of finding him. These past few weeks I found him in a variety of ways.

Diamonds increase in value according to their size, and their intricate cuttings which in turn refracts light in a rainbow array of colors. Recently, I found a diamond of tremendous value. I did not find a material stone, but a spiritual gem. My priceless diamond was the Holy Spirit refracting his beauty and presence in a variety of ways.

Looking at this precious diamond from one angle, I saw the Spirit of God, poured out on those being confirmed. Opening their hearts to the Spirit, they received the powerful gifts of the sacrament, praised and thanked God, and celebrated the Eucharist most enthusiastically. They went forth recommitted to follow Jesus more faithfully; they were new cuttings in the diamond of the Holy Spirit refracting the beauty of God.

The next day, I saw this priceless diamond, the Holy Spirit, at a completely new angle. For the first time in my life, I celebrated Mass inside a prison; what a celebration, what a revelation! Truly, the Holy Spirit was present as we sang, prayed, and enthusiastically celebrated the love of Jesus. The residents worshiped with a vitality that would make most parish liturgies pale in comparison. There I beheld the "rough cut" diamond, of the Spirit, under the capable hand of God, the "artisan," being delicately and finely cut to refract the incredible love of Jesus.

That day the words of St Paul, "There does not exist among you Jew or Greek, slave or freeman, male or female. All are one in Christ Jesus," took on a new and fuller meaning. People of color, Hispanic and white; male and female, residents and visitors, young and old put aside all barriers and were united in Christ Jesus. The "diamond" of the Holy Spirit refracted the brilliance of compassion, acceptance, forgiveness, and love. If God was playing "hide-and-seek," the residents certainly found him in the spectacular team sharing with them at the facility, and the team recognized him in the faith-filled residents. I was awestruck, humbled, and personally blessed as I found him in both. That "diamond" would far surpass the hope diamond in size and value. How sad we fail to see the light of "the diamond" and mistakenly judge it as worthless "glass"!

Later in the week, I detected still another facet of the "diamond." Called to the bedside of a dying man, the son of God refracted beautiful rays of light, his grace and presence, as the Holy Spirit brought peace and comfort through the loving care of his wife, family, friends, and the hospice ladies.

Each time you turn a diamond, it exudes a new color. The colors are all hidden in the diamond, waiting for us to find them. The presence and working of the Holy Spirit is hidden in every person and thing around us, but the light of Christ present through our faith is necessary to perceive their beauty.

Without the light of Christ, we are unable to see the assorted colors of the diamond refracted in our young people, those incarcerated, or in the people and circumstances associated with the dying. Truly, God is not hiding from us, but sometimes we must seek him in unusual circumstances, people, and places. Neglecting to do so, we fail to see the most precious "diamond" of all, the Holy Spirit: the perfect diamond.

October 26, 2003

Lost and seldom found! Every church and school has a huge bin of lost articles and people seldom come to claim them. Several years ago when I lost my yellow jacket, I went to great length searching for it but never found it simply because I could not remember where I last wore it. It was a great disappointment for me.

Since our society is so affluent, we have become quite indifferent about losing things and simply replace articles with little concern about the loss. Material loss and waste is extravagant, but spiritual loss and waste is devastating.

In my kitchen there is an automatic coffeemaker. Over the years, the water line has become so corroded that the coffee barely dribbles into the pot. It will likely be replaced unless it can be cleaned.

My coffeemaker reminds me of so many people who judge themselves as having lost their value because they are not as agile or capable as they were in younger years. The "lost" bin is full of such people who have a hard time coping with the changes in their lives. They are abandoned, unclaimed, and unwanted as a result of a spiritual draught in our secular society. We have lost our "family" value—our appreciation of earlier generations. Faith alone enables us to respect and treasure aging members of our family. When we fail to acknowledge the specific purpose and important role they play in our lives, they become a lost treasure. We suffer both a material and spiritual loss. Try as we may, they cannot be replaced because they are so unique.

Even though my coffeepot responds at a much slower rate, it still performs its task faithfully. The coffee is good and satisfying. Our "seniors" burdened with the limitation of memory, sight, hearing, and energy need to be encouraged to actively participate in the faith and community life of their families and parish to sustain their identity; failing to do so a great source of wisdom and experience will be lost, never to be found.

In conjunction with this devalued segment of society, our secular culture has also affected another great spiritual loss; we have lost the value of our name. We are known by our number more than by our name. Criminals and war prisoners are given numbers; service people are numbered; driver's license and credit cards are registered by numbers and everyone has a social security number. This might be justifiable to avoid error due to a duplication of names, but why are parents failing to give a Christian name to their child at baptism, a saint to become their guide, model, and pattern of life?

We know the difficulty in finding a desired location when the street sign is torn down or the country road has no name. A child lacking a Christian name or knowledge about their patron saint has lost valuable guidelines for a life pattern.

As we celebrate the feast of All Saints, we pause to recall those holy, saintly people whose example has drawn us closer to Jesus, especially those "seniors" in our parish family, lest their wisdom and value be lost, and to teach our children more about their saint in order to imitate them.

Our concern today is about more than lost clothes or malfunctioning coffeepots; it's about people, the neglected elderly and the young who need spiritual role models. Just as every church and school has lost and found bins, so will our homes and parishes if we become oblivious to the value of the spiritual. Look around and see if someone is forgotten in our "bin" and then search for a way to find them.

November 1, 2003

A house that makes me cry is slowly dying from the ravages of time. When I pass, my heart weeps, for this once stately structure perched atop a rolling hill facing the ultimate end of demolition. How similar to our lives!

Sitting on a little hill all alone, this house has a most wonderful view of the glorious rising sun. Not hidden amidst a multitude of trees, it experiences the warmth and the brightness of the sun throughout the day, and then the glories of the colorful sunsets.

Thus situated it enjoys the panoramic view of the countryside displaying the beauties of the seasons. It has much to offer, but no one is willing to make the difficult changes. Here we see a parallel with ourselves.

I can vividly imagine the life of this grand place housing a happily married couple whose children filled the place with laughter and love, adversity and adventure, success and sadness, but always a place of reconciliation and revitalization—a reservoir of life.

Secretly I pray that I could repair and replace its brokenness and restore it to its former beauty and active life. The very thought of my inability to do so fills me with pain and stirs within me a greater disappointment when I compare the disrepair to this house with the neglect of our souls.

We are that stately "house" atop a rambling hill. We experience the beautiful "son" rise at our baptism, which brightens our faith journey and guides us throughout our lives if we are careful not to allow the trees of materialism and secularism to block our view. We will behold the glorious sunset when Jesus invites us to share in the fullness of life at the Resurrection. Our "house" built on the "hill" or "rock" of our faith enables us to enjoy the beauties of our Catholic Liturgical Seasons as they refresh us with their beauty, newness of life, and spiritual energy.

This beautiful house is dying because the family was attracted by the enticements and conveniences of our fast-changing world. The dying house has so much to offer but difficult and costly changes are needed to replace broken windows, missing doors, and to refurbish the house's extensive interior and exterior deterioration. But more important is the need of a family to give it life and purpose.

So too our "house," soul, abounded with life as we received the sacraments frequently and carefully. The "son" of God showered his light upon us, and we matured in wisdom, knowledge, and true love of God and one another. We laughed and enjoyed our family, our faith, and our loving relationship with Jesus in our "house" and found love, forgiveness, and newness of life. Sadly, with the passing of time, the quest for knowledge surged ahead and wisdom diminished and some neglected their house as the pleasures of the world, the flesh, and the devil lured them away. Slowly they accepted the disrepute of their "house," their soul, and in some cases abandoned it in search of fleeting pleasure.

The "death" of my stately country house will eventually happen. It has already been forgotten. The "death" of our "house" (soul) must be avoided. We will never be forgotten by Jesus. No sacrifice is too difficult or costly to repair, renew, or restore our "house." We must ask Jesus, the master carpenter and artist of the blueprints of our house for guidance and help and get busy now before it is too late.

November 9, 2003

Once upon a time there were two islands. One was called Covenant and the other Lepsog. The two islands were separated by a dangerous sea called Satan. The people of Covenant were greedy and always trying to overpower one another. They lived in a huge city known as "Evil" and were known as the Rag-o-muffin people.

The people on the other island of Lepsog were kind, loving, and caring and they were called the Country Bumpkins. Their little village was called "Evol" and for as long as they could remember life remained unchanged.

Then one day the loving and wise king of both islands decided to offer them a chance to change, and he sent his son to build a bridge over the sea of Satan making it possible to travel from Evil to Evol and vice versa.

So the Rag-o-muffins from the city of Evil from the island of Covenant and the Country Bumpkins from Evol from the island of Lepsog were able to cross over the sea of Satan by means of the bridge if they were willing to make that choice.

Some of the youth of both islands gathered and shared all kinds of stories about who was the best, greatest, most powerful, happiest, and most loved.

The youth of Evil from the island of Covenant told how much they were loved because they were protected by police and curfews; how strong their houses were with powerful locks because they were afraid of each other and did not know or trust each other.

The Country Bumpkin youth from the island of Lepsog were shocked by their stories and spoke of the true love they experienced. Their parents and grandparents loved them and carefully watched over them so they needed no policing. Nor did they need a curfew because in their loving country village of Evol, everyone knew their neighbor and often stayed at relatives" and friends" homes over night. They did not lock their doors because they shared everything with others. They did not live in fear because they were all one loving family community.

The Rag-o-muffins could not believe this and had to check it out; they were surprised to see that love could be so real and lived. Slowly, the Rag-o-muffins from the island of Covenant (when pronounced correctly it is Covenant) realized they were living by laws and rules, namely the Ten Commandments, while the Country Bumpkins from Lepsog (when turned around spells Gospel) lived the beatitudes and had gone beyond commands and laws to experience happiness and the rewards of loving.

So the Country Bumpkins invited the people of Evil to turn their lives around, for when Evil is turned around, it spells live, as those from Evol had turned their lives around, and it became love.

Thus we see the two islands represent the Old Testament Covenant calling us to live the Ten Commandments, and the New Testament Gospel inviting us to live the beatitudes and works of mercy. The Ten Commandments assure salvation, while the beatitudes lead to an intimate friendship with Jesus.

God gave the Ten Commandments, but we were foolish, hard hearted, and fearful so he sent his Son, Jesus, to *bridge* the Old Testament guidelines to the Gospel message. Thus kept safe from the sea of Satan, we pass over to a fuller life of love, peace, and sharing by living the beatitudes and works of mercy. The critical question remains: are we willing to cross the bridge?

November 16, 2003

The fields were empty and desolate; the trees in the woods were stark naked and the animals were searching for protection against the bitter cold, which cut like a sharp knife, while the howling winds chased leaves around silent machinery resting in the outbuildings. Amidst all this, the neighborhood field mice were gathering in the attic of our old farmhouse to celebrate the safe return of those mice that had been accidentally flown to foreign countries in cargo planes.

The pumpkin which just a few weeks ago was trying to scare me was now a delicious pie; the apples which adorned the trees in the orchard like Christmas ornaments added bright red color to the spacious dinner table; the proud turkey that ruled the yard all fall was stuffed and roasted brown waiting to be carved, and the finely decorated table was piled high with an abundance of other delicious foods.

The hustle and bustle of family hurrying home from distant and not-so-distant places filled our house with life and merriment as we gathered to celebrate one of the greatest of family holidays, Thanksgiving.

Following a most bountiful harvest from our fields, orchards, and gardens, we had filled our bins and tables. We gathered as family to enjoy the plenitude of God's cornucopia of gifts and blessing, too numerous to list. Earlier, our family participated at Mass and celebrated our greatest blessing, Jesus present in the Eucharist and throughout day we offered prayers of thanks and asked for continued blessing and protection.

While we were enjoying food, family, and prayer, our little furry creatures, huddled among the rafters, were busy sharing adventure stories as they awaited the leftovers from our table. Slim, one of the field mice was complaining about how difficult it was to find food since the fields were empty after the harvest.

Then Pug, his city cousin, who had just returned from a horror trip to Iraq, spoke up: "Our fields are empty and desolate and our trees are leafless and barren of their fruits because they have been harvested and not bombed, burned, or destroyed by war. True, they along with the other animals had to search for food left in fields and woods, but at least, we have not been killed in the endless skirmishing of soldiers and gorilla forces. Furthermore, they could rest as the silence of winter envelopes the sleeping machinery but the noise of tanks and war machines was inflicting fear and destruction, killing loved ones, destroying crops, and property causing poverty, starvation, and death." Hearing of these atrocities, the mice paused quietly to thank God for their safety and blessings.

Will we, like Slim, continue to complain about the hardships of life or, like Pug, rejoice and thank God for his protection and generosity?

Our fields are empty but our tables are full; hopefully our lives are empty of greed and our hearts full of love, for God has blessed us more abundantly than the field mice or the animals in the woods. Besides peace and freedom we enjoy prosperity; we dine luxuriously, live in spacious houses, and enjoy health and employment. But that is not all, for those who share of their abundance and even of their "little," Jesus blesses one hundredfold in this life and forever in the life to come.

November 23, 2003

The hour was late, the house was dark, and the room was cold as Slim and Pug, our little friendly mice, more stuffed than the Thanksgiving turkey, with great effort strained to squeeze through the tiny hole in the closet and climb back to the attic to rest. Tomorrow life would return to normal as Pug ventured back to the city and Slim remained on the farm; neither had great plans for the coming year.

The hour is late, the world is dark, and the days are cold as we come to the end of another Church year. We, who have been greatly blessed throughout the year with the love and grace of God, are now on the brink of a new year. Will we, like Slim and Pug return to our routine pattern of life or do we look forward to a year of opportunity?

No one knows the hour on our "clock" of life; the hour is of little concern. Our concern is how we use the time remaining. We face a world of darkness but in a spirit of hope. We endure the "cold" of the present times as we expectantly await a year of opportunity.

It is Advent! It is time to act—a time to remove our blinders of apathy; our "rose"-colored glasses that we may see clearly. Moving about in the dark can be dangerous; putting off necessary conversion in our life, be it physical or spiritual, can likewise be disastrous. Rationalizing our sinful actions, like "rose"-colored glasses only disguises the truth, which eventually we must face; for we are sinners, and we make mistakes.

"Advent" means, "to come to." As we begin a new liturgical year, the church reminds us of the urgent need to come to our senses—to come to an awareness of who we are, where we come from, and where we are going; to come to Jesus, who offers us another year of opportunity.

Slim and Pug were so stuffed that they could hardly get out of the room through the tiny hole back into the safety of the attic. Is it possible that we are so "stuffed" with the things of the world that we have difficulty returning to the safety of the "spiritual"? Our furry friends had one thing in mind and that was to rest in the attic. We cannot rest.

During the coming weeks, we are to prepare ourselves. We must make room in our lives for Jesus. We may not have a splendid palace; it may be nothing more than a stable, but we are to ready it to welcome Jesus, our Savior. Enveloped in darkness, in the spirit of hope, we await the coming of Jesus, the light of the world. Paralyzed from coldness of heart, we prepare for the coming of Jesus who will warm it with his love. Only one barrier remains; our unwillingness to come to him.

Jesus in humble obedience to his Father left the glory of heaven to come to us, to be born in a dark, damp, stinky stable; a presence that changed that stable into a magnificent temple. He comes to save those willing to be saved. Putting off our "rest," we are to come to Jesus to invite him into our dark, cold, dirty lives that he may save us and make us glorious temples of his Spirit.

Slim and Pug, our little friends, doing what was natural, returned to their routine way of life. We can no longer do what is natural; it is time to put on the "supernatural," that union of our "coming to" Jesus and welcoming his "coming to" us. Thus united we enter a year of opportunity.

November 30, 2003

Pete and Len left the arena amid the deafening roar of hundreds of spectators. The tournament was over, and they had lost by a small margin—the reward of months of strenuous practice and many hard fought games. As they boarded the bus to return to their small town, Pete was sullen while Len was exuberant. Why the difference? Pete was always competing, but Len was striving to excel.

When competing, someone must lose and Pete did. When excelling everyone can win and Len did. Competing is not always the best thing; it means always comparing yourself to everyone else, and winning only if you've beaten everyone else. To excel is an entirely different concept. One who excels gives their best effort because it matters to them personally; they emphasize their strengths and manage their weaknesses; they are focused on their own accomplishments without being conscious of anyone else. To truly excel, one must figure out what they need to do; do your best and forget the other person.

Pete was disturbed and bitter because they failed to win the trophy. Len was content and in good spirits because he was satisfied with his efforts to develop his personal skills, to become a team member, and to excel in sportsmanship over the year.

Families are broken, communities are divided, and countries are fighting because they are in competition—seeking to be the greatest, to have the most, and to dominate. This could be avoided if everyone gave more time and effort to personal excellence and less time comparing and competing.

Jesus came into our world not to compete, but to excel; not to be the greatest speaker of all times, but to speak the truth at all times; not to acquire possessions, but to trustingly share with all in need; not to become the most powerful, but to serve everyone; not to forcefully control our lives, but to offer us the opportunity to choose to love. He was never in competition with others, but always excelling in virtue. Jesus created us all different, uniquely different. It was not his plan that we be in competition because of our many differences, but he hopes we will excel in developing into the person he created us to be—to be excellent, to become perfect, and to be saints.

Pete may rank among the most competitive players and acquire a room of trophies, but in the end, he will always lose because someone will eventually surpass his abilities. Len may not be ranked among the elite sports idols, but he will achieve an ongoing sense of peace and satisfaction knowing that he has spent himself cooperating with God striving to excel—using what he has and being who he is according to God's plan.

Society has us sparring with one another in a variety of "rings"—climbing the company ladder, keeping up with the "Joneses," manipulating the lives of family, friends, or employees, resulting in ulcers and heart attacks. Jesus invites us to excel in virtue, to focus on his will, to stop comparing ourselves to others, and enjoy true peace.

How we live will win for us a crown of glory; will it be one of passing glory, like Pete, to be lost in competition or one of eternal glory won by excelling in virtue like Len, who sought to develop his strengths and manage his weaknesses? Don't compete, excel!

December 7, 2003

On the corner of my cram-packed desk is a little pumpkin. Yes, a pumpkin which someone gave me at Halloween. It stands out, truly out of place, since it is nearly Christmas—with Christmas songs and lights and decorations becoming more visible with the passing of each day. It is there simply because I did not want to throw it away. Each time I look at it, I am reminded of what we as Catholic are expected to do.

No, we are not expected to be pumpkins, but we are expected to stand out in a way that we seem as out of place as a pumpkin under a Christmas tree. A follower of Jesus, one who truly lives their Catholic faith, is always a "pumpkin" and does not change into a squash, gourd, or cucumber when around them, simply to fit in or to prevent notice. Fidelity in living our Catholic faith takes a lot of courage. It does not fluctuate with each new trend or fad and frequently is not the fashionable thing.

To be a Catholic one will always stand out and frequently be out of place; refusing to buckle under peer pressure, to blend with the current trend, or to change our moral values and ethical principles. We cannot be pumpkins when pumpkins are around, and then change to a squash, gourd, or cucumber when they are in vogue in order to avoid derision. Our model, our pattern is Jesus who never changes and neither can we.

Next to the pumpkin on my desk is a little word picture quoting Mother Teresa: "We cannot all do great things but we can do small things with great love." That is the challenge of followers of Jesus. "Pumpkin" Catholics may not always do great things, but they will always do everything with love; they will love the lovable and the unlovable; love all stages and phases of life; love their Catholic faith when beneficial and when inconvenient. Their foundation is the solid, immutable "rock," Jesus.

The little pumpkin on my desk has black and orange ribbons tied to it; the black signifies the times of suffering and trials, which Jesus promises all his followers and the orange represents the glory and joy offered to those who endure to the end. We are in need of more "pumpkin" Catholics in our church today so that when someone expresses views contrary to the plan of Jesus, they would stand out like a "scarecrow" in a pumpkin patch.

A scarecrow is attractive, like the propaganda of our contracultural society, but soon it loses its attraction when it no longer scares away the birds and danger lurks in the pumpkin patch. Likewise the enticements of our modern world are most attractive until we accede and realize their inability to fulfill their promises and confront us with grave danger. "Pumpkin" Catholics don't need scarecrows to protect or attract them, we have Jesus who protects us from all harm and attracts us, like a magnet, by his love.

Jesus chooses our "black ribbons" careful not to overwhelm us, for every follower of Jesus must expect crosses. When we accept them and allow Jesus to help us carry them, he will also robe us in "orange ribbons" as he fashions our crown of glory. Whether we do great things or small things, we do everything with great love—courageously living our Catholic faith, willing to be different, and to stand out, is to be out of place like a pumpkin under a Christmas tree.

December 14, 2003

During our school Christmas Program, I heard several little "trees" talking; their message was so applicable to each of us. As Christmas was approaching, each wanted to be chosen to be a Christmas tree. All the trees were various types of evergreen trees except for one; it was a popular tree. The evergreen trees made fun of the popular tree because it was different; its branches were pointing upward and were bare while theirs were soft and green and reaching down to everything around them.

As the children came searching for a Christmas tree, the evergreen trees vied to be chosen first. One by one they were chosen and carried away by happy children leaving the popular tree sad and disappointed, all alone.

Each Christmas tree was delighted to be the center of attention, to be decorated with lights, tinsel, garland, and ornaments and to have Christmas presents piled at their feet. But immediately after Christmas, they were no longer the center of attention and the excitement ended as they were tossed out into the cold and quickly forgotten.

Broken hearted, the Christmas trees returned to the woods with empty branches, which only recently had reached to take everything they could get. Being vain, they had selfishly vied to become a Christmas tree while making fun of and ridiculing the popular tree and ignoring its desires. Consequently, they had been pushed and shoved and abused by the crowds celebrating the Christmas Holiday. How surprised they were to see the popular tree had become a tree of "Christmas"!

While they were busy seeking for themselves, God had chosen the popular tree and sent his angels to transform it into a tree of "Christmas." The popular tree with raised branches offered all to God and God's angels filled them with the real gifts of Christmas—love, peace, forgiveness, abundant life, and eternal life.

Ashamed, the Christmas trees came to realize that Christmas is not a time to seek for self, but to recognize God like the popular tree; not a time to seek to become Christmas trees, but rather to become a tree of "Christmas." Sadly they came to realize that Christmas trees are simply a part of the Christmas holidays, but a tree of "Christmas" offers the gifts of the season all through the year.

These little trees represent many of us as we get so involved in the hustle and bustle of the Christmas Holidays. We are anxious and stressed as we spend much time decorating our homes, purchasing gifts, participating in holiday parties and busying ourselves with worldly demands. We enjoy the excitement and the involvement of the Christmas Holidays, but then like the Christmas trees we experience a big let down when the holidays are over. We have missed the "reason for the season."

God did not make us to be Christmas trees to be showy but to become a tree of "Christmas" to share love and life. Each of us is unique with greater differences than between the trees. Some are more acceptable and more sought after than others because of external appearances just like the evergreen trees, and unless we are careful, this may lead to pride or vanity as we pursue our selfish goals while forgetting the needs of others.

The "Reason for the Season" is the coming of Christ who transforms us into a tree of "Christmas" if we raise our "branches" (lives) to him. When we focus on God and welcome Jesus into our lives, he fills us with peace, love, mercy, and abundant life so we can share it all through the year and not only during the holiday season.

A Christmas tree is used for the Holidays and discarded, a tree of "Christmas" gives life and love all year and is highly treasured. Jesus came to make us a tree of "Christmas"!

December 21, 2003

Jesus said, "Let those who have ears, hear." What does he want us to hear—his message of life and love? Do you hear? Jesus speaks in unique ways, but his message is powerful. Some of you may have heard Jesus a few Sundays ago when he spoke at the school Christmas Program. He spoke through "little prophets" as he made his final plea for a place to dwell.

How clever of Jesus to use a children's play as a means for our conversion; we have ears, did we hear? Joseph and Mary were desperately looking for a place to stay; a place for the birth of Jesus. Inn keeper after inn keeper turned them down for various reasons.

The weary travelers in the children's play were turned away from every Inn; the "No Trust Inn," the "Last Chance Inn," the "Too Busy Inn," the "Procrastination Inn," the "Status Quo Inn," the "Good Life Inn," and the "Care Less Inn" until at last they were compelled to spend the night in stable.

Via the "little prophets" we realize that Jesus experiences the same difficulty today; as many have no room for Jesus. Do we heed his plea or which "Inn" is our excuse?

God sends Jesus to show us how to live and reveal the promise of eternal life, but some are more inclined to listen to the voice of others, not trusting in his pattern of living or his promise; those at the "No Trust Inn" are too satisfied with worldly pleasures to trust that Jesus's promises will be more fulfilling. There are some who have taken a room at the "Last Chance Inn" feeling the need of immediate gratification, for tomorrow may never come. Their misconception of God causes them to "live it up" now; there is always time for Jesus after we die. The "Too Busy Inn" is overcrowded because the time saving technological gadgets only causes them to extend themselves to other projects, depriving them of room for Jesus. It is unlikely that Jesus will ever find lodging at the "Procrastination Inn" because they have become proficient in rationalizing how they live—planning time and room in our lives for Jesus when they retire or get old. Thinking they can do that tomorrow, they fail to realize that their last tomorrow may be today. Jesus will never find room in the "Status Quo Inn," the Inn for the elite, those satisfied with their lives and disturbed about how he wants them to live. The Source of all life, Jesus, is unwelcome in the "Good Life Inn." Those in high society vie to improve materially, mentally, and physically but refuse to make room for Jesus who offers spiritual transformation. Certainly, Jesus will not find room in the "Care Less Inn" for he would make everyone most uncomfortable. It is unreasonable to expect that selfish, uncompassionate, "all for me" group to see any benefit for making room for this poor, vagrant, share all you have radical into their lives. Finding no room in any Inn, Jesus is once again shoved out into the darkness and forced into the "stable," the humble.

Christmas has come and gone, but Christ remains; looking for a place to dwell, he knocks at your heart. Do you have room? Listen to the message of the "little prophets" and prepare a place for Jesus in your life all year and not just for Christmas, even if it is only a humble stable; the presence of Jesus transforms it into a palace of glory.

December 28, 2003

Looking out my office window last week, I saw a storm fermenting in the south. Slowly the warmth and the brightness of the sun disappeared as the clouds pushed and jostled their way across the sky. Like an ongoing wrestling match, the clouds and sun battled; at times the sun had the upper hand, only to be overpowered by the clouds, which in turn were tossed aside by the brilliant sun until at last the clouds won. Temperatures were rising and falling like a yo-yo, so it was hard to know what to expect; would it rain, sleet, snow, or simply send angry clouds scurrying past?

Examining our lives, we find much the same pattern: Positive and negative experiences are grappling for control. Life is pleasant and enjoyable when suddenly someone or something clouds the beauty and excitement of family or work and we question the outcome of the particular situation. Turning to God, we can weather the storm, trusting that the clouds will soon pass revealing the love of Jesus. The storms of life can destroy, or they can increase and strengthen our faith to trust in his plan of salvation.

As we look back of the past year, we recall bright sunny days filled with the light and warmth of Jesus's love when things went well and we remember those days when the storm clouds of pain, disappointment, sickness, and the death of loved ones blocked our view of the "son." The year is completed, its storms are past; the "son" has returned and life goes on. The world, the flesh, and the devil will continue to "cloud" our lives and block our view of the "son."

Reviewing our life experiences makes us confident that just as the sun always eventually overpowers the clouds and storms of nature, so will the graces of Jesus help us to endure our spiritual storms. A new year is God's gift to us; a year of expectations, excitement, and one in which we can anticipate clouds and even some storms.

When the clouds drop down rain, then new life springs forth; if sleet results, then there may be need for some trimming and repair, but if it snows, we behold beauty and newness. Rain, sleet, or snow is generally the exception; most days are simply overcast, days when we long for the return of the sun to brighten our lives.

So when confronted with spiritual rain clouds, try to see an opportunity to bring forth a new and stronger faith life; if the rain turns into sleet, then allow Jesus to trim away any ugly damage resulting from the storm, and if God showers down upon you beautiful snow, then thank him for the newness and beauty of your sanctification. We are able to endure these occasional tests of our faith, but frequently we succumb to the overcast dreary days when nothing seems to be happening. During such time we can only pray and long for the return of the "son" to enlighten us and empower us to accept his plan.

Storms of nature and difficulties in families or at work can be destructive but nothing as devastating as the storms of the spirit. Storms of the soul unless squelched early can develop into a tornado, which will destroy our faith and relationship with Jesus. Jesus is offering us the warmth of his love and the light of his plan, but the devil perpetually clouds our minds so as to foster fear, guilt, and confusion. Natural storms take their toll; so do storms of family or work, but each time they are followed by periods of renewal.

Trusting that God will protect us from storms of nature and help us resolve our family or work differences, we believe he will help us live his plan of salvation this New Year!

Happy New Year! Trust God to Bless You.

January 4, 2004

Thank God for gravity; these weeks and months have been passing with cyclone speed, which I believe would spiral us into space were it not for foundational gravity holding us in place. What's the rush? What are we gaining by this whirlwind lifestyle?

Entering the new year with the speed of a bullet, we glance back to see where we have come from and what have we accomplished that has lasting value in order to see where we should aim and determine how to attain our goal.

Several weeks ago, I received a beautiful ceramic figurine of Jesus surrounded by little children for Christmas. I can easily visualize Jesus's love as he embraces them, and I can almost hear him teaching to them in a caring, compassionate, child-level way.

Back in the "ole" days we were taught the three "R"s, but today with the modern technology of videos, computers, and calculators, many can hardly read; very few write legibly and only rarely can someone competently work with figures. This modern catastrophe affects countless people, but it is quite insignificant when compared to our obvious failure to teach the three "R"s essential for spiritual growth—relationships, respect, and responsibility. They were valuable assets in the good ole days; the foundation of your "good" name which was the most important asset you could possess.

With the increase of family dissension and war between nations, along with the shocking number of teenage pregnancies and innumerable abortions, and the appalling divorce statistics, is it not time to reevaluate the morality of our relationships? Jesus respects us, invites us into a loving relationship, and listens carefully to resolve our difficulties. Would Jesus be pleased with the spousal relationships today, or those between parents and children? What about our relationships with friends?

Relationships stand or fall on our respect for one another. In the "good ole days" men respected women, tipped their hats, which were never worn in the house, opened the doors for them, and were gentlemen. In days of yore, women were ladies and added much feminism to the wholeness of the family and together with their husbands taught their children obedience and respect. Respect evidenced love for the whole person and great sacrifices of self-control were expected by all.

Relationships built on respect produce responsibility. Today's secular society seeks to undermine the very basis of responsibility, religion, or the rightful place of God in our daily lives. Religion fosters respectful relationships accountable to God. Commitment to God's commandments and his Gospel message compels one to acknowledge the responsibility of their actions.

We need to enter a "cyclone" cellar seeking shelter from the rushing world, which makes us spiritually dizzy to discern where we are going and if we are gaining in our spiritual life as each year jettisons us closer to eternal life. My figurine of Jesus and the children reminds me of the urgency to teach the three "R"s essential for spiritual growth today: relationships, respect, and responsibility. We need Jesus as our point of gravitation so we won't be destroyed by the cyclone of the secular society. This requires deep faith.

January 11, 2004

Last Saturday evening, I was privileged to see God painting. The sun set as a huge fire ball, the fish-scale clouds, kissed by the sun, were blushing and the crystal blue sky was marred by nine streakers; planes playing tag so high that only vapor trails chasing tiny silver balls were visible. As the sun melted, its final rays silhouetted the bare trees and the motionless farm buildings along the western horizon. As his final touch, God completed his pastoral painting with a huge flock of geese slowly gliding into the lake nestled amidst the darkening hill through which I was passing. God's works cannot be verbalized nor painted on canvas; God's presence can be appreciated in its fullness only with clear vision, which at times may require the help of glasses.

Often times glasses are tinted so a person never sees things as they really are; others refuse to wear glasses for a variety of reasons, and some need to have their eyes checked and have their present lens changed. The person wishing to see things as they really are will take the steps necessary and undergo the inconvenience required to achieve the truth.

The same is true regarding our spiritual sight; maybe we need to go to our spiritual optometrist, Jesus, for a soul checkup. Anyone who has gone for an eye check will recall how you were required to read the letters as the doctor continued to change the lens settings to determine which gave you the best vision. Some settings made it worse while others offered clear perception. Jesus likewise strives to improve our spiritual vision. He uses the various lenses of the sacraments, Mass, prayer and sacred scripture to achieve a sharper view of his plan.

Frequently, we view people with tainted lenses resulting from prejudiced views of others; at times, due to lack of interpersonal relationships we are too far removed to see their inner beauty clearly. Occasionally, we are too proud to wear glasses even when we know they are needed; pride can also prevent us from spiritually doing what is necessary to see Christ in those around us, or perceive his plan.

Without the proper spiritual "lenses," sanctifying grace, and sacramental grace, we will never appreciate the "art" work of God in nature, nor be capable of seeing clearly enough to recognize him in the least, the unloving, the marginalized or anyone different from ourselves. Without the "frame" of faith to hold our "glasses" firmly in place, it is impossible to distinguish the work of God in the people and happening around us from things of chance. Wearing the "glasses" prescribed by Jesus, our spiritual optometrist, we are able to see clearly enough to walk amidst the sufferings and trials of "twilight" as the light of Christ silhouettes the dangers of darkness to be avoided and keeps us focused on the truth, the way and the light as we instinctively, like the geese, follow Jesus to eternal life.

Fuzzy vision, misunderstanding the directives of Jesus; stumbling in the darkness of sin resulting from misplacing your spiritual glasses or being lost in the confusion of faith "blindness" are indications that you need to have your "eyes," your inner spirit and your soul checked and new "grace" glasses prescribed. Do you need an appointment with Jesus?

January 18, 2004

This past month I have been doing some experimental cooking, and this past week I even made an apple pie. My cooking and baking will never win me any Betty Crocker awards, but it was a growth experience, a challenge, and fun.

This week we celebrate Catholic Schools' Week and Catholic Schools are meant to be a growth experience, a challenge, and fun for the students, teachers, parents, and entire parish. Each year is designed to produce a growth experience, or we fail to achieve the purpose of education. The subject matter progressively expands throughout the year and each successive year to challenge everyone involved in education both in the classroom and in the home. A well-balanced academic schedule is one which also intersperses fun amidst routine experiences of mental development.

When I was cooking, much of what I prepared was done without a recipe but simply guesswork and for the most part, it turned out quite well. Baking the apple pie was truly a challenge; I had never done so before. The apples were droppers from an orchard I gathered last fall and had seen better days; the pie crust was not fresh, and I could not find a recipe for an ordinary apple pie, so I improvised. And to make matters more challenging, I had never baked with a gas oven.

Our Catholic School is truly a great blessing to our parish; the channel through which we capably nurture and pass on our priceless gift of faith. United, the parish, teachers, and parents assist and enable the students to experience not only superior academic growth, but more importantly spiritual and faith growth—the main purpose for a Catholic School. Certainly, we are challenged academically in this technological age, but we face an even greater challenge to our faith by today's contracultural society. Both challenges are accomplished by our capable, faith-filled teachers, who embellish the academic requirements with fun moments of rejuvenation.

My pie was edible and even delicious. It shows that good results are possible when one is willing to take the risk and put forth the effort. All our students are not equally qualified but with loving attention and heartfelt compassion our teachers help them to develop to their best potential. Our Catholic School standards are high and the requirements are demanding, but the results are most gratifying as each student is encouraged to do their best.

Catholic Schools foster intellectual and spiritual growth not only of the students, but also of the parents. Catholic Schools implant the seedlings of faith which will survive only when the parents, like a strong "crust" containing the pie filling, support the Catholic Schools' teachings of church doctrines and morality in their home life and their active participation in the faith life of their parish community.

Together, we, teachers, parents, and parishioners should take each student, like I did with each apple, and remove what is not good and then add "sugar and spices" as in my pie, that is, personal and special love, attention, and help so they will become "delicious" and pleasing to God. Add the "heat," the love of Jesus, and our students will come out of our Catholic School, God's spiritual oven, baked to perfection and with parents and parishioners, bring nourishing, spiritual sweetness to the community—a living faith.

This week, in a special way, we thank God for the marvelous blessings of a Catholic School. It leads us not by guesswork, as my baking experiences, but with the certitude of Jesus's Good News, and not to a questionable result, but to eternal life with Jesus.

January 25, 2004

It's a bird, it's a plane, it's superman! How I used to be thrilled at hearing those words on a battery radio as each exciting program started. It was even more exciting at the movie screen when Clark Kent would change from a human to superman and do such remarkable things and always for good. But it was only a story of pretense.

Things are not always what they appear to be. In our modern technological world, we can be easily fooled. The TV, video, and computer have so drastically affected us that we tend to live a life of pretense in our dealings with family, friends, and at work, and even in our relationship with God. We are not superman nor TV or movie characters living pretentious lives, but we are living real lives in a real world with a real God. As a consequence, we must examine our lives and avoid judging others to determine whether or not we are a "great pretender." It is easy for us to fool those around us for they only see the outside, but we cannot fool God who sees the heart, the real us.

Last week when I took a potato from the refrigerator, it appeared to be good, but when I cut it, I found that I had been deceived, for most of it was spoiled by dry rot. Is it possible that some of us, either consciously or unconsciously have become like that potato? Perhaps some emotional injury or a spiritual mishap has bruised us internally or maybe our faith has lain idle for so long that we have dried up inside and no longer truly live our faith. We may pretend to be Catholic or give the appearance of being one to those around us, but we know and God knows whether we are truly living our faith.

The media loves to demean our religion, our moral, and ethical principals as it gradually undermines our faith foundation. Consequently, Mass attendance has dwindled, and many go only when they find it convenient justifying their actions with pretentious and false excuses, and they know it is wrong. Young couples are living together before marriage pretending it is necessary for economic or other reasons; they are sinning. Premarriage sex and abortions may be secret, but not from God; he sees the "dry rot" beneath the external façade. The list goes on. Each of us is responsible to give good example in the way we personally live our faith.

Parents and all of us must witness to our young people the innate value of our faith, not only by teaching, but by living it internally as well as externally. Solid lived faith has more power to change us from weak humans than any power that superman possessed; and it is not pretense, it is real. This faith empowers us to do superhuman thing that are always good.

We are not "superman" pretending to be human like Clark Kent nor are we human pretending to be superman; we are humans who have been elevated to the "superhuman" by the indwelling of the Holy Spirit as a result of our living faith. We may not overcome our human weaknesses as quickly as Clark Kent changed into superman, but we know that if we persevere in living our faith, Jesus will change us. Our faith protects us from "dry rot" and empower us to share in the "superhuman." We are not potatoes which cannot prevent their "dry rot"; we are followers of Jesus who can remain whole and holy by living our faith until Jesus welcomes us into his eternal kingdom of life and love.

February 1, 2004

"The weather outside is frightful but the fire is so delightful, but as long as you love me so, let it snow, let it snow, let it snow." These beautiful words from an old familiar song are most appropriate today as it is snowing, sleeting, and disagreeable out. But as the song states, it is love that keeps us going.

On my desk sits a cuddly snowman with a carrot nose, charcoal eyes, and smile, topped with a bright red cap and a candy-stripe scarf around its neck. Unlike the ice and snow outdoors, it is exuding love and longing to be loved.

New fallen snow is beautiful and inviting, at least for children; it wants to be played in, and it transforms the ugly world into a fairytale land of mystery and beauty. When the temperature is right, it can be formed into a snowman or the snow-covered hills can become a place for much fun, but with time it tends to harden and become dirty.

In a sense we are like the snow. God creates us and we are beautiful and lovable and when we remain close to Jesus, we can be formed, like the snowman, into the person of beauty we were created to be longing for love and offering love to others. Living deep faith we, like the children who see goodness in the snow, can see the good, beauty, and mystery in others as God transforms us and graces over our prejudices. Covered with the love of Jesus, like snow-covered hills, we bring joy and peace into the lives of others; we are fun to be around.

When the snow begins to melt and refreezes, it becomes cold, hard, dirty, and dangerous. Likewise when we wander too far from the love of Jesus, we become hard hearted and dangerous. Separated from Jesus we grow cold and hard; no longer able to be molded into another Christ. Ceasing to be lovable or loving and smudged with sin, we cannot reflect the beauty of Jesus or enjoy the mystery and beauty of his plan for us and danger lurks.

Fresh snow covers the black, bleakness of the ugly winter landscape until the heat of the sun returns to destroy this spectacular beauty and once again reveal the true reality of the dead terrain beneath. The redemptive grace of Jesus, like snow, covers over the ugliness of our sins until we become too involved in the "heat" of worldliness and allow the deadly effects of sin to become visible. There will be times when we will harden like old snow because we have wandered too far from the warming love of Jesus as well as times when we will be blown about by the wind as dirty snow when we fail to control our prejudices or selfishness and so reveal our inner ugliness.

We are not a cuddly soft stuffed snowman, nor are we a frosty one in a snow-covered meadow; we are a special work of God. We will not always be loved or loving. Jesus loves us anyway. Jesus makes beautiful snow; he melts dirty snow. Jesus makes us good and allows our sins. He longs to renew and reconcile us. He does this when we, with eyes of faith, behold the mystery and beauty of his plan in everyone.

The weather outside may be frightful; the world, the devil, and the flesh, like ice, sleet, and snow, may be making life miserable, but the fire, "Jesus" is so delightful as he continues to warm, guide, and protect us. As long as he loves us so, let it snow!

February 8, 2004

Have you checked your "vital signs" lately? I do not mean your physical vital signs, but the vital signs of your spiritual life. If not, then why not? We spend fortunes and go to extremes to preserve our lives, which we know will end soon regardless of what we do to maintain it, but we seem to be a bit careless about caring for and developing our spiritual lives, which are to last forever.

On the table in my office there is a poinsettia; it has been there since before Christmas. It seems like a plastic representation since it has not lost any leaves or blooms, nor has it grown. This plant adds color and beauty to my room, but it does not add any new life. Too many of us are like this poinsettia, we never seem to change, to show new life; we need to check the vital signs of our spiritual life.

A sensible person, following a visit to the doctor, will take the necessary steps to remedy any disorder, or possible life-threatening danger resulting from high blood pressure, cholesterol, or heart rate. The prudent and wise patient will change their food, get proper rest, and engage in healthful exercises to improve their health.

Maybe it is time we listen to our "spiritual doctor" Jesus and improve our spiritual life.

Jesus warns his followers of their inevitable fate if they fail to listen. Our faith is not plastic or something stationary which merely looks good to those around us; it must be changing, growing, and showing signs of new life. If we have not grown closer and more like Jesus since last year, we need to have our "vital signs" checked immediately.

After a quick look at your soul, what do you see needs to be changed? What are we feeding our spirit? Hours and hours of "fats" from crude and immoral TV, regular overdoses of "sugary computer desserts," and unhealthy amounts of "fried foods" from trashy papers and magazines? Jesus tells us to substitute these with prayer, scripture, and other wholesome spiritual reading if we are to avoid a spiritual heart attack.

Have we become complacent in our faith life? Is there a need for more activity, some exercise to strengthen and bring real life to our spirit? Works of mercy, both corporal and spiritual, will go a long way in helping to get us in shape; removing excess fat, strengthening our spiritual muscles, and helping the body of Christ to develop and become rejuvenated. Walking, spiritually walking away from temptations and occasions of sin—doing push-up, that is promoting the well-being of others over self; and chin-up, raising your head when things tend to get you down in the dumps are excellent exercises to keep yourself spiritually fit and growing.

We would benefit much from periods of rest by going away to a deserted place as Jesus frequently did for a day of prayer, a retreat, or at least making time in our busy schedules to "check in" with Jesus via a quiet visit before the blessed sacrament. We are such a noise-craving generation and action-packed society that we panic when we find ourselves alone, in silence and not busy. What a tragedy! Physically it leads to a stressful breakdown, and spiritually it leads to despair.

We are not a poinsettia or a picture-perfect Catholic; we are the body of Christ and vitally alive. We are to give new life to others by dying to self, "losing our leaves," rising to life in Jesus, "blooming his reflection" and sharing his love and compassion with family, parish, and community, always "growing" in faith. Now is the time to check our vital signs.

February 15, 2004

169

The missionary had hardly begun to speak when heads started bobbing; no they were not falling asleep, they were wide awake; dodging the sporadic flight of a bat. As long as the tiny creature maneuvered its dangerous flight pattern throughout the church, everyone remained alert, but as soon as it docked high above in the rose window, the usual calm resumed. Life quickly returned to routine.

This momentary experience during the mission talk could easily represent a passing "flick" of our daily lives. Each of us follows a routine pattern of life; not too exciting and not overly boring, varied only by some unexpected or shocking turn of events. This by and large applies to our work life as well as to our spiritual life. We need a "bat" to disturb or rouse us from time to time if we are to break the routine.

If a tiny bat could excite or bother a church filled with people so quickly and easily; imagine what a person or an entire parish could do for a community if we truly lived our faith, were concerned about peace, equality, and justice for everyone and worked to achieve it in a loving manner. We are all good people; we have our weaknesses and failures, but we are good, even special to Jesus and truly unique. Our greatest difficulty is that we do not appreciate who we are; we continue to compare ourselves to others. Imagining that we are less talented or capable, we fail to expand our potential and quietly and quickly develop a routine lifestyle. Bring on the "bat."

Fear is the impetus for our reaction; uncertain of what the bat is going to do unnerves us. From time to time God allows a "bat" to disturb our routine lives. Does God's "bat" cause us to break from our routine or is the effect only temporary? God just released a "bat," our parish mission. Some people were afraid to come near the "bat," others were unable to; but what will be the reaction of us who were blessed to see and hear the message of God?

Receiving the truth, the Good News of salvation, and shown the way, let us follow the light of Christ as we live his message in this dark and broken world where danger lurks and terror abounds. It will be difficult but Christ will prevail. People in darkness are unable to see the "bat" and go undisturbed. We are to carry the light, Christ, into their lives so they will be disturbed with their routine lives and become excited by the truth.

Faithful Catholics and Christians are like "bats," their lives make people nervous. Mindful of the needs of others and responding to them with generosity and compassion in the imitation of Jesus makes many people uneasy. Their lives bother or change people.

We have been graced by the Holy Spirit this past week; we should never be the same. Our work lives may remain routine, but our faith lives cannot. We have been rejuvenated, enlightened, and have been called and commissioned by God to proclaim the Good News in word and action. Hopefully God's "bat" has not filled us with fear but has excited us to live our faith and change our homes and community into a place where Jesus is welcome.

We are not bats; we have power to overcome a little bat darting about in our midst. Jesus spiritually empowers us to overcome all evils in the world. In time of emergency we dial 911 and hope help will save us. In your spiritual emergency dial 473 (*God*) and be assured that God will save you.

February 22, 2004

It is said that you are what you eat. Is it possible that you may also be what you hear? From little on an infant hears the word "no" so frequently that one of the first and most used words of their vocabulary is "no." As a result of this negative priming many people develop a negative attitude. We see it during the terrible two years, again during the teenage transitional years and sporadically at various stages of later life. With this well-developed insubordinate nature, is it any surprise that we dare to even say "no" to God?

We, who dislike hearing no from others, do not hesitate to say no to God. The created foolishly demanding "freedom" and rebelling against the Creator challenges the plan of the all-knowing God. That is sin!

Lent, a season in our church year is comparable to spring in our calendar year. Each spring the lifeless, dry grass begins to grow with the return of the sunlight and refreshing rains only to be trampled underfoot, devoured by animals, and cut down each time it grows. Catholics are like grass. When we are deprived of the light of the son and the nourishment of the sacraments, we dry up and become lifeless. Lent is the time to welcome the son, Jesus and to restore our spiritual lives by means of the sacraments.

For the most part, we all are willing to return to Jesus during Lent by means of prayer, fasting, or discipline, and almsgiving—caring for the less fortunate. The six weeks of Lent we can endure because we know that it will soon be over; the rest of the year is problematic. During Lent we are repentant, reconciled, recharged as we allow Jesus to renew our faith. All goes well until someone tramples us underfoot, devours us, or cuts us down at work, home, or in our community.

Like the grass bursting forth each spring, we may be trampled down by those taking advantage of us at work, school, or in the community and even at times at home. The grass does not give up and quit growing when trampled because it is firmly rooted in the rich soil; neither will we abandon our Catholic faith since we are deeply rooted in Jesus.

When animals devour the grass, it simply deepens its roots and shoots up a new blade. Catholics who live the Gospel Message will be devoured by people who refuse to accept the truth. They will try to achieve their personal, selfish freedom by attacking any messenger of the truth. Deep roots are needed to stand firm and witness the truth under such destructive and persistent attacks.

Each time the grass grows up and looks beautiful, someone comes along and mows it down. Similarly when one practices their faith, performs works of mercy, and becomes involved in the parish faith life, they are likely to be cut down by someone envious or jealous of their accomplishment or unintentionally due to misinformation.

During the hot dry days of summer, the grass withers and during the cold of winter it appears to die, but because of its root system it will respond when the temperature and moisture are improved. "Grass" Catholics will experience the same effects in their spiritual lives, but Lent is the time to allow the son of God to improve the temperature of our love for others and to welcome the moisture of the Mass and sacraments to soften the hardness of our hearts.

February 29, 2004

The posters are up and the platforms are clear as the candidates vie for your vote. Who are you going to choose? I am not referring to the political campaign which is most confusing, very unclear, and at times a bit deceiving; I am referring to the only vote that really matters, Jesus or Satan.

During Lent we take time to evaluate the campaign issues along with the promises assured if you choose a particular candidate. There is no question that the issues facing our spiritual life are far more important than any put forth on the political forum. Even though political issues touch the spiritual, for the most part they are ignored or minimized by the candidates.

The campaign speech of Satan is very tempting, very inviting as he offers the easy life—sexual pleasure, material security, political power, and prosperity. His drawing card is immediate gratification. But he says nothing about the damage to your life as a result of selfishness, greed, and pride, nor does he mention that this immediate gratification is only temporary and the evil effects are disastrous.

Jesus's campaign speech is the Gospel message, which calls for a life of sacrifice, love, and forgiveness. His platform requires strong faith, perseverance, and crosses. He promises to bless and strengthen us with all the grace we need to follow. There will be exhilarating and difficult experiences, which will pass quickly but his trump card is that he guarantees a life of lasting peace, love, and happiness if we vote for him.

Satan's platform stands for pleasure, and Jesus's builds perfection. Satan makes tremendous promises to please the desires of the body; Jesus guarantees salvation. Satan pledges to provide for temporal desires, while Jesus provides for our eternal needs. The choice may be difficult because as physical entities we have an innate inclination for the tangible. Satan knows this and uses it to win over the weak. He is also quite efficient in his smear tactics as he misconstrues and misuses the promises of Jesus to cleverly undermine the truth. He will stop at nothing to get your vote.

Jesus on the other hand simply states the truth, the Gospel, shows the way, his life and offers light, the guidance of the Holy Spirit and lets us make our decision. Jesus does not force us; he gives us a free will. He does not deceive us; he blesses us with an intellect. He does not threaten us when we make a bad choice, but sends the Holy Spirit to realign our vision. Anyone who listens to the truth realizes that Jesus loves us with an unconditional love—a love so compelling that he sacrificed his life to save us.

The voting polls are now open. We must choose Satan or Jesus; there are no other options. For some, this Lent will be their last time to vote; a choice which may determine their eternity. Succinctly put, Satan offers lust, greed, power, and empty promises which lead to death, while Jesus empowers his "constituents," his faithful followers, to love, sacrifice, and humbly submit to his will, assuring them of inner peace, the grace of reconciliation, true love, and eternal life. Still many make the wrong choice!

Our political choices in the coming weeks and months will require prayerful decisions and the guidance of the Holy Spirit if we are to ascertain candidates determined to uphold our moral and ethical principles. The political campaign speeches may boggle our minds; the promises may be camouflaged, but if we choose Jesus as our spiritual representative, he will guide us in choosing our political representatives. *Vote for Jesus!*

March 7, 2004

Death has died! The hills are alive with the sound of music. One sunny warm day while taking the Eucharist to the home bound, I had to stop to listen to God "sing" through a variety of song birds. It was so uplifting and exciting to experience the "death" of winter rising to new life in the greening of the grass, the beauty of the flowers, and the songs of the birds. I was deeply moved by God's song as he restored life in nature.

God sings and speaks through the birds and nature, but he also sings and speaks through people. At the DCCW meeting, God spoke to us as together we sang "The Reconciliation Song" in which we were invited to be the generation of reconciliation and peace. God loves the praise of the song birds, but we praise him far more when we choose to serve him in unity and to build on one foundation until he comes and wars shall cease. Oh, let us share the love of Jesus without hypocrisy so others will believe!

Each bird sang a different song which resulted in a harmonious melody; so must we.

This beautiful "Reconciliation Song" asks, "Have we not one Father, one faith, one calling to be one holy race?" Each one of us sings our "life song" in different ways but "let us keep our hearts from evil, and cling to what is good; let us honor one another, and love our brotherhood." The cardinals, robins, chickadees and song sparrows live and sing together, and so can we as we become the generation of reconciliation and peace.

God sang again at the school Mass in the song "God has chosen me." God chose each of those birds to sing to me on that bright springlike day, and God has chosen each of us as that prayerful song proclaimed. Why God has chosen us is a mystery, but he has. Has God chosen me (you) to bring the Good News to the poor or to bring new sight to those searching for light; to set alight a new fire, to bring to birth a new kingdom on earth or to remove oppression and break down fear? God has chosen each of us to tell the world that his kingdom is near. God is singing if only we listen.

The hills are alive with the sound of music; the next few weeks the hills will echo the sounds of the machines, which is music to the farmers' ears as they work their fields and plant the seeds of new life. The fruit of their labors will assure life for them and people throughout the world. Certainly, that is a necessity, but what are we doing for the assurance of the greater life, eternal life? Do our lives sing melodies of praise and thanks as we become the generation of reconciliation and peace—bearers of new life?

Spring is nearing with new life. Easter is approaching, will we experience new life? Let me use a hibiscus plant as an example. For several months this plant had been growing rapidly and blooming profusely which resulted in its death. Trying to make sure it would continue to prosper, I over watered it and it drowned. We do the same in our daily lives; we find something we really like, we overindulge and consequently destroy our health and worse still, damage our spiritual lives. Lent is a time to reflect on the condition of our lives, physical and spiritual—a time to eliminate overindulgence and to live in moderation with our focus on Easter—not Easter Sunday, but that day when we will rise and enter into the glory of eternal life. Now is the time when God has chosen us to witness to others that his kingdom is here—a time to listen to his song as he invites us to be a generation of reconciliation and peace.

The hills are alive with the sound of music, the birds are singing with joy, and the fields are humming with new life singing praises to God. Death has died in nature as life returns.

Sin is destroyed and we live anew; it's time we sing; sing of God's goodness and love. Sing a Resurrection song!

March 14, 2004

Have you ever had to "eat your words"? A few weeks ago a friend of mine told me about a Lenten practice of a coworker, which seemed like a good idea. Apparently the person had difficulty with exaggerating and controlling her tongue and consequently had to eat her own words when proven wrong. Aware of this bad habit, she decided to place a dry navy bean in a jar each time she deviated from the truth so that at the end of each month she could take those hard dry beans and soak them in water and eat them hoping that eventually she could break the habit, and in the meantime they would be edible. How many beans would we have to eat if we did the same? Hopefully so few that we would be hungry, hungry for the truth, the Word of God.

Her plan to place beans in a jar certainly was better than placing rock in a jar because she could eat the beans; the rocks could only be used to build a wall separating us from those we tried to deceive, or worse still, be used to throw at one another. When the time comes to eat the "beans" or words, we can turn to the sacrament of reconciliation, and Jesus will soften our hard dry hearts; but when we refuse to repent or be reconciled, we continue to bury ourselves under the "rocks" of unrepented sins.

Sad to say the minds of some Catholics have become obese from overindulgence in the endless use of worldly words too full to digest the Word of God. Radios, TVs, CDs, DVDs, videos, computers, magazines, papers, and books have cluttered our minds, and we find little room for words of value. Words of eloquence may win us degrees, position, or fame in the world; Words of life alone will win us the crown of eternal glory.

It may be time for us to check our diet before we do irreparable damage to our spiritual life. We justify our lack of intake of the "spiritual" because of lack of time, but that is a façade because we spend hours devouring the secular propaganda via a variety of ways.

Our spiritual diet is much like our physical diet; we know what is best and necessary for sound physical health, but we choose that which is more delectable even though harmful. In like manner, we know the truth in the Bible and reading good spiritual books will enable us to maintain our spiritual health, but an inner craving for the enticing news of our sinful world take precedence over spiritual "health food."

This addiction to the worldly often leads to the need to "eat our words" as we fail to imitate Jesus in his dealings with others. The word of the world is "fight." The Word of God is love. Fight has become the battle cry of the worldly—fight against abortion, fight against drugs, fight between political parties, fight for peace, and fight for life. The very connotation of fight means to battle and destroy. God on the other hand says that only love will preserve life, overcome addictions, bring unity among people, assure peace, and foster life, for love means to care for.

Jesus came into the world, to witness, suffer, and die for our sins because he cared for us; love is stronger than death. He did not fight his enemies; he did not destroy them. He cared for them, forgave them, and loved them. When we learn to love, we will no longer need to place beans in a jar in case we have to "eat our words," for we will know the truth, speak the truth, and love the truth. The truth will set us free; it is the Word of life. Now is the time to check your diet; what you are feeding your mind will be revealed by your tongue. Will it be "rocks," beans, or the Word of truth; your eternal life depends on your choice.

March 21, 2004

It's spring! It is a season of excitement and new life, but it is also a time of danger and fear. Spring requires much courage and determination just like living our faith. When the tender shoots break through the ground, it takes a lot of courage because of the dangers lurking about. The possibility of a late freeze and the danger of some rabbit devouring it for lunch calls for much courage, but each time it suffers a setback, it perseveres and shoots forth new leaves. Sometimes the beauty of the flower is destroyed, but it continues to grow hoping the next year will be better.

With the passing of Lent and the rapid approach of Easter, hopefully we are excited and anxious to share in new life, a renewed life in Christ. The option to share in the life of Jesus is a tremendous blessing, but it requires much trust. Unlike the flowers, we hesitate because we are afraid of possible dangers. We try to live under the cover of a security blanket, a hidden faith never daring to visibly express our trust in God. We are afraid to live our faith in a visible way lest someone say or do something that will cause us to "freeze" or "devour" us; we are governed by peer pressure, more concerned about personal relationships with so called friends than with Jesus. We neglect to witness signs of our faith in order to avoid ridicule or rejection.

We hesitate to pray outside of church whether it be in restaurants or other gatherings, neglect to verbalize our needs in the prayers of the faithful during Mass, refuse to drink from the cup for fear of disease, and refrain from singing lest someone comment about our choral ability. Faith is not a security blanket under which we are to hide, but a catapult, which launches us into action. Faith without action is dead.

Many talents and gifts of God remain undeveloped, unused, and wasted simply because we are afraid that we may make a mistake or may not do as well as someone else. The ministries of Priesthood or Religious Life, Lector or Eucharistic Minister, choir or server are no longer perceived as positions of honor. Few respond to these challenges, signs of weakening faith.

Unused muscles shrivel and unused faith weakens. To develop muscles takes perseverance and entails pain but the result is a healthy body. To grow in faith, we must dare to act, to take risks to witness our trust in the power and protection of Jesus; that's the fun of spring, the surprises.

Jesus endured the trauma of his passion and death and most everyone present went away overwhelmed with grief, nearing despair, but Jesus surprised us all by his rising from the dead. Living our faith will require discipline, perseverance, and pain. We may be disappointed, confused, and face suffering, but if we persevere, we will experience surprises. Like the spring flowers, we will bring excitement and new life to others.

I cannot imagine spring without the customary beauty of flowers; nor can I remember a spring that some of them did not suffer from freezing temperatures or a hungry varmint. A faith-alive parish family evidences active Catholics praying, working, and sharing; such faith draws others to Jesus as we share in his cross. Each time we practice or witness our faith and encounter some repercussion, we, like the flower are challenged and empowered to try again expecting and hoping this time it will be better.

It's spring, a time for excitement and new life. We are not flowers, which bloom and fade; we are children of God excited about a life that will never end. Daring to live our faith, we trust God will protect us, use us, and reward us with eternal life. It's Lent and time for our faith to grow and blossom so all may share the new life of Easter.

March 28, 2004

The silent page of the calendar proclaimed that spring had arrived, but the thermometer diplomatically debated the reality of its arrival. Despite their argument, my winterized ears were thrilled to hear the tenor croaking of little frogs awakening from their listless winter nap this past week, for with their return I knew the spring of life was underway. A day or so later, I went into the woods for some quiet time and to enjoy the beauty of new life in the first spring flowers and the trees pregnant with buds about to burst forth their God-given beauty. The greening of the trees, bushes, and grass revealed the marvelous way in which God worked methodically to remove all signs of death. In the midst of this beauty, the clear water of the recent rain jumped from rock to rock making noises like a bunch of giggling girls darting through a meadow. Life was filling the woods!

What an exhilarating experience! Yet even without the perceptive eyes of an eagle, the sad results of winter were evident; trees broken by the ice and winds, dead leaves littering the path underfoot and sharp, lifeless briars attacking everyone daring to come near. The woods await the raking of leaves, the removing of dead briars, and the disposal of the fallen trees to augment its God-given beauty; and that will require time and effort.

The message of Jesus tells us that he has come to free us from sin, but the news media, the "thermometer" of worldliness, readily disputes his Word as it claims to be gaining momentum. Say what they will, we followers of Jesus know that the present "cultural death" is slowly being conquered by the life-giving presence of Jesus.

Hearing the increasing cries for justice from our young people energizes, motivates, and awakens others from their sleep of apathy as they see new hope and life arising to carry on and reinforce their efforts. The spring of social justice is a sign that the spring of life is underway; there is hope for all phases of life.

Walking through the "woods" of Lent, I see new "flowers," our Catechumens, ready to bloom as they receive life from Jesus through baptism; "bushes," our Christian Candidates, are budding as they prepare to share in the fullness of our faith; and "trees" are flowering as "prodigal" Catholics return to participation in the sacraments again. This "greening" of faith life evidences the mysterious ways Jesus touches us, destroys the effects of death, and renews his people with grace.

This spiritual renewal like the birthing of the woods is a result of the flowing waters of baptism, so necessary for life and the nurturing of the sacramental graces, especially the Eucharist. The beauty of our faith life requires the endless effort of removing all the debris, which clutters our lives so God's masterpieces can be more fully appreciated.

The woods, open to the will of God, are being renewed as spring life bursts forth in breathtaking beauty. New members, guided by the Holy Spirit, are being born through the waters of baptism, Christians are being welcomed into the fullness of our faith community, and broken branches are being grafted to Christ the vine as they experience a conversion of heart. This new life is the result of hard work.

During the final week of "walking in the woods" of Lent, let us take some quiet time and examine the condition of our spiritual life; how deep is our faith, is there life still budding, have we come closer to Jesus through our efforts to remove all the "debris" of sin, are we, like the little frogs, telling the world that "spring" is underway? Sing it, shout it, and show it! Jesus has conquered sin, risen from the dead, and new *life* abounds.

April 4, 2004

High above the church there is a hornet's nest hanging from the arch of the bell tower. It is empty. It is hard to imagine how much time and effort it took for them to fabricate their wondrous work of art, and now it is empty. It is finished! The hornets used it for only a short time and now have moved on in search of a better place to live.

Atop a barren hill stands a heavy, rugged, blood smeared cross. It is empty. We will never fully realize the suffering and pain expended in that horrendous journey. It is empty now. It is finished. The body has been carried to a place of rest.

Deep in the side of the hill is the cave where they laid the body. It is empty. Much hard labor and many days were needed to hollow the rock in preparation for a burial and now it is empty. It is finished. Jesus used it for a time and now has gone on to a greater place to live forever.

Within each of us there is our soul; the most unique work in all of God's creation. It is not an abandoned hornet's nest, nor a rotting piece of wood. It is not a cold, dark, damp empty tomb, but a glorious temple of God. Is it empty? Is it finished?

These past forty days in the "desert" of Lent, we have been praying, fasting, and caring for the needy. During our faith journey with Jesus, we have prayerfully attended to his message; hoping to become more loving, accepting the differences of others, forgiving, and asking forgiveness. We have deprived ourselves of legitimate pleasures by fasting in order to strengthen ourselves against temptation and sin. In imitation of Jesus, we sacrificed to relieve the sufferings of the poor. It is now time to exhume our soul in order to see if it is empty; if it is finished.

As a faith, people we have emptied our souls of worldly pleasure and attachments; making more room for Jesus and his spiritual blessings. Our souls are never empty; either they are cluttered with the earthly or filled with the spiritual. God's work in our souls is never finished on our earthly pilgrimage, we are always developing. It will be finished only when we enter that new and lasting life.

We celebrate that new life this Easter as we see so many signs of life abounding around us in nature and in the grace life of the church. The abandoned hornet's nest reminds us of the emptiness of life without the presence of Jesus who alone can fill what is lacking in our lives. If your life is empty, then welcome him. The rotting ugly cross keeps before us the realization that to be a follower of Jesus means to accept the cross he believes will best help us achieve our salvation. Are you overburdened and fearful? Then trust him. The cold, dark tomb now open and filled with light empowers us to face the dark moments of life confident that Jesus will open the way and be the light leading to glory.

Easter is a special time for celebrating and praising God with our Alleluias as we recall the incredible truth that Jesus loves us unconditionally and will never abandon us as the hornets abandoned their nest, and that he carried our cross while we complained, opened the tomb to free us from death of sin, and longs to dwell in the temple of our souls. He has conquered sin and death and risen from the dead; he promises the same to us.

Jesus's life on earth is finished, but his work continues on through you and me. We are a "Resurrection" people; he is alive and so are we. Life is not empty when Jesus fills it. He will never abandon us, and we must never abandon him in search of something "better." Happy Easter!

April 11, 2004

As the anesthetic was being administered in preparation for the heart transplant, the doctor said, "you will come back a new person." Total trust is required to place one's life so completely in the hands of another person; yet we hesitate to trust in God who is in complete control of our lives.

Walking through a garden of brilliantly blooming flowers on Easter Sunday afternoon, I encountered two beautiful butterflies flitting about like two kites tossing in the wind. With precise accuracy they landed on a beautiful hyacinth. Engrossed in deep conversation, completely oblivious of my presence, they were greatly concerned about a former friend, a caterpillar, who was afraid to enter the "tomb" of the cocoon and so would never be free to fly about and enjoy the beauty and blessings of the life they now experienced, but would eventually die a wasted life.

They reminisced about the times they shared basking in the sun and enjoying the tasty morsels of plants and flowers—a life of self-centeredness and destruction, thinking not aright that this was the epitome of life. Never in their wildest dreams had they imagined the incredible change that had taken place as a result of their dying to self in the cocoon; God brought them back as new and more beautiful creatures.

Elated at their transformation, they were in a quandary as to how to convince their fuzzy caterpillar friend to take the risk. The wonder of their transformation was evident; no longer were they preoccupied with satisfying their every need, but now they spent their time airily flitting from plant to plant gently and carefully so no harm resulted as they pollinated the plants empowering them to bring forth new life. Along with this valuable work, their erratic flight patterns, and exotic colors brought much beauty and gaiety to all who visited the gardens; they found this far more satisfying and fulfilling than their former self-centered lives. After much dialogue, the butterflies realized they could only encourage their friend to take the risk; the choice was his; all they could do was flying around him and witness the uplifting blessings of their new life.

All of us at times are "caterpillars" selfishly seeking to satisfy our every want; at times even hurting those around us. Focused solely on the things of this life, we frantically strive to fulfill all our needs, material, and spiritual, and it cannot be done. Foolishly trusting others, we neglect to trust in God's plan; we shun our "cocoon," that period of dying to self and sin vitally essential for new life. Consequently, like the untrusting caterpillar, we face the possibility of dying a wasted life.

Life is dull and empty as long as we remain "caterpillars" seeking only personal gratification. Excitement and meaning fill our lives when like the butterfly we are free of self and joyfully reach out to enhance the lives of others; our beauty is magnified as we reflect the love of Jesus through our works of mercy.

A malfunctioning heart results in death; surgery offers a chance to "come back a new person." Even with the new heart ultimately our physical life will end. But God offers more for he says, "I will give you a new heart and place a new spirit within you, taking from your bodies your stony hearts." When we trust God, he transforms us "caterpillars" into beautiful "butterflies" replacing our worldly hearts with spiritual ones by means of grace freeing us to enjoy the beauty and blessings of eternal life where we truly become a new person.

April 18, 2004

Have you been brainwashed? This past week I was walking in the woods, and suddenly I encountered my first snake of the year; my immediate reaction was to crush its head with the stick I was carrying. After my first impulse and panic reaction, I reasoned more clearly and decided against it; why should I destroy this creature?

The Bible story of the fall of our first parents has so influenced my life and so brainwashed my mind that I automatically condemn every snake and on impulse am inclined to kill any that cross my path, be they large or small, dangerous or harmless.

When my heart rate returned to normal, my thought process went into play, and I realized that this snake had done nothing to me; that I was intruding on his territory and that God had created both of us for a reason. I had no justification to destroy it; only prejudice and fear of the unknown warranted such a drastic solution.

It is a known fact that some snakes are dangerous, poisonous, but that does not mean that all snakes are a threat to our safety and thereby should be destroyed. It is likewise true that some people are a danger, but that gives us no right to brand or condemn entire races or nationalities.

Brainwashing results in indoctrination in the truth or justification of devious actions through rationalization. Careful indoctrination in the truth is necessary for the spiritual maturity necessary to avoid sinful rationalization.

Brainwashing is devastating, and truth is trampled when we neglect to discipline our actions, lose patience with others different from us, or become intolerant of diversity.

When, because of devious brainwashing, we are instinctively inclined to destroy someone who we mistakenly judge to be a danger or threat, we must strive to counteract our ignorance lest we brainwash others, thereby fostering misunderstanding or prejudice. Our conscious or unconscious comments and example can inadvertently but profoundly influence others. Discipline, patience, tolerance, and a search for truth are vitally important for a Christian.

The trend of modern society is self; achieve your selfish goal regardless of the effects or consequences on others. If someone hinders or appears to be a threat to our plan, treat him like we would treat a "snake" and simply destroy him. Our political campaigns, our business promotions, our community projects are all victimized by people who seek their goals by destroying others rather than by proof of personal capabilities.

Time and time again my Sandals will wander into the woods aware that the snake may still be there. I will certainly watch for it, but it will not prevent me from enjoying the quiet and beauty of the place. In like manner, when we meet people who disturb us, we must adjust and continue our faith journey without destroying them. Jesus gives us the model. Trusting in his Father's plan, He endured the "snakes," even the poisonous ones, plotting his destruction to prove that he would prevail in the end.

People are not snakes. We must not destroy others. Care must be taken to assure we are brainwashed in the truth; then we can walk safely through the "woods" of life, undaunted by possible dangers while enjoying the beauty surrounding us and trusting Jesus to protect us.

April 25, 2004

On my desk is a cheap pair of binoculars, which I received for making a donation to the National Audubon Society; they are designed to help detect birds more easily amidst the brush and enable one to see them more clearly even at distance. The intent is praiseworthy, but their power is quite limited and the result is minimal. As I analyze this situation, I realize that we often face the same difficulty in our search for Jesus.

If I hope to succeed in getting a clearer and closer view of the birds or other wildlife on my treks in the woods, I will need more powerful binoculars; failing to do so will result in frustration. Many people on their faith journey experience the same frustration.

The woods are full of creatures and color for those who take the time and use the proper instruments helpful to appreciate the beauty of God's creation. Life is full of the marvels and miracles of Jesus but all too frequently, we fail to use the proper means available to see clearly and appreciate his presence in our midst—in our lives.

To many, Jesus seems so far away and blurred; they find it hard to see him acting in their daily lives. It is time for some binoculars—spiritual binoculars. People of every age have had difficulty recognizing Jesus, even his closest friends, the Apostles, because they were using the binoculars of the world.

When our view of Jesus becomes blurry, it's time we stop and refocus our spiritual binoculars if we hope to draw close to him. Jesus never changes; he never walks away from us, but we fabricate our blueprint of him and so misconstrue the truth, or we go wandering off looking for him in the wrong places. More time in prayer is necessary getting to know Jesus. Reflective reading of the Bible, like readjusting the lenses of one's binoculars, will sharpen our view of Jesus and bring us closer together.

One can walk in the woods without binoculars seeing only what is near at hand; others may carry weak, useless binoculars and feel frustrated because they cannot clearly see things at a distance, while a few will be able to see what is close as well as focus on things far away because they have been wise enough to bring powerful binoculars.

In like manner, there are Catholics who walk their faith journey failing to bring their spiritual binoculars; hearing the beautiful message of God but unable to see Jesus, they give up their search. Many are greatly frustrated on their faith walk because their binoculars are too weak to keep them clearly focused on Jesus; thus they become attracted to the things close at hand, the world. A few, however, aided by their powerful spiritual binoculars, the Bible, truly enjoy their "walk through the woods of life." They hear the Word of God and are clearly focused on Jesus. They are able to see things at a distance—the future, which promises a new and perfect life, while enjoying the sounds and sights in the mysteries of deep faith.

We are not looking for the colors or sounds in the woods; we are searching for Jesus. Binoculars may help on our nature walks, but our spiritual binoculars, the Bible, is absolutely essential if we are to appreciate our spiritual heritage; walk faithfully with Jesus in the present, and look to the future life with assurance. Only with our powerful spiritual binoculars, the Bible, can we see clearly the past, present, and future, for it alone keeps our vision focused on Jesus and his plan of salvation for us. Get your binoculars!

May 9, 2004

While digging the soil preparing new flower beds, this past week I came across several earthworms—a welcome sight. Seeing these industrious creatures renewed my hope—working underground, loosening up the soil, they would be a help to the plants and seeds I was planting. Blessed with these underground cultivators, working silently and steadily, I felt my work would not be in vain, but new life would soon abound.

In the early centuries, the Catholic Church became an underground church because of the persecution by the pagans opposing Christianity. In order to preserve and foster new life in the church, Christians gathered and celebrated the Resurrection of Jesus in the catacombs, underground rooms, and tunnels known only to Christians. The church suffered much, but it continued to grow because of its "roots," which were developing secretly and rapidly underground. The blood of martyrs nourished the faith of those risking everything by meeting "underground" as faithful followers of Jesus.

The catacomb Christians were the "earthworms" of the early church. They dedicated their lives to teaching the Gospel Message and remembering the holy lives of the martyrs thereby keeping the soil of faith loosened and more susceptible to receive the message of salvation. The world today needs more "earthworms," Catholics, who are willing to work tirelessly and with little recognition sustaining the "roots" of our faith.

The church is being persecuted or attacked today from all sides; Catholics are hesitant and negligent in practicing their faith. The rich soil of our faith is becoming hard and dry; we need some "earthworms" to loosen it up and restore that former richness to our faith. We have experienced a shocking decrease in religious and priestly vocations, a breakdown of solid Christian marriages, a notable decline in the size of our families, the ever increasing desire to acquire material possessions, and the degradation of our moral and ethical codes; we desperately need more spiritual "earthworms" to renew our faith.

We look for "martyrs" too—those willing to suffer for their faith on a daily basis. In the early church, Catholics shed their blood to prove their love and faith in Jesus. Today only a privileged few will experience martyrdom for their faith, but more and more will be challenged to be "white" martyrs, enduring the ridicule and worldly "put down" of our secular society. With the world in a tumultuous condition, confusion has caused some to judge our faith to be too demanding, and they turn to the softer ways of the world. The church lacks "earthworms" and "martyrs"—people willing to live "tough love."

God did not make us earthworms, working underground keeping the soil loose and life giving, but he has empowered us to be dedicated Catholics believing and living personal faith solidly rooting ourselves in the teachings of Jesus and capable of helping others draw life from the richness of Catholic teaching.

During these turbulent times we are challenged to live our faith; we must not lose hope. Christians of the first centuries deeply rooted in their faith witnessed even to the point of death; we can do no less. At baptism we committed ourselves like "earthworms" to living deep personal inner faith, and like the "martyrs," we have agreed to proclaim the Gospel message, not counting the cost.

With every new generation, Jesus continues to plant new seeds of faith. May they sprout and flourish because of the richness of our faith and bear lasting fruit as a result of our witnessing!

May 16, 2004

Sitting listlessly on a country bridge one afternoon this past week enjoying the bright sun and deep blue sky and listening to the meadowlarks and the red-winged blackbirds, I watched the water of the small creek pass beneath me flowing to the river and on to its final destiny. The plan of God in nature was being carried out to perfection.

Perched on the bridge high above the water, I realized that I had no part in this beautiful schema of God's work; I was not involved. The bright sun, blue sky, singing birds, and flowing water were actively sharing to make the day beautiful while I did nothing.

How similar to our faith journey! At baptism we enter the stream of life, our faith journey; Jesus is our light; the Spirit is more glorious than the brilliant sky and the lives of the saints living among us and those gone to the new life, like the birds, resound in perfect harmony. Jesus has formulated a perfect plan for us, but at times we choose to sit on the bridge constructed by the world high above the stream of life, refusing to have any part in God's plan. Enthralled with the material world we live for the day and ignore God's spiritual plan. We neglect or refuse to get involved.

Relaxing in the sun and watching the stream below, I noticed dead leaves and sticks drifting aimlessly downstream; occasionally I spotted a fish swimming against the current searching for better things. The same is true of us once we get off the bridge; we drift aimlessly wherever the stream wishes to carry us, or we have to fight the current of the world and become involved in the stream of life to achieve salvation.

In the coming weeks, schools and colleges will laud the academic accomplishments of thousands of graduates. Our society leads us to believe that our academic achievements are all we need for happiness and tempts us to try crossing on the bridge of fame, fortune, and power while avoiding the stream of life, living our faith. Academic achievements have value only to the degree that they partnered with faith. We can no longer sit atop the bridge and watch the stream of life flow beneath us, hoping to cross on the bridge to happiness, eternal happiness; we must enter the stream of life and become involved in sharing our faith and gifts with others.

Frequently, we do not want to swim because the water is too cold—people are very unloving; the current is too swift—peer pressure and the fast pace of life; the water is too rough—the ridicule and rejection of today's society; or the water is too deep—the fear of the mysterious and future. But we must swim in the stream of life allowing Jesus to strengthen our faith, or we will drift aimlessly through life carried by the current of the world, away from Jesus until our lives end in complete waste.

The beauty in God's nature can only be appreciated by those who live deep faith; otherwise we will waste and even destroy it. Similarly, the value of our academic achievements is evidenced in the way we live our faith and become involved in bettering our community and the world, or they are wasted and become destructive.

Each of us has a part in God's overall plan of salvation. We cannot simply rest atop the bridge enjoying God's blessings; we must get involved in living deep faith and spreading the Good News. Experience proves that the happiness attained by crossing the bridge constructed by the world is unsatisfying and passing; true happiness is attained by those willing to enter the stream of life so the spiritual plan of God may be brought to perfection in eternal life. Get off the bridge; it is time to swim!

May 23, 2004

From time to time, sending a particular mail or bulk mailing requires a trip to the post office to determine the cost. Every time you wish to send a letter in the mail, there is a cost depending on the size, weight, and the country to which you wish to send it. Without the stamp of approval, it will not reach its destination. If there is no stamp or not enough postage, it will return to the sender; if the address is incomplete and there is no return address, it will go to the dead-letter bin, and if you use the stamp from the wrong country, it will not be delivered. A stamp of approval is necessary for delivery.

A stamp of approval is a requirement for salvation too. The church, realizing the strict requirements for sending a soul to heaven, begins early on to assure that everything is prepared correctly including the mailing address along with the stamp of approval. The correct address is our responsibility; Jesus has paid the postage.

It is important that we address our letter of life to God and not to the world, the flesh, or the devil. The size and weight of the letter determines the postage; God requires more postage according to the length of our lives; babies and infants require only the stamp of baptism; as we grow in size it costs more—Reconciliation, Eucharist, and Confirmation. A few need a special stamp depending on their vocation; be it matrimony or holy orders. There is also an airmail stamp that some people choose, namely, anointing of the sick.

God has determined the cost of the various types of mailings, and Jesus has paid for the postage, but living moral lives is required in order to receive his spiritual stamp of approval on our letter of life.

At times we forget that God is our creator and loving Father, and that he has written the life letter for each of us, sent it to earth to be lived, and eventually returned to him. Careless reading of his letter of life causes people to direct their lives to the wrong address, choosing the world, the flesh, or the devil instead of God. There are some who put an incomplete address on it and simply end in the dead-letter bin of wasted lives. Others, even when offered the required stamps by Jesus through his Church, neglect to use the correct postage—failing to use the necessary sacraments. Some will try to use foreign stamps—the things of this world, instead of those Jesus offers—the sacraments, and so they fail to acquire the proper stamp of approval; they will not return to the Father who placed them in this world.

Our postal service issues various types of stamps: the plain ordinary ones and the commemorative stamps, which often are more elaborate and beautiful. Either type will carry your mail if the amount is correct, but the more elaborate one adds more beauty to the envelope and brightens up the moment for the receiver. We too can live ordinary lives, which fulfill the requirements of salvation by merely covering what is necessary to save our souls; but it is more exciting and rewarding when we choose to live elaborate and grace-filled lives for they help to brighten up the lives of those around us and certainly are more beautiful and pleasing to Jesus.

The content of our letters, regardless of how important or beautiful it may be, will never be received or appreciated if mailed with an incorrect address or if we fail to place the proper stamp on the envelope. Regardless of how important and beautiful our lives appear to us or others, unless they are carefully addressed to God and have the stamp of approval of Jesus, they will never arrive at their proper destination—eternal union with God. We know the cost; we know the address; let us live so that Jesus will place his spiritual stamp of approval on our letter of life.

May 30, 2004

Shortly after I was ordained, on my day off, I came home to help my brothers to bale hay. It was a hot summer afternoon, and I was riding on the baler tying the wires as each bale came into the compression chamber. Late in the afternoon, we passed over a bumblebee nest in the ground; they were disturbed and came swarming out and stung me several times. Soon after, I had to leave and return to the parish. While driving home I became dizzy or light headed, so I pulled over and stopped; after I regained consciousness, I drove on stopping periodically until I got to the rectory where I collapsed and was rushed to the hospital. After a night of treatment I returned to normal life.

This past week, one of the school staff noticed a bee in her car. She realized that a bee loose in her car would be distracting and make her driving dangerous. Unable to chase it out she eventually killed it—a wise choice to prevent an accident and possible injury. Safety is an important factor in making the right decisions, but frequently we take risks that evidence immaturity.

A bee sting hurts momentarily and in a few cases it may have an even greater physical effect, so we are cautious, but we do not seem to have the same concern with regards to our spiritual safety.

One bee is usually manageable, but when you have a swarm, disaster lurks unless you have a capable beekeeper who can control the bees. It is time we recognize that we have a growing problem with spiritual "bees" and unless we act quickly and wisely, we will experience an increase of spiritual devastation.

We are facing a growing problem of improper and even risqué dress, which is far more dangerous than any bee in a car. My Sandals have traveled to many parts of the world from golf courses to mosques in Israel, to the national bishops' meeting in DC, to St. Peter's Church in Rome, where people are refused entrance due to improper dress. And I have seen a huge amount of people who come to Mass would not be allowed to enter. People say: It is better that they are there than not to come at all or Jesus doesn't care what they wear. Certainly Jesus welcomes everyone—the poor and the rich, but he does expect us to wear our best and to dress decently. Plunging fronts, no backs, bare midlines, and short shorts for women and T-shirts and grubby blue jeans or shorts for men are inappropriate dresses. Such attire that leads to temptation are the "bees" swarming around us. We need more parents and parishioners to act like "capable beekeepers" to control our young and not-so-young by word and example to avoid a great spiritual disaster.

We are very careful to protect them from the dangers in the physical world so their lives will be safe, peaceful, meaningful, and fulfilling; why aren't we willing to do as much for their spiritual life?

It is time we "pull over" and recover from our "dizziness" resulting from the repeated "stings" of the world before we collapse. A bee is a creature of God, beautiful in itself, and created for a good purpose, but when it finds itself in a bad situation, physical harm results. We are special creatures of God, beautiful and created for good, but when we find ourselves in a bad situation spiritual harm results.

Things of beauty, including bees, when properly used give glory to God; things of beauty, like our bodies, when carefully used prepare us to share in his glory. Bumblebees harm the body temporarily, but "spiritual bees" can destroy the spirit eternally. Wise beekeepers avoid unnecessary dangers and live healthy lives.

June 6, 2004

Why is it that weeds flourish where flowers barely manage to survive or that a seed will die where you plant and want it to grow, but will sprout up where you don't want it?

Several weeks ago, I planted a variety of seeds beside the church where I had removed the grass and weeds. Now that they have sprouted, I cannot tell if they are flowers or weeds. In a few weeks when I can determine, I will begin weeding removing all the unwanted plants to make room for the good.

My yard is green, but much of the "green" is due to a variety of weeds and not grass; there is a conglomeration of buckthorn, dandelions, creeping Charlie, wild strawberries, and other undesirable, space-taking greenery. Periodically I spend time removing these unwanted plants to make room for a better grass coverage.

We have a mind-set of the perfect yard adorned with hybrid flowers but many times the wilderness areas offer a greater variety of beautiful plants than we can in our carefully manicured yards. This is a result of God's infinite plan of life. God knows what grows best in every situation while we are still experimenting and searching. The same is often true in our spiritual life.

People are intrinsically good, but they have a hard time achieving spiritual growth. We try to imitate Jesus, but we experience such little progress, while the "weeds" of sin nearly overwhelm us; evil vices pop up in the most unexpected ways and unwanted places, while virtues root only with extreme effort. We are still foolishly experimenting with temptations and searching for ways to satisfy our spiritual needs by means of the worldly as we ignore God's plan for us.

The church is forever sowing good seed, which will produce beauty and lasting fruit but modern society has become so confused that the seeds of worldliness, materialism, and atheism are flourishing and choking out the good plants of Christianity. It is time we begin weeding. It is hard at times to discern when a plant is a weed, but as it grows and begins to crowd out the good plants, we as Catholics must rise up and unite in our efforts to remove them.

Jesus has empowered us with the seven powerful gifts of the Holy Spirit to choose the good and to avoid sin, to live our Catholic faith and to conquer evil. When we mow our yard, we cut down the grass and the weeds, but both will continue to grow and the weeds will continue to spread and choke the grass unless we remove them. It is only by their removal that we are able to make space for the grass; so too, it is only by the removal of sin in our lives that we can make more room for Jesus.

Wild flowers growing in the wilderness give praise and glory to God just as much as those which adorn our yards. All people are created to glorify God, both the sinner and the saint. To be special to God, let us love one another as he loves us. Together we form a priceless spiritual bouquet.

When we uproot weeds from our flower beds, we must take care not to uproot the flower. When we weed sin from our lives, we must be careful lest we destroy ourselves or those around us. While working to remove sin from our lives, let us call upon Jesus for help and trust in his grace; we should never give up even when it seems impossible. Special care must be taken when we unite to weed out the evils of worldliness, materialism, and atheism not to destroy the sinner along with their sin. Our challenge is to make room in our lives for Jesus who wants to forgive us and welcome us into the Garden of Paradise, eternal life.

June 13, 2004

Have you ever seen a "handicapped" wheelchair? No, I don't mean a wheelchair for the handicapped. This motorized wheelchair had some mechanical problem preventing it from going forward or backward in a straight line; it went round and round in circles. I think there are times when some Catholics function in like manner.

Our faith, in some sense, is a motorized wheelchair. We are all a bit spiritually handicapped. God created us intrinsically good, but occasionally we experience some "spiritual" handicap and need a "spiritual" wheelchair. The condition of our wheelchair is the issue of scrutiny. Those who live a deep and solid faith make progress straightway to Jesus; those with weak and uncertain faith will find themselves going in circles; their lives will be burdened with endless confusion and frustration.

Confronted, while on retreat, with this frustrating situation wherein a malfunctioning wheelchair caused a handicapped person to go in circles, it became quite clear that all of us should check our "spiritual" wheelchair, our faith. Many spiritual wheelchairs malfunction due to anxiety, for the center of "anx-i-ety" is "I."

Faith focused on "I" is truly a malfunctioning wheelchair, and it will never carry you to God; it causes us to spin dizzily around our concerns ignoring God's plan as well as the good of others. We need some major repair work on our "spiritual" wheelchair. Faith is healthy; our "wheelchair" is in topnotch condition when focused on God. Faith in God removes all anxiety and restores peace; it enables us to accept God's plan for us. It fills us with compassion for others; it puts "I" in its proper place.

We are all bothered with "spiritual" handicaps of varying kinds throughout our lives but our "spiritual" wheelchair will carry us through as long as we trust in Jesus who is ready to repair and willing to strengthen our faith if only we let him.

These past few weeks Jesus has been checking our "spiritual" wheelchair by testing our faith to see if it is alive and carrying us in a straight line to the truth. We celebrated: the death and Resurrection of Jesus where he paid for our sins and restored us to life; the glorious feast of Pentecost when Jesus sent the Spirit of Truth upon his Church filling us with the powerful gifts of the Holy Spirit; the mystery of the Trinity where he proved his "Godliness," and then last Sunday Jesus showed his love and desire to be with us as we celebrated the feast of Corpus Christi, his presence in the Eucharist. Have these mysteries sent us spinning spiritually or have they strengthened our faith in the omnipotence of our God?

If our faith enables us to believe and rejoice in these manifestations of our God, then we need not fear; our "spiritual" wheelchair will carry us straight to Jesus. But if our faith is in the world, such a handicapped "spiritual" wheelchair, like the world, goes round and round in confusion. We may be confronted with "spiritual" handicaps, but our "spiritual" wheelchair, our faith, when clearly focused on Jesus will never allow us to go in circles. Faith in Jesus guarantees us the way, the truth and the light necessary for salvation.

A handicapped "spiritual" wheelchair, that is faith in the world, weakens or destroys faith in God, but deep faith in God is a wheelchair for the spiritually handicapped which assures us of eternal life; which do we choose?

June 20, 2004

It's summer time. It's fair time where there is beauty, competition, exhibition, entertainment, food, and a fun time for all. Sad to say the ole county fair is not what it used to be, but it is still a time to share and build a community spirit. When I was young, the fair was much later in the summer, and people were able to exhibit various fruits and vegetables, which are not available this early. A county fair was more farmer-centered—that is the time when men gathered to tell their yarns about their great abilities and spectacular accomplishments and competed in horse-pulling contests and physical fetes, while women displayed the delicious bakery goods and sewing achievements and kids were just kids having fun at the fair which for many was the highlight of their summer along with a visit to grandparents or relatives for a couple of weeks. Life was much slower, and we took time to enjoy people and the simple things of life.

Today we have beauty contests, tractor pulls, horse racing, some exhibits of baked goods, and needlework but no home-grown fruits or vegetables. It is quite different from the good ole days when there was plenty of food and other attractions; the media and the ability to travel far and wide were too great a competition for the ole county fair.

In many ways this is analogous to our spiritual life where we experience beauty, competition, exhibition, entertainment, good food, and fun. Many of our parents saw the beauty of their faith embellished in mystery and marvel and competed in a quiet humble way to become a better Catholic. They were willing to live it in a visible manner. They were not afraid to live their faith even when the social and financial demands were costly. Their church was the source of their spiritual and social life, their weekly gathering was often the highlight of their week and a time for fun and entertainment, and there was no question that their spiritual food, the Eucharist was longed for and greatly appreciated.

But sad to say that is often not the case today. The endless competitions of sports, the cancerous eroding of our moral code along with the worldly perversion of our ethical guidelines have tarnished the beauty and value of the faith for many Catholics. The competition to "get ahead" in the world has overpowered our motivation for sanctity and we are afraid to witness our faith, which has become a "God and I" secret relationship. Many are so stressed and stretched trying to keep up with the fast track that they fail to see the Church community as a place for entertainment, let alone fun. Their ability to go everywhere and see everything has become too great a competitor for the "ole Catholic religion," which is no longer the highlight of their lives.

Whether we go to the county fair or not, whether we find meaning and fulfillment there really doesn't matter, but it is quite a different story with regard to our faith. God has given us this gift of unsurpassable beauty—holy men and women down through the ages have exhibited this truth and have competed against all odds to preserve and spread that faith by means of religious orders and communities. We, today, share in the fruits of their sacrifices, and it is up to us to educate and encourage faith communities to appreciate the great beauty of our faith, to live it more faithfully, to nourish ourselves on the Eucharist to greatest "food," which brings joy to our lives now and forever.

It's summer time. It's fair time. It's faith time. It's "heir" time. Summer time is a time for immediate gratification; faith time is a time for eternal sanctification. Enjoy the fair, but live as an "heir."

June 27, 2004

A fly is a tiny insect whose value is questionable, except maybe as food for frogs. This was my thinking until God sent me a "prayer fly." Some people have prayer shawls to aid with their praying; others have prayer mats. Many find using a rosary helpful to keep their prayer focused on God and using a prayer book is quite common, but only a rare few are blessed with a prayer fly.

One day recently while I was attempting to pray in church, I kept dozing off, but each time, God sent a fly to awaken me. With the help of this fly, I was able to refocus on God and finish my prayers. What instrument do you find helpful in your prayer life or how has God chosen to keep your attention?

Several nights back I shared a "lock-in" with about two dozen "frogs," the youth from All Saints Parish and surrounding communities. They are dubbed "frogs" because they have resolved to Fully Rely On God. God used this group of potential leaders as an instrument to help my prayer life. These "frogs" participated in a variety of activities, which required trust, sharing, perseverance, sacrifice, community building, character development, and celebrating their faith life in a meaningful and personal way.

As the night progressed, it became clear that these young people and the youth leaders were there by choice and that they enjoyed witnessing to each other their faith as they formed a community of caring and sharing people. Some activities were easy, some more difficult, but all called for a deep trust in God and their peers. The spiritual message cleverly conveyed by means of balls and balloons accentuated the importance of character building, emphasized the importance of Jesus in our lives, and stressed that even though we were not the best or most capable at what we were doing did not mean we were any less a person or less loved by Jesus.

These young people, Fully Relying On God, were a great inspiration. All of us need to trust more the mysterious but marvelous plan of God, as these young people did, and we too will find excitement, satisfaction, and great joy in our unusual and unique faith journeys. The "lock-in" was a great success; everyone did not excel in every event and even failed in some, still they knew they would be accepted, welcomed, and loved by their peers regardless of the outcome. Those who fully rely on God likewise realize they will be accepted, welcomed, and loved by Jesus, not for their successes, but for their enthusiasm and perseverance, simply doing their best and leaving the rest up to God. These young people experienced a variety of things that helped their prayer life and some surprising ways that got and kept their attention.

A few days later, while enjoying the Fourth of July fireworks, I suddenly became aware that they too were a means by which God caught my attention and led me to prayer. The smoke, noise, and crying children had little effect on the crowd, but a TV flashback reminded me of a drastic contrast, for the families in Palestine and Iraq were suffering from deadly "fire works" and the destruction and cries were stained with blood. So God can use anything, even the most mundane, to get our attention and lead us into prayer as I quietly thanked God for our freedom and safety.

Flies, *frogs*, balls, balloons, and fireworks are certainly not the usual things most people use to focus on God, but they are among the many unique things he uses to get our attention; once that happens, the rest is up to us to use them as a springboard to prayer. I am confident that each of us has a routine way of praying and special objects to help us focus, but we need to be alert to the out-of-the-ordinary ways that Jesus offers to give newness to our lifeless, wordy recitation of prayers.

We need to be open to the movement of the Spirit who longs to renovate our prayer life and our faith life so we can experience meaning, joy, and fulfillment by Fully Relying On God's plan, even to allowing him to send a "prayer fly."

July 11, 2004

One afternoon I took some time off to spend a few hours outdoors pulling weeds on a huge vegetable farm. It was a wonderful outing—the sun was bright, the ground was soft because of the recent lovely rain, and the solitude was a blessing. The huge variety of vegetables, differing in size and shape, were flourishing, but so were the weeds who were rapidly invading their territory; the plants welcomed the removal of unwanted weeds.

As I worked among the different plants pulling weeds, enjoying the rustling of leaves, and the songs of the birds, I noticed some dissatisfaction and criticism between the groups. The turnips were discontented because they had to work underground while the corn was able to rise above everything to enjoy the view, the cool breeze, and be seen by all who passed; the corn was disgruntled because it always had to stand at attention and could never rest on the cool earth like the peas. The green beans were jealous of the yellow ones; the peppers were proud because they came in more colors than the egg plant. The peas and beans were grumbling because the cantaloupe vines were taking up too much space and infringing on their area. The tomatoes were unhappy because the corn was blocking the sun and no one liked being next to the onions because of their odor. The pumpkins were unhappy because the rest of the plants were jealous of them simply because they would become the biggest and would soon ostentatiously show off their bright color long after the rest had died. No one seemed to pay any attention to the few strawberry plants that were crying concerned about their future for most of them had been eaten by the deer. Truly, their concern of the future had some justifying foundation while all the other dissatisfaction simply steamed from pride and selfishness, for God had protected and blessed every other plant abundantly.

The complaints of the prosperous plants stifled the weak cries of the strawberries, but screams of the weeds overpowered them both. Their cries were for justice and life, for God had created them and placed them in the garden too, yet they were being harshly cut down based on man's perception and definition of weed.

Can you imagine such folly among your garden plants? It may seem a bit far-fetched, but how reasonable is it for people to act in a similar manner—foolishly ignoring God's many blessings and envying talents and accomplishments of others? We dislike those who are different from us or jealous of those who are more talented or academically endowed, criticize those recognized for greater accomplishments, tear down those who are more popular, and those who are more handsome or beautiful than us. We ignore the cries of those who have less, those who are weak or suffering, and disregard those who do things quietly and secretly and destroy people out of prejudice as weeds in a garden. Our misperception weeds them out of our lives, depriving ourselves of blessings and graces, which God wishes to bestow upon us through acceptance of those who are different.

Every vegetable offers something different, valuable, and delicious, which it alone can produce, whether it is the tall corn high in the sky, or a vegetable near the ground or underground, small as a pea or large as a pumpkin, colorful as a pepper or drab as a turnip. Each person God places in our lives is likewise different, valuable, and unique and no one can accomplish what God created them to do. To believe otherwise is pure folly. Vegetables don't fight; so why do we?

July 18, 2004

Following a wedding, a funeral, a week-long vacation bible school in Carrollton, and the one day in White Hall, a dozen Masses, and the regular busyness of the week, my Sandals meandered off the beaten path through pastures, fields, and woods, seeking peace and quiet, into a three-dimensional experience of the presence of God.

Strolling down a cowpath I heard a choir of tiny frogs worshiping harmoniously in a little pond—frogs never to be seen by anyone and heard by only a few privileged like me who happened to pass their way. Their part in the creative design of God might seem very insignificant when joined to the total schema of the universe, but they add much to his glory, day after day, totally in conformity with his plan.

Moving on I was inundated in a sea of green corn, so thick and tall that I quickly sank out of sight, unable to be seen by anyone, and I was able to see but a few feet in front of me. I had disappeared into oblivion lost among thousands of giant stalks of corn, too many to be counted, and unconcerned about my intrusion, consumed totally in glorifying God.

Eventually, I emerged from the sea of corn and entered a woods where I beheld the huge skeleton of a tree, which had given many years to nesting birds, scampering squirrels, and offering shade to any animal, which rested beneath its vast branches raised in praise of God, both in life and in death. Its dedicated service had ended through death and no one cares. The hillside was covered with trees, so who would miss this one? Unknown, unseen, and unappreciated by most everyone around it, that particular tree played a significant part in God's overall plan.

Walking through the flowering weeds, beautiful yellow butterflies showed the bright colors as they darted from plant to plant, and dragonflies, with the brilliant, translucent blue wings, hovered "angel-like" atop the swaying water plants besides the lazy stream, systematically going about their business of carrying out God's work. Numberless and nameless, unaffirmed and unrecognized, they never hesitated to fulfill their God-given function in nature.

As my head rose above the hilltop like a periscope rising from the water, I saw two deer dining in a field of flourishing beans. I thought of the words of the psalmist: "Like a deer pining for running water so my soul longs for you O Lord." Pausing in this three-dimensional shadow box depicting the creation of God, I was suddenly aware of the awesome unprecedented presence of God in our lives.

In our moments of despondency, we may compare ourselves to: the frogs, never heard of; or the corn, one among so many; or the dead tree, never appreciated; or the butterflies and dragon flies, unrecognized for our work; or the deer wandering lonely through a flourishing world, but we, unlike any of them, share our value from within—the unprecedented presence of God.

An intelligent person can see the "work of God" in other creatures, but only a wise person can see Jesus's presence in all people. Realizing how unique we are, we become consumed with Jesus and are no longer anxious or disturbed when we are lost among the many, receive little recognition, and are not known far and wide; depression, dislike, discouragement, and disappointment find no place in our lives. Our value in no way results from what others see or say but flows from this unprecedented presence of God.

July 25, 2004

High above the church roof on the side of the bell tower hangs the remains of a hornet's nest. Last year it was a busy place with the hornets shaping the cone and inhabiting it all summer. For whatever reason it was abandoned, the remarkable work of those industrious creatures is gradually deteriorating and disintegrating; it is no longer a thing of marvel but an ugly sign of abandonment.

The hornet's nest weathered the elements of nature, even the most severe storms, as long as the hornets inhabited it because they kept it in good condition; but once they neglected to rehabilitate it, devastation resulted. Things weaken and gradually are destroyed from lack of use—both material and spiritual.

In the sacristy is a costly piece of equipment for playing tapes over the sound system, but due to years of nonuse, it is no longer any good; the components have dried up and rotted. A valuable instrument, abandoned and neglected, has been destroyed. How like our faith life! A most valuable gift of God, but when we neglect to practice it or keep it in good condition, it too dwindles and dies.

Great care is taken by parents at the outset of their spiritual journey to assure our children of spiritual protection; we baptize them, prepare them for reconciliation and the Eucharist, and generally encourage them to receive confirmation. Spiritual formation and faith life are fostered in the early years of their lives and all goes well; then gradually by neglecting to require them to actively live their faith and allowing them to abandon the important things that keep their faith growing, like the hornet's nest, their faith becomes lax, and their lives begin to fall apart. Forming a solid and safe "grace" wall in the early years is vital, but it must be kept strong with the passing of time by means of the sacraments, Mass, and prayers and the personal witness of parents and adults; otherwise the storms of the world, the flesh, and the devil will weaken and destroy their faith.

Catholics are doubly blessed with powerful sacraments to build a solid faith structure and a Catholic school to help us maintain a close check on and rebuild our faith when it becomes weakened or damaged. But they are of no avail if we neglect to use them.

The hornets may build a nest, which is a masterful work of nature, and the tape player may reproduce marvelous sounds but neither measure up to the unique value of our faith.

Material things can be replaced with new and maybe even better things, but that is not the case with the spiritual; nothing can replace our faith life and personal relation with Jesus.

Our faith flourishes only if we live it actively all our life. It may be tested by trials and crosses of life, but it will never be destroyed if we strengthen it by frequent use of the sacraments, daily communing with Jesus in prayer, and uniting our sacrifices with Jesus at the weekend liturgies.

Unlike the hornet's nest, which cannot be repaired following the ravages of the elements, or the tape deck, which may be irreparable even with costly parts, our faith life can be renewed and restored to an even better condition than before we neglected or let it fall into disuse. That renewal depends on our personal choice.

As we appreciate the works of nature and the accomplishments of man, let us not overlook the miracle of God; our soul made in his image and likeness will live forever if we never abandon our faith. Where your treasure is, there is your heart. Where your heart is, there is your faith. Where your faith is, there is your God! Does your faith, your God assure you of salvation?

August 1, 2004

When the families passed through the gate of Christian Family Camp, they entered the time machine and marvelous and mysterious things began to happen as the pace and lifestyle underwent a remarkable transformation; the rush and pressures of the world disappeared along with modern media as family living took their place. For nearly thirty years I have enjoyed this remarkable experience, which always reminds me of the scripture passages describing the early Christian community who held all things in common and shared what they owned with others.

Prior to the invasion of the woods by these humans, the animals have been anxiously preparing—the adults frantically trying to convince their little ones of the dangers that will confront them in the coming week. The snakes aware that their very life is at stake simply slither into the depths of the woods out of sight; the mice parents caution their children not to become careless, but to go about only at night; the parents of the lizards are distressed because the little children love to capture any type of creeping critter for the great critter race held at the Olympics; and the mosquitoes fear the poison gas and crushing hands, which only human animals seem to possess; while the younger animals are filled with excitement at the approach of Christian Family Camp week.

Life at Christian Family Camp does not offer the luxuries we feel we need at home, such as TVs, radios, computers, video games, microwaves, electric stoves, soft beds, air-conditioning, but it offers much more; it's time to get to know and share with your spouse and family and other families. People quietly reading, groups discussing, individuals praying, and families celebrating the liturgies replace the noise of the media. Silence is broken not by blaring boom boxes but by joyful noises; the chatter of excited children and the laughter of adults enjoying time together. This wilderness silence allows the songs of birds to announce the new day and the noise of the night creatures to lull one asleep; the sounds of nature are a pleasant blessing of God unknown to most humans.

Wholesome meals, time in the pool, hiking and biking kept us physically in shape; the beautiful Masses and prayer services renewed our spirit; enjoying the beauty of God's natural cathedral was an awesome experience; and bonding with our family and forming a community with other families provided a well-rounded week for spiritual renewal.

Time did not stop nor did we go back in time, but we did grow in faith becoming a more loving and spirit-filled person more appreciative of our family and God's love.

Everyone loves the week at camp including the animals—the mice have their big summer get-together at this time because there is always plenty of food in and around the cabins when all these families bring loads of goodies and sweets. The squirrels play hide-and-seek with the dogs who chase them around and around the trees; lizards have races with the younger children who try to capture them for the critter race but usually outrun them and hide between the stones, and the mosquitoes vie for the "gold medal" for drawing the most blood from the campers.

Christian Family Camp gives one a taste of how the early Christians shared all things; the families became one large family watching each other's children, working together to plan entertaining skits and prayerful liturgies, answering the needs of young and old alike. Life for the humans was an experience of living love, compassionate caring, and in-depth bonding of family members. Life for the animals was quite different, but the experience resulted in a clearer understanding of the mystery, majesty, and marvels of God in nature and in families.

August 8, 2004

Two little mice, high in the abandoned choir loft, watched the people rushing into church for Sunday Mass. Finally Holly turned to Polly and said, "I thought we were going to Mass." "We are," said Polly. "From the looks of their dress, it appears they're on their way to the beach or a party," retorted Holly. "I know," said Polly, "there was a time when people had special "dress up" clothes, which they only wore for Mass—clean, neat, and decent, but now they have braided the spiritual, secular, and sports activities so tightly together that one can hardly distinguish the spiritual from the secular."

After listening to the singing and the prayer participation, Holly whispered to Polly and said, "They get more excited and enthused at their sports events, hoping to win a trophy, than they do in worshiping their God, who offers them a crown of glory." "It's sad, but what's even worse is that far too many do not even come at all," replied Polly.

When the "Our Father" was finished, Holly could no longer contain herself and she blurted out, "Do they mean what they say? Why don't they say what they mean? They say "hallowed by thy name," then weakly offer praise to their God who loves them unconditionally; they say "thy will be done" and yet we know how unhappy and angry they get when he does what is best for them; they rebel and do as they please. How can they say "lead us not into temptation" when they dress in ways that are so revealing and tempting? It appears they don't mean what they say." "I know," said Polly. It looks like they need to be open to the Holy Spirit and set their priorities: God, faith, family, friends, work, and relaxation in order to live moral faith lives."

Leaving the church quite perturbed, they entered the shed where they lived. There they noticed the article in a discarded *Catholic Times* about the eleven-year-old girl who was urging retailers to sell more modest clothing. Polly admired the little girl and said she hoped the retailers would offer more decent clothes for people.

"That would be a start," said Holly, but why do Catholics and other Christians continue to exploit the precious gift of their body in tempting ways—ways which will likely lead them into sin as well as those around them?" "How sad that today's society condones advertising via exposing the human body," said Polly, "but we cannot give up. Everyone can do a little to promote decent dress. We must keep in mind the lesson Ella learned from her campaign, namely, that you should speak up, because you might be heard."

Resting on a sack of feed, Holly and Polly continued to discuss the problem of decent dress; quite baffled that parents are furious at all the sex abuse but seemingly unconcerned about how they and their children dress. Shaking her head, Molly said, "Don't they realize those plunging necklines, the spaghetti strap dresses, the bear backs, the bare mid-drifts, the short shorts, or the miniskirts certainly are temptations, as well as the low hip-huggers, the pants with holes, the sideless

T-shirts, or sweatshirts, and the skimpy shorts the men don are likewise an invitation or temptation?"

"All we can hope for," said Polly, "is that more eleven-year-old girls, like Ella, will stand up and protest; that parents will realize as purchasers, they set the styles, and that decency will prevail if they want it." "And until they do, it will be difficult to find modest clothing," Holly said as she entered her house behind the box of rags to fix dinner, and Polly made her way up the wall to her house in the loft.

August 15, 2004

One morning Sammy rushed into the kitchen, waving the local newspaper, where his wife Tammy was preparing breakfast. Excitedly Sammy showed Tammy the huge ad announcing the formation of a new airline: "WANTED! Pilots; no flying experience necessary; all that is required is that you want to fly. We are willing to agree to any of your personal desires. You will be accepted regardless of age, mental capacity, or physical ability. Hopefully you will find joy in your new adventure and endure the problems that go with it. If interested call 463-728-3968 immediately."

Tammy could not believe what she read and said: "Sammy, that is ridiculous! Who would be so foolish as to fly with you since you have never flown before? Furthermore, you would be risking too much in hopes of promised benefits; it's not worth destroying your life and the lives of others."

Sammy, a bit frustrated, protested, "We need the money, and besides I can learn as I fly a few times." "That's bizarre, Sammy, you have to be prepared before undertaking such a responsibility; the gamble is far too dangerous."

"I appreciate your good intentions, Sammy, and I realize we need the money and benefits, and I know you are willing to try anything to make me happy, but no one would ever fly with untrained pilots. That airline is doomed to be a failure." "You can't be a doctor, teacher, or lawyer, or hold any position of responsibility without careful preparation, or someone will be hurt seriously. The same is true of marriage."

"You remember how our friend complained that the church made too many demands and married outside the church. How sad that people will undergo years of strenuous education and training, difficult examines, and pay tremendous fees in preparation for a worldly career, but complain about marriage preparations! Proper preparation for marriage is far more important than any other vocation. It is permanent until death and the pathway to salvation for couples."

"You are right, Tammy, it would be sinful for me to endanger my life and that of others for personal gratification, just as it is sinful for a couple to marry without careful and prayerful preparation. There is too much at risk—their lives and that of their children, their happiness, their faith, and their very salvation. Can't they realize the church is helping them prepare for what lies ahead, encouraging them to appreciate and live their faith and understand the need of Jesus as the center and end of their marriage?"

"It is only sensible that I find a job for which I am prepared because good intentions are not enough, the risk to others is too great, and I would not be happy working under such tremendous stress," muttered Sammy as he left the room to continue his hunt for work.

Peeking around the door, Tammy said, "While you are searching, remember to pray that engaged couples may recognize the value of the church's guidelines or requirements for good intentions. Just wanting to get married and be happy is not enough, the risk is far too great and someone will get hurt when the marriage fails. Marriage is life giving and life sustaining, both spiritually and physically, so we must prepare carefully for this life-long commitment. People would not fly with a pilot who was not prepared, so why do they expect they will be able to live a life-long commitment of love and fidelity without preparing? Marriage makes greater demands of a person than what is required for flying, but the blessings and reward are also greater."

August 22, 2004

Sitting in the duck-blind and giving my sandals a rest after tramping through the "Wetlands," which were now dry and hard due to the lack of rain, I heard two crawdads discussing their plight, concern for themselves and the young ones.

They were greatly concerned about their future; whether they should stay or move. Most of the year their area is a delightful place to live—it is cool, muddy, and covered with water, and there is ample food along with their other needs. Gradually as the summer progresses and the rains are few and far between the Wetland begins to dry up. At first the ground is soft with occasional pools of water and a small supply of food, but when it hardens and cracks, life becomes very difficult. When that happens, they have to travel for water and food and become vulnerable to birds and other hungry predators.

As more crawdads gathered, some were suggesting that they migrate to a place where the problem could be eliminated. Some had heard of a pond not too far away and others were telling about the new levy being constructed to contain the water all through the hot summer. Still a number were hesitant to leave their homes speculating that maybe next year would not be as hot and dry and favored staying where they had always been. The heated discussion continued as I made my way across the parched and barren swamp knowing that some would stay and die while others would choose to better themselves.

Maybe we should all go and sit in the duck blind to do some serious thinking as we examine the future of our lives like the crawdads. What is the condition of our soul; is it dry and hard lacking in life and in danger from spiritual predators? God created each of us and brought us to the pool of water, baptism; he nourishes us on the bread of life, the Eucharist and protects us from spiritual dangers by means of reconciliation. If our spiritual life is drying up and our hearts are hard, then we need to welcome the refreshing waters of the Spirit. Deprived of the graces of the Spirit, we, like the crawdads, will need to search for food and turn to the things of the world for our nourishment. Neglecting to use the sacraments will endanger our spiritual lives as we expose ourselves to the spiritual predators of the world, the flesh, and the devil, which are continually waiting to devour the weak and those far from the safety of God and their faith.

Realizing that our spiritual lives are drying up or that we are becoming hard of heart, it is time for us to consider looking for a better place to live; maybe we need to change jobs or choose better friends, maybe we need to spend more time in prayer, or return to a more frequent use of the sacraments, or participate more fully in the Mass as we offer our daily sacrifices with Jesus. Each person must discern what is needed to avoid aridity of soul and to secure their spiritual safety.

Like the crawdads, some will stay where they are amidst all the danger within their hearts and around them, thinking not aright if they can survive or things will change; to die from lack of spiritual food or be destroyed by spiritual predators; others will talk about making a change later, but only a few, fully understanding the destructive result if they don't, will choose to return to the safety and life-giving sacraments essential for faith.

Let us find a spiritual "duck blind," before our soul becomes too dry and hard to change, or we are destroyed by some spiritual "predator," so Jesus can renew and refresh us by the life-giving sacraments which keep us safe and lead to eternal life.

August 29, 2004

Looking across the playground I saw a huge pile of strong cardboard boxes stacked against the garbage dumpster, sentenced to death. What had they done or failed to do that should warrant such a sad ending? I am quite certain that if they could talk, they would bemoan the injustice of this atrocity; after all they had accomplished their mission faithfully and carefully and protected the contents transported within them. Had they failed they could accept their fate, but they hadn't. So what was the reason for this decision? Could it be that we are too affluent and carelessly wasteful and no longer perceive the need to save? We have become a "throw away" generation both in the material and the spiritual realms of life.

We spend more on garbage disposal today than our grandparents spent on the basic necessities of life; only a few things in our lives grow old, aside from ourselves, because we are in endless change; lasting commitments are passé.

I realize that we cannot keep every box, but we can become more aware of our waste. Our waste of material things is a sad reality, but it is more disheartening to note how we waste human lives, talents, and friendships. Abortion is our response to inconvenience, avoidance is our view of the handicapped, and institutionalizing is our answer for aging. These are not boxes with little value; these are people with eternal value.

As Catholics, followers of Jesus, how can we "use" people? When their talent or their friendship benefits us, we cling to them, but once they are no longer useful to us, we discard them like empty boxes. To "use" people is to abuse them; to develop a friendship is a priceless treasure.

Living in a mobile society we tend to belittle the value of friends. Time was when we treasured friends and developed life-long relationships. Today we move about so much that many friends simply fade into oblivion; we find a new "box" to answer our passing need and dispose of the old one. Only a few believe that friends are forever.

Waste is disturbing. Losing a friend is disheartening but reckless abandon of God's spiritual gifts is destructive. Our planet is suffering ecologically because of our careless waste. Our society, even our basic family, is deteriorating from the increasing lack of respect for life itself. This should not surprise us since our culture no longer has a need or place for God; we have thrown him out of our schools, our courts, and our homes. Our faith has been trampled by the secular world. We have forgotten that God alone gives and sustains our material and spiritual needs. Spoiled and pampered by a material world, we neglect the blessings of the Mass and sacraments and avoid any personal encounter with Jesus because that requires making room in our lives for others.

There may be another cardboard box or plastic bag to replenish the one we waste, but we are poor stewards of God's treasures; the number of people we abuse through broken friendships may not run out in our life time, but we are not good stewards of God's talents; but to abandon God in our foolish efforts to satisfy or glorify our ego with the material is a clear sign that we are inept stewards of his precious gift of time.

When we see an empty box sentenced to a wasteful end, stop and see if you know an empty wasted life longing for a welcome and build a friendship. Check to see if yours is an empty lifeless soul who has abandoned God; if so, recognize your need for him, make room for him and don't waste your life; you are not a disposable box.

September 5, 2004

Have you ever collected cicadas' shells, empty locust's shells, and lined them up like a covered wagon train heading west? As autumn rushes upon us, you can find them hanging on various trees or bushes; one of the mysterious ways that God reminds of the empty tomb and that life continues on in a new way. These Cicadas are a great example of our life cycle.

The Cicada or Locust, spends years underground only to come forth and live a short time beginning in late spring through summer into early fall. After years of being underground, where it endures the bitter cold of winter and the extreme heat of summer, it hatches and climbs up the tree where it breaks loose from its plastic thin shell and flies freely, unless it happens to be the unfortunate one, which is eaten by a squirrel. It hardly seems worth all the years of suffering and waiting to live for such a brief period and then leave only a dry empty skin as a reminder.

But what is the comparison with our lives? We live most of our lives underground or unknown, as babies, little children, and youth until we finally mature and begin to affect those around us for a few short years, and then we, like the locust die, appearing to leave only an "empty shell" or memory behind.

During that short time of "freedom" and life on earth, the Cicada also lays hundreds of eggs, which continues the cycle of life, first underground for years and then rising to new life and freedom.

So too, we, as Christian Catholics spend many years quietly preparing ourselves to witness our faith, undergoing the "cold" rejection of the world or the "heat" of persecution living a few years on this earth; then we die and rise to a new and lasting life. Those few years often go unnoticed, and we feel we have done so little that we fear we leave only an empty "shell" or soon-to-be-forgotten memories behind, but in truth, our lives can result in a spiritual legacy if we plant the seeds of faith in family, friends, and acquaintances.

Most everyone is familiar with the noise the cicada makes when breaking out of its shell to achieve its freedom and carry out its mission. Catholics too must be heard as they speak out against the moral evils of the world while breaking away from sin and carrying on the mission of Jesus.

We are tired of the endless monotonous noise of the cicada and wish they would quiet down or go away; so too, we will bother the world if we live Catholic lives, and they will try to quiet us or drive us away ignoring the message of Jesus's mission.

One may feel the cicada that was eaten immediately by the squirrel was a waste, but it is all part of the ecological cycle. In like manner, we are inclined to judge the death of a child or young person is a waste, but in God's plan every situation is an opportunity for us to grow spiritually and no life is a waste regardless of how brief.

Likewise when we are facing death as a result of aging and think our lives have been useless, and that we have done nothing noteworthy and are leaving behind empty "shells" like the cicada, we need to recall that as faithful followers of Jesus, we leave a spiritual legacy. When we cast aside the chains of sin and plant the seeds of faith, we free ourselves to enter a new and lasting life; our life is changed, not ended.

People may be unaware of the good work we have done; some may judge our lives as an empty "shell," but Jesus knows the extent and the benefits of our efforts to live and pass on our faith. The shell of the locust may be empty but new life has resulted; the tomb may be empty, but Jesus has risen; our body may be lifeless, but our spirit lives forever.

September 12, 2004

A broken brick lay atop a heap of crushed bricks. Looking at the wall above, which was slowly deteriorating and dropping loose bricks as the months passed, it recalled its structural beauty of former years. Companion bricks buried in the rubble were venting their anger because no concern was shown to them after all the many years of service. Other bricks, dangling high above, were alarmed aware of their immanent fate. There was nothing they could do by themselves; they were built on each other, the upper bricks were supported by the lower and now they were gone, a carelessness leading to destruction. They needed the help of a caring person to reinforce their foundation if the former beauty was to be restored; otherwise eventually the entire building would collapse.

Note the parallel between the breakdown of the building and God's plan of salvation.

God created a beautiful world with a marvelous plan of sharing his love, but our first parents failed to care for his work of creation. Over the years, due to misuse and lack of concern on the part of his people, it was destroyed as "brick by brick," generation after generation, fell from the truth and broke away from his loving embrace.

God in his loving compassion, aware of the inevitable destruction, readily sent his son to repair the damage. Having repaired his temple, renewed the life of his mystical body and established his church, he left it in our hands to maintain.

Just as the brick cannot do anything to repair the falling wall by itself, but needs the cooperation of the other bricks and a good bricklayer to repair the collapsing wall, so too, we need the help of each other and a good "bricklayer" Jesus, to assure a responsible maintenance of his church.

Over the years people have removed spiritual "bricks" until the wall is dangerously precarious. For many have pulled the "brick" of matrimony from the wall; they are simply living together or in a civil contract. Modernists have weakened the wall even more by tossing the "brick" of reconciliation into the pile of spiritual rubble, no longer acknowledging sin in their lives. Many underestimate the value or need of the "brick" of baptism; physical life and tangible things have buried this important "brick" beneath the rubble of secularism. That cornerstone "brick" of confirmation no longer is a prime option for others greatly weakening the structure. That essential "brick" of the Eucharist has fallen, as increasing numbers question the real presence of Jesus. Family life is being choked by abortion, its limited size, divorce, and that innate desire for "more" so that the special "brick" of holy orders is seldom encouraged or chosen, greatly limiting the church's ability to minister to the multitudes. The "brick" of anointing has been broken because of misunderstanding the value and purpose of the sacrament. Our "anti-God" culture is destroying the very foundation of the church; the walls are toppling as more and more people remove spiritual "bricks" from the beautiful temple.

Apparently the owner sees little value in the collapsing building and has lost all hope of restoring its original beauty. That is not the case with God; he has not given up, but offers us his spiritual "bricks," the sacraments, firmly united by our deep faith to rebuild his church under the guidance of the Holy Spirit. The time has come; the need is urgent, for us to rekindle our faith and with the help of the master "bricklayer," Jesus, carefully use all his "bricks" to restore his church to its original beauty. Let the work begin!

September 19, 2004

As we begin this lovely season of fall and the crops and leaves please our eyes with a variation of yellow, tan, orange, and red, you must also be on the lookout for a moving "yellow," a small bee known as the yellow jacket or their sting will also turn you red.

One glorious sunny afternoon, recently, my Sandals headed for the country to enjoy some quiet time amidst the beauties of nature. I entered the woods where I began chopping weeds and apparently disturbed a bees' underground nest whereupon I was met by some unwelcoming yellow jackets, which immediately stung me a couple of times, so I left the woods and went for a walk in the "bottoms" where I came upon a flock of wild turkeys, while aloft in the cloudless azure sky was a beautiful hawk drifting on the gentle breeze—a pastoral scene of peace beyond word expression.

That same afternoon, I rode the corn picker as it devoured the tall stately stalks of corn saving the grain and shredding the stalks abundantly rewarding the farmer with grain, the fruit of long and hard labor, while building up the soil with the refuse left behind.

So many experiences in our physical life parallel those of our spiritual life. Frequently on our faith journey we have plans and suddenly we encounter danger—"yellow jackets," we are tempted and will get stung unless we move away to a safer place. If we are willing to do so, we will experience peace and beauty just as I did in the "bottoms"; there we will share in that intimate friendship of Jesus, which far surpasses explanation.

Overcoming temptations and developing a meaningful personal relationship with Jesus is comparable to farming. It takes time. You begin by resisting a temptation over and over as your spiritual life grows. It's not easy. Just as some crops suffer from draught or bugs or weeds, so we can expect difficult times as we "put on Christ." The farmer sometimes needs to spray his crops to kill the bugs and weeds or to irrigate to counteract the shortage of rain; so too, we need to use the sacraments and Mass to eliminate sin and restore fullness of life to our souls. If we fail to do so the "yellow jackets" temptations will lead us to sin and death just as multiple stings of the yellow jacket can kill us.

Changing our plans and moving on to something new, living according to Jesus's will, brings not only safety, but also that inner sense of peace and tranquility, which comes only when we are sharing an intimate friendship with Jesus. Accepting the will of Jesus does not free us from hardships, but we can be sure he will furnish us with the "spray" to kill all "bugs and weeds" in our spiritual growth so we can produce abundant and lasting fruit.

Our lives much like the corn stalks will be shredded and cut down by the passing of time, but we will produce bountiful and lasting fruit as God, our Father, welcomes us and shares his happiness, peace, love, and lasting life, and those who have known us will be better people because of the legacy of faith we leave behind.

Life from birth until death, like the year with its changing seasons, offers beauty and newness and excitement interspersed with "yellow jackets"; those mysterious hardships by which God channels grace into our lives motivating necessary changes to improve our spiritual life. Watch out for the sting of Yellow jackets, but avoid spiritual "yellow jackets" as God leads to conversion and lasting life.

September 26, 2004

A good teacher is one who captivates the student through innovative means. Jesus, the teacher, did that when some of us spent several days picking grapes as a fund raiser to better our school and parish. While enjoying the beauty of the outdoors, I saw a similarity between the grapes and us as Jesus silently expounded his truths.

We harvested different kinds of grapes—white, slightly red, and blue. Some grapes were large and tender, some were smaller and firm, and some were still green and sour; yet each one had value and something unique to offer. Next to these were several rows of purple Concord grapes, which were most appealing to the eye and extremely sweet to the taste, but we were not to pick them.

God is not concerned with color; he loves all his people and the variety of nationalities adds much to the beauty and charm of his creation just as the color of the grape enables the owner of the vineyard to produce a variety of wines.

The ripe grapes are chosen for their juice along with some more green ones to vary the taste, and then by means of a carefully guided process of fermentation, the wine master develops dry or sweet wines, red or white wines to please the palate of his customers.

In like manner, Jesus uses each of us to fill a specific need in our community and church in this present day; we are gifted differently and are selected to use our times, talents, and treasures according to his plan, the salvation of all.

The Concord grapes were exceptionally sweet and very enticing because they were the largest, most colorful, very delicious, and seedless; being such they are a great temptation, just as so many worldly pleasures, and can lead to problems. They cannot be used for making the other types of wine; they are very exclusive. Jesus teaches us to be moderate in our use of all things and offers us the wisdom to make right choices, thus avoiding all exclusivity.

By showing us that all grapes are good and each is destined for a specific purpose, Jesus reveals a greater lesson; no person should be labeled or rejected—not even the least among us or those the society so readily brands as "the marginalized." History, both secular and religious, has given us evidence to prove that oftentimes the least, the weakest, or the sinner has become the light and the strong leader to save a nation or the church.

We cannot and will not all become Concord grapes—the greatest, most famous, or most loved; but God does not want that; his mysterious majesty is more evident when he accomplishes his transformations through the not-so-perfect. It is difficult for the first to be last, the greatest to serve the least, or the exalted to be humble, but that is the message Jesus is trying to teach us through the harvesting of the different grapes—every person, just as every grape, has a special mission.

There is need for differences in the grapes in order to produce the many types of wine; so too God has populated his world, as only a genius could, with endless possibilities. No two are alike; everyone is unique and essential in his plan of salvation. No one is a "Concord" and no one is useless; all are to be blended together in ways, which produce the end result for which God created us—endless peace, love, and life.

Not all are married, not all are religious; some live the single vocation. All three walks of life are blessed by Jesus, and each has something to add to the flavor of the "wine," the faith life of the church.

October 3, 2004

When my Sandals ended a busy day this past Sunday, I was surprised to see an opossum running across the driveway in front of my garage; it was totally out of its natural habitat; it reminded me of so many people I had seen that afternoon.

An opossum is known for its attempts to play dead when danger approaches; it is a great pretender; it often gets hurt or killed as a result of its false pretense. A large number of our youth and several adults took part in the "Life Chain" defending the right-to-life of the unborn. We stood along the highway in silence for an hour, silently praying, holding signs condemning abortion and defending life while hundreds of cars passed by.

A few honked, waved, or smiled and gave us the thumbs-up sign; fewer still gave us some sign of ridicule; but most people imitated the opossum. They, like the opossum, just pretended we were not there; they seemed to be out of the natural habitat, ignoring that human life from the moment of conception is endowed with a soul made in the image and likeness of God, which is to live forever; they were taking life for granted and were not caring about the abortion situation. Their almost total ignoring of us and our cause is a result of apathy; their indifference will eventually lead to suffering in their own lives or those of others when someone close gets hurt, and a child is killed through an abortion. The time has come to stop pretending that abortion is not wrong; our Supreme Court judges have immorally legalized abortion; our politicians have condoned it; the weak and misguided Christians have come to personally accept it.

Danger lurks when an opossum pretends to be dead; when danger presents itself, its pretending may well end in death. We can get judges, organizations, or political parties to endorse the pro-choice theory and pretend that abortion is not killing or destroying life, but playing opossum before God will not work; it will end in death.

The beauty of the day was to share with our youth this hands-on experience, a moment of grace, and a teaching of the truth about all life. Hopefully they will remember this as they face their choices in years to come and realize the impact their presence had on those who drove by; they may be the cause of some mother choosing to give life to her child.

Later that evening at a youth meeting, I took part in a discussion on responsibility: to minister to others, to be accountable for your commitments, to protect all life, and to encourage others to live their faith and actively participate in Mass.

It was a great inspiration to see so many youth aware and alert to the stumbling blocks of society; they were not playing "opossum," but were challenging each other to practice what they claimed to believe.

Our young people are good in spite of all the muck and mire they face via the media and the corruption of today's society. We as parents and leaders need to be more positive and affirmative of their efforts, more open to mature and sensitive discussion of the problems they encounter, mentoring their lives with loving discipline, and careful to witness by our lives what we know to be God's will.

Our young people pattern their lives after us. If we play "opossum" to God's plan and teaching, pretending they do not exist or do not apply to us, then we can expect our young people to do the same. Drinking poison while pretending it is medicine still has a deadly result. Living undisciplined, immoral lives pretending it is the will of God leads to the same end. The opossum must get back to the woods for safety; we must go back to God's plan if we are to live healthy lives now and eternal ones to come.

October 10, 2004

With the upcoming elections, everyone is wondering who will be filling the place of our president along with many other political positions. It's that time when people seem to become experts expounding their knowledge, limited, biased, and even at times wrong, in selecting who should fill the place of our president, senators, and representatives. It is also time we check and see if we are in the "right" place in our relationship with Jesus.

A few weeks ago while taking the Eucharist home, a lady gave me this poem entitled "My Place."

"Master, where shall I work today?"

And my love flowed warm and free!

Then he pointed me out a little spot and said, "Tend that for me."

I quickly answered, "O, no, not there.

Why, no one would ever see—no matter how well my work was done.

Not that little place for me?" And the words he spoke were not stern;

He answered me tenderly: "Oh my child, search that heart of thine, art thou working for them or me?

Nazareth was a little place and so was Galilee!"

—Alice Barbour Bennett

We may not be running for office, but God has a special place for each of us to serve him. Do we trust Jesus enough to ask: "Master, where do you want me to work today?" or are we afraid of the risk and so tell him where we are going to work. Are we ready and willing to serve him in the most inconspicuous place and without any fanfare or recognition even when it requires suffering, or are we doing things to be noticed and applauded?

During our diocesan "Called by Name" program, it would be well for parents and single men and women to ask God, "Where do you want me or my children to serve?" Many people are unhappy with what they are doing but afraid to make a change; this may be God nudging you to reevaluate your lifestyle to see if Jesus may be leading you to a different and more fulfilling place and manner of ministering.

Happiness and peace of mind is far more important than enduring the misery of some demoralizing job, which is financially attractive but physically, emotionally, and spiritually depressing or destructive.

Each of us is to discern how we can best fit into Jesus's plan, whether it is in some insignificant or in a major role. We can't all be the wheels of the plane on which everything must move; or the jet motor, which propels everything. We may be the door through which others may find their way to Jesus or something as simple as a cup of water, which refreshes the thirsty passenger. We might even be a small key, which begins the process of empowering the plane to move, fly, and carry happy passengers safely to their destination. In a similar manner, we are to do our part to help Jesus transform his people; he is the one who moves everyone, propels them to act, and carries them to their Goal. He is the Savior, not us.

Every part of the plane, big or small, must be in its proper place and functioning harmoniously or disaster will result. Each of us must be in the place Jesus has prepared for us and working cooperatively with all parts of his mystical body, the important and insignificant people in our lives, so his plan of salvation can be accomplished.

Are we in the right place? We question whether our politicians are working for us or for themselves; now is the time to discern the place where we can best serve God, working for his glory and not ours. No one can choose our place for us; Jesus will reveal it if we ask and trust him. There we will find happiness in our relationship with him; there we will best perform our role in God's plan which leads to salvation.

October 17, 2004

I just enjoyed a week of dancing with God—a week where I went back in time, a place where there was no time, and a revelation that at the present time I am to be an emissary commissioned to teach others how to dance with God.

How quickly we forget the past, and how sad that so many never experience the past so as to appreciate the present! We are so incredibly blessed, yet so discontented with life. I participated in a Mass that was conducted in a language, which I could not understand, in a church where there was no air-conditioning, where ladies wore dresses and men wore shirts and ties much like the past when I was young. The seats were uncomfortable, the temperature was hot, and there were no missalettes, but the community sang verbosely. There was a sense of the divine presence, an awareness of the mystery and mystique of God shown in their humble worship and the willingness to sacrifice. They may be back in time, but they had time for God.

Aside from this prayerful experience of sacrifice for God, I shared days with throngs of people who lived without time. They were simply enjoying the moment, not caring what time it was—sleeping late, eating when they chose, doing whatever they were inclined to do, no real beginning or end of the day since time vanished into endlessness, having satisfaction and personal gratification, and were seemingly devoid of responsibility. One could almost sense the void resulting from the absence of the divine and sacrifice was a no-no amidst the surplus.

There appeared to be no time, not even for God.

Reflecting on these two situations I became aware that Jesus's commission was not to lead his people back in time nor to allow them to rest in self seeking, but to unite the past with the present. How could this be done? How could I convince people of their need to sacrifice, to appreciate their many blessings, and to use the present time in a way to foster a permanent and intimate union with him?

The answer was revealed to me through an e-mail message; I was to teach them how to dance with God. People today desperately need spiritual guidance. When you consider the word *guidance*, you will notice "dance" at the end of the word. Doing God's will is like dancing. When two people try to lead, nothing feels right. The movement doesn't flow with the music, and everything is quite uncomfortable and jerky. When one person realizes that and lets the other lead, both bodies begin to flow with the music. One guides and the other follows and the two become one, moving beautifully. The dance requires surrender, willingness, and attentiveness from one person and gentle guidance and skill from the other.

Look at the word "guidance." "G" stands for God, followed by "u" and "i" and "dance." God, you, and I dance. If we are willing to trust that God will guide us and let him lead us, then the "dance," life, will flow smoothly filled with blessings and mercies according to his plan. Then we will appreciate the past sacrifices of those going before us, be more willing to make sacrifices ourselves while carefully using the present to develop an intimate union with Jesus. Life is time—time to "dance" with God.

We cannot live in the past; we can learn from the past, have we? We cannot selfishly relish our surplus; we must share it, do we? God has invited us to dance with him and he wants to lead. I have enjoyed a life-long "dance" with God; he now commissions me to invite you to join in the "dance."

October 24, 2004

Halloween is here; that is "All Hallows Eve" or the night before the holy day of All Saints. We enjoy and chuckle at the little children dressed up in their funny or ugly costumes pretending to be someone other than they are in real life; most of us would be too self-conscious to wear such ridiculous costumes; we don't want people laughing at us.

We are not disturbed when people, young and old, do it at Halloween and in fun, but we become quite concerned when it is ongoing; yet many adults and children "dress up" and wear a "mask" trying to fool others pretending that things are going quite differently than they really are. They hide behind their masks because they do not want people to know the truth and their attempts bring them more pain and ridicule than any ridiculous Halloween costume.

People burdened with addictions, confronted with marriage tribulations, faced with serious health problems, suffering from extreme loneliness, tempted to despair and even suicide, refuse to reach out for help and persist in wearing "the costume" pretending all goes well, and they are happy. The pretense of Halloween can be fun; the false pretense in our mode of living can be depressing and even fatal.

Our Halloween "wee" ones are innocently pretending to be a pretty princess, superman, an ugly witch, or a monster and everyone knows they are acting and time will reveal who they are and reality will resume; but that is not true of those afraid to reveal they are hurt and seek help. They have worn their masks so long that they have almost forgotten who they really are, the beloved children of God, those he wishes to heal and forgive if only they will remove their "mask" and ask for his help directly or from others.

Vanity is the popular mask for many and deception completes their costume. People are unwilling to let anyone know they have problems, so they try to deceive themselves and hopefully those around them. For a time it may be possible, but forever it is impossible; what begins as a little problem, capable of being resolved, is covered over out of vanity until it burst forth like a volcano erupting, no longer capable of being disguised and their deception ends in shame and ridicule.

We are all weak; we are sinners. Those who pretend to be otherwise are merely wearing a mask, which either they must remove and seek a resolution if they are to find peace and wholeness of life, or eventually someone or something else will in time crack their mask and expose the truth to their shame.

The children are not afraid to remove their Halloween costumes because then they see the good person they are; so too we should not be afraid to remove those "costumes," which burden us because when we do, we see how good we are, even with our imperfections, capable of resolving those problems with the grace of God. Then we shall experience a freedom and wholeness and surprisingly too, the acceptance and welcome of others who were willing to remove their "mask," revealing that we are all sinners, forgiven and dearly loved by Jesus.

Halloween is followed by the feast of All Saints; that is *our feast day* if we are willing to remove our false "masks," admit we are redeemed sinners, and persevere in following Jesus while imitating the holy lives of family and friends who lived deep faith, shared his love, and walked humbly with their God.

The witches, goblins, ghosts, and masks must go with the passing of this pagan feast; so too must the masks of vanity, deception, and pretense be put aside with the celebration of the Catholic feast of All Saints. A Happy Halloween prepares us to be joyful saints.

October 31, 2004

I slapped myself; I must be dreaming. Wake up, it can't be real! God is too wonderful! This past weekend the young people of All Saints, in conjunction with the celebration of priests' appreciation, gave me a book entitled *God Loves You Very Much!*—a book of extreme depth, yet one even a small child could read and enjoy: a book of "VeggieTales."

VeggieTale books and videos use vegetables to teach moral values in a manner in which young and old can comprehend and be entertained at the same time. They make it quite clear that God loves us all equally regardless of our differences. God does not love the powerful leader any more than he does the little, totally dependent baby in our arms, just as he loves the tiny French pea as much as the huge pumpkin. He loves the hot pepper equally with the sweet watermelon; so too, he welcomes the sinner along with the saint. He loves everybody and has a plan and purpose for everything and everyone; and that's the part of the VeggieTales and of life that is extremely difficult to understand. Only by faith can we come to appreciate it.

Even before I read their book, I was aware of his love for me, all his people, and creatures. In the first book of the Bible, the book of Genesis, we see God calling the universe, vegetation, animals, and humans into being. Then he called Adam and Eve to enter the life-giving union of marriage. At The Last Supper, we see Jesus calling his Apostles to become priests empowered to represent the sacrifice of the cross at each Liturgy, to forgive sins in his place and proclaim the Good News of salvation.

We have reason to appreciate our priests, but we have equal reason to appreciate couples living out their marriage commitment, cocreating life in union with God. Likewise, the religious men and women who answer God's call to a life of prayer and sacrifice deserve our appreciation along with single parents and those called to the single life; he loves us all equally and unconditionally. Therein lays the depth of Jesus's love.

I know I am not sleeping, and I know the reality of God's love; I have experienced it in powerful and miraculous ways. I thank God for the countless ways he shares his love, with me as a priest, directly and indirectly, sacramentally, and through the lives of the people he places in my life. It is because of this love, and my desire to share this love with others that I suffer much. I cannot adequately express the pleasure and satisfaction of being a priest, nor am I sufficiently able to thank you for your prayers, love, and support; I only wish I could convince others of the peace, happiness, and love, which flows from the priestly life and leads to a deep sense of fulfillment.

Certainly there are sacrifices demanded; but that is true of every vocation. Every vocation is challenging, filled with blessings and a personal "call" to eternal life if we share our journey with Jesus. As you appreciate the priesthood, appreciate your "call" and live your life in a way that helps you and others to prepare for the final "call" to that greater and lasting life to come. Every vocation results from God's call; every vegetable is a consequence of God's plan; both show his unconditional, personal, unique love, and exhort us to love him above all and others as ourselves.

When difficulties or failures tempt you to doubt his love or cause you to withhold your love for others, then read VeggieTales and the Bible; both make it quite clear that "God Loves You Very Much!"

November 7, 2004

Have you ever seen or met an angel? I have! In a magazine *Angels on Earth* there are faith-filled testimonies of people who have encountered angels—messengers from God sent to guide, protect, or help them in some mysterious way. God uses animals, noises, nature, people, and other unusual things as angels, bringing his message of life and love.

This past Sunday night, God sent three angels to speak to our young people; one spoke of the love of God, clearly revealed in the Bible and his desire for their safety and happiness, another spoke of the dangers resulting from failing to live the Gospel message and making bad self-centered choices, and the third assured them that God never gives up on us sinners, but continues to love us and forgive our sinful mistakes.

Truly, they were angels from God; they carried the truth of his message clearly, and honestly; their humble sharing of life experiences revealed the emotional, social, physical pain and suffering, and spiritual guilt resulting from misusing the great gift of "free will."

Angels sent by God from the "Arms of Love" facility, they embraced our young people with arms of love, just as Jesus welcomed, taught, and blessed the little children, and offered them hope and sent them forth with a positive attitude about their personal value and urged them to make the proper choices.

The following morning as I drove to Greenfield, I saw a huge, beautiful "angel" cloud; powerful and aglow with the sun rays reflecting through and around it—a sign from God that the message of the "three angels" would have a powerful effect on our youth who in turn will transform our parish.

We fail to recognize or see angels among us because we are looking for some angelic being with wings and wearing dazzling white garments much like the glorious "angel" cloud; we need to focus our spiritual eyes on the happenings in our life if we are to experience the mystery and magnitude of God's angels working in our daily lives.

On the shelves in my office, there are three or more figurines of angels, and there is a picture of my guardian angel above my bed; they are productions of an artist's imagery. They are like a picture of a loved one in our billfold or hanging on the wall, living or dead. Not unlike the picture of our loved ones, they can do nothing for us, but that does not mean that angels and our loved ones do not exist or that they are not concerned about our well-being, praying for us, guiding, and protecting, and interceding on our behalf with God.

Throughout the Bible in both the Old and New Testament, we find many references to angels and their important missions, as well as Jesus stating that everyone has an angel guarding them. We are no less important in his plan of salvation than any of those to whom angels were sent in the Bible; we, weak in faith or fearing to be different, tend to resolve the mystery by merely relegating it to chance.

Overshadowed by a materialistic world, a world devoid of God, one solidly set on power, wealth, and genius, we try to explain everything, even the miraculous, by way of some human or physical solution. In a Christian world, acknowledging God is basic; we need God, his guidance, and protection; and angelic messengers are a reasonable way for him to communicate with us to live a faith-filled life.

Angels do exist, and they are acting in our daily lives; those mysterious and marvelous happenings and unexpected people answering our needs and leading us to God are not mere chance or an accident; investigating them with the eyes of faith quite likely will reveal the work of some angel.

November 14, 2004

Let all the earth cry out with joy to the Lord. The earth, all of nature, and all creatures cry out with joy as it praises the Lord; what about us, those special creatures made in the image and likeness of our God? When something goes wrong in our lives like sickness, failure, disappointment, or death, do we praise the wisdom of God? Nothing can happen in our lives without God directly planning it or indirectly permitting it; if that is so, how can we not thank God, for God knows what is best and does only what is best; he loves us with an unconditional and infinite love.

Only people of deep faith experience that peace, which comes from the awareness of the presence of Jesus in all situations of life and consequently are capable of thanking him for their "cross" of suffering and "crown" of glory; he is the strength and joy of life.

In order for Thanksgiving to be truly meaningful, we need to thank God for giving so bountifully to us, and then give to others of what we have and who we are to express our thanks in a practical way, for . . .

Holy, happy, spiritually healthy people help to make our lives more
　Attractive and enjoyable as they support us and willingly bear
　　Part of our daily burdens and consciously
　　　Plan surprises and ingenious ways to relieve
　　　　You of those things which dampen your spirit.

Treasure those wonderful people our loving God
　Has placed in your lives this day
　　And realize the graces he pours upon you through them
　　　Never asking or expecting any return but love.
　　　　Knowing what is best for our every need, God
　　　　　Spontaneously and with unbounded measure
　　　　　　Gives us everything we could possibly need;
　　　　　　　Indeed even more than we desire or deserve that we may be
　　　　　　　　Victorious in overcoming temptations and sins of the world, flesh, and devil;
　　　　　　　　Inspiring us to recognize and accept him as our dearest friend and Savior so
　　　　　　　Nothing in the world, not even the entire world can take the place of our
　　　　　　God who longs to share unending life, love, and peace with each of us.

Today, in a spirit of awe and filled with gratitude, my Sandals approach Christ our King—no golden throne, but a rugged cross, no crown adorned with precious stones, but one of blood-stained thorns. His attendants are criminals; his followers are not the powerful royalty but the lowly sinners. He beckons us to dine with him, not at some lacy dining table but at the altar of sacrifice, to be servants with him to the least among us. We are heirs of the kingdom; our inheritance is not gold and jewels or passing pleasures but love poured out for the remission of our sins and life renewed and eternal.

Jesus, our humble and loving King, promises new life to those who appreciate their blessings and share their time, talents, and treasures to benefit others. Thanksgiving is a time to express our gratitude to family, friends, and parishioners for the wonderful ways they have shared their lives with us—a time to cry out with joy to the Lord, a time to acknowledge Christ as our King, a time to give thanks to the Lord for his love is everlasting!

November 21, 2004

Once upon a time, a few days before Thanksgiving, a loving father took his little son with him to the barn to feed the animals. While his father fed the livestock, the little boy sank into a pile of sweet-smelling hay. In the distance, he could hear the animal thanking God for the warm barn and his father who was feeding them; in front of him he saw Tom, the turkey strutting and showing off his prowess to do the turkey dance while fanning his colorful tail feathers. In another area of the barn, he was shocked at the pandemonium between the pumpkins, apples, sweet potatoes, and corn: the pumpkin bragging because it was the biggest, the apples were claiming to be the prettiest, the sweet potatoes were sure they were the sweetest, while the corn argued it was the most necessary. The rivalry was so great that he hardly heard the cranberries crying in the corner; they were so small; no one noticed or wanted them.

When the father had finished feeding the animals he returned to carry his son back to the house. On the way back the little boy told his father about the events in the barn; he felt sorry for the unwanted cranberries.

Once inside the house, the father sat the boy down and told him that they would have a special place on Thanksgiving. The proud turkey would lose his beautiful feathers and be baked; the big pumpkin would be cut to pieces and baked into a pie; the shining apples would be peeled of their color and baked as a pie; the sweet potatoes would be mashed and baked, and the corn would be ground up, made into bread, and baked; only the tiny red cranberries would be placed on the table, unchanged, to add color and beauty to the meal. All those who were so proud would be humbled while the humble cranberries would be exalted. This made the little boy very happy.

Then he told him another story about a loving father who sent his son to a far off country, but when he arrived, the king did not welcome him for he was proud and tried to impress others; the governor did not welcome him because he was big and looked down on people; the scribes and Pharisees did not welcome him because they tried to shine before others in their knowledge of the law; the self-righteous would not accept him because they felt better than him; and the high priests rejected him because they felt they were more necessary than he was. He wept because he was unwanted, but at the first Thanksgiving, at the Eucharistic table, they were humbled when his father used him to bring beauty and life by exalting him on a cross. This made him very happy.

We just celebrated Thanksgiving; are we humble and truly thankful or are we proud like the turkey trying to impress others instead of humbly thanking God? Has power or position turned us into pumpkins? Have our accomplishments or degrees turned us into shining apples? Do we live sweet potato lives pretending to be faithful followers of Jesus, when in reality we are not, or do our lives witness that we, like the corn, think we are the most necessary person around?

We need more "cranberries," humble people who see Jesus in everyone. If not, it will lead to our being "cut up" and "baked" and humbled; only the humble will share in the true Thanksgiving; the eternal Eucharistic banquet. God has blessed all of us abundantly; He has gifted us with gifts we are to share with others. If we are truly thankful we cannot be turkeys, pumpkins, apples, sweet potatoes, or corn but humble cranberries aware of who we are, who made us, and why he made us.

All of us were stuffed this Thanksgiving Day. Was it food only, or were we filled with the love and presence of Jesus appreciating everyone and everything around us?

November 28, 2004

Today my Sandals stand before the Western Wall in Jerusalem, a remaining portion of the Temple of Solomon. Jews come here to pray longing for the reunification of the Jewish nation and the rebuilding of the temple. I stand before the Western Wall, now known as the Wailing Wall, along with our peace-mission group, praying for peace, which grants freedom to the Palestinian people (along with the Israeli people), whose ancestors were the shepherds at the manger that first Christmas welcoming Jesus, the Prince of Peace. Christians and Jews gather at this wall, praying with a sense of hope for a better future—a hope that is weakening with every passing year.

There is another wall—a wall of protection being constructed by the Jewish leaders—a wall of despair, which is not only unjustly confiscating Palestinian land, but fomenting bitterness, impeding true peace, and justice for the country.

Earlier this morning, we celebrated Mass with the Latin Patriarch who thanked us for our efforts to achieve a just and lasting peace by keeping the plight of the Palestinian people before the world. This afternoon, we will meet with a Palestinian peacemaker, Zoughbi Zoughbi, followed by a meeting with Yheskal Landau, a Jewish peacemaker; I pray that God will guide both men and help us all to honestly discuss the problems and prayerfully seek methods to restore a just and lasting peace between the Palestinians and the Jews.

Jesus, born in this land, preached his message of peace; the holy, humble people heard it and sacrificed for it, while those in power ignored it and destroyed him. The same thing is happening today; the Israeli and Palestinian people long for peace while their leaders, out of greed and prejudice are destroying those favoring peace.

Each day when moving from area to area, we see signs of hope along with much destruction and are reminded of the walk of Jesus offering peace, hope, and life, only to receive hate, rejection, and death. Following Jesus from Galilee to Jerusalem, we see how he suffered emotionally, spiritually, and physically, but he loved us unto the end; he conquered sin and death and offers peace, love, and life. He exhorts us to do the same.

It is difficult to visit this land of Jesus's birth with an open mind; the suffering and overt injustice to the Palestinians is so overwhelming that one must strive continually to control becoming prejudiced against all Jews.

Soon we will be celebrating the birth of Jesus. He came precisely because of prejudice, pride, greed, and selfishness, which has been dividing his kingdom since the creation of the world and is still prevalent, not only in Israel, but all throughout the world. We cannot continue to build walls of defense and walls of separation; we need to build bridges. We cannot stand alone; we are morally challenged to unite God's people.

Tomorrow we will visit a Bedouin camp where poor shepherds are living in tents among their sheep on the hillsides beneath the skies just as they did on the night the angel announced the glad tidings of Jesus's birth. Our visit will be good news for they see in our humble efforts some attempt to tell the world of their horrendous atrocities. Following our visit with them, we will visit the Basilica of the Nativity where "Peace" was born; Advent is a season of longing for the Prince of Peace—a time to discern how we plan to live and carry peace into the world by humble service and generous sharing.

Hopefully our "peace" trip will show our solidarity with the suffering Palestinians. May their lives inspire and motivate us to strive for peace between nations, in our parishes, and in our own lives regardless of the cost! Prejudice precipitates punishment; peace promises paradise.

December 5, 2004

Exhausted, exasperated, and overwhelmed we rush through this prayerful, grace-filled holy season of Advent. Frantically we shop, bake, decorate, mail Christmas cards, and labor to prepare everything for Christmas—everything that is, but ourselves. Struggling under the burdens of societal views of Christmas, material peer pressure has become the grinch that stole Christ from Christmas and seeks to substitute glitter and gold in place of true love.

I recently read a short story, "The Selfish Giant," by Oscar Wilde. The giant had a beautiful garden filled with blossoming trees, blooming flowers, and singing birds where the children loved to play. One day the giant chased them away and told them it was his garden and only his. After that the flowers and trees would not bloom and the birds no longer sang; it was too cold and ice, snow, and winter prevailed, and the giant was sad; he missed the beauty of the garden and the singing birds.

One day when the children crawled through a hole in the wall, the sun returned, the flowers and trees bloomed, and the birds sang. The giant was happy to see his beautiful garden alive and to hear the birds sing. When he went to see why, he saw the children climbing in the trees, which were all blooming except for one. There was small boy, who was most beautiful and loving stood crying because he could not get up the tree. The giant went out and lovingly held the boy, lifted him up the tree, and the tree blossomed. Every day all the children returned but not the little boy, and the giant missed him. Years later, when he returned, the aging giant slowly made his way through the garden to meet him and was shocked to see his bruised and broken body, the nail marks in his hands and feet and was surprised to hear him say, "you raised me up and gave life to the tree when I was unable to climb, and now I come to raise you up to a new, beautiful, and lasting life because you welcomed the children into your garden and shared your love and life with them."

Like the giant, we get caught up in the possession we have and life is cold and empty; when we open our hearts and let people into our lives, we find warmth and fulfillment.

Often we try to give material things to show our love—many and costly, but we withhold ourselves, and they fail to satisfy for love.

The garden was cold and dead when the selfish giant refused to share; the flowers bloomed, the trees blossomed, the birds sang, and the garden came alive when he was willing to share with the children. But only when he reached down and lovingly raised up the little boy and placed him in the tree did the entire garden truly come alive. Nothing can take the place of our love—our willingness to give ourselves to others.

All the material gifts we give are only letting people into our garden, not our lives; it is essential that we reach out to them, raise them up, and share ourselves with them if we or they are to experience true love—that love which brings Christ to our lives.

Advent is a time of waiting and longing for the coming of Jesus, our Savior. He offers his friendship and his love. Advent is a time to make room for Jesus in our lives—not a stress-filled month of crowding people into our "garden" with the end result that no one, not even Jesus is welcomed to share our love, our real selves, at Christmas.

Christmas is the day when Christ was born into our world, in each of us. The wise men brought gold, frankincense, and myrrh; let us give Christ, in others, gifts of peace, compassion, forgiveness, acceptance, and ourselves in true love. Learn from the "Selfish Giant," guard against the Christmas Grinch of today! Give yourselves this Christmas!

December 12, 2004

My Sandals have just left one of the largest "prisons" in the world, Palestine. It is absolutely impossible for me to convey the full impact of that experience. My heart goes out to those lovely people who are being taunted, tortured, and killed unjustly by means of a carefully organized process to break their spirit emotionally and strangle them financially by means of closures, check points, and physical threats—all under the blanket of security.

How sad it was to see the latest "security" effort of the Israeli government—a twenty-eight-foot high cement wall enclosing the Palestinians thus preventing them from getting to their farmlands, to their place of work, to their family in other cities, or to any of the holy shrines! Thousands of homes have been destroyed, olive trees have been killed, and land for farming or the grazing of sheep by the Bedouins has been confiscated for security—a disguise for a methodical land possession.

I have taken part in five peace missions to Palestine, shared my views in many discussions with Israeli and Palestinian leaders, listened to their disheartening stories of families, prayed with and for them, and supported and encouraged them to trust and hope, yet each time I receive far more than I am able to give.

Besides visiting the sacred places, the Holy Stones, which were uplifting to our faith, we also visited the "living stones," the people, who in a sense did far more for my faith life. We are so used to conveniences and immediate services that this mission became a time for a humbling reality check. When we have to wait in line for service, we are disturbed; but they may be forced to wait in line for hours or days. We complain about our garbage removal service, our utilities, our highways; they are deprived of such services or receive them on a most minimal basis. They persevere under daily hardships and live in hope; a most humbling exposure to us who have everything we need and to excess.

As we approach to the birthday of Jesus, the Prince of Peace, it is hard to understand how people can be so selfish and inhumane. I am not condemning the Jews but questioning the morality of those in leadership roles, both in Israel and the United States and throughout the world when they misuse their power and destroy life; the Jews and Arab Palestinians are good people desiring peace.

As faithful followers of Jesus, we have a grave responsibility to work and pray for peace. The angels' message that first Christmas night was "peace on earth to men of good will," if we are not experiencing peace, could it be that we are not a people of "good will"? We can no longer ignore the cries of the poor; nor allow our leaders to satisfy their greed or the selfish desires of a few at the price of blood and enslavement; we must be of "good will" toward all, or we will be forced to build more walls of "security" which only foster fear, division, and destruction. Security comes only when people live in love.

As our peace mission bus made its way throughout Israel, we reflected prayerfully on the incredible truth that the son of God became man; he was born into a world longing for peace, lived amidst the poor, suffered because of corrupt leaders, died because of sin, ours included, and rose from the dead in fulfillment of his promise. This loving Jesus brought hope!

This mystery is still evolving today in the Holy Land, in our lives and throughout the world. We, like the Palestinians, are called to be a people of hope trusting in the plan of God. Peace will come when world leaders selflessly are willing to free the Palestinians from their prison; when we are willing to free those we imprison by power, greed, prejudice, or other injustices. We believe Jesus's message that love, peace, and freedom are the fruits of justice. We are and will always be a people of hope, freeing the imprisoned!

December 19, 2004

This past week Santa came to our school with his reindeer and sleigh. Some were able to believe what they saw; others did not. The little children saw and believed, but the "worldly wise" who had lost their sense of imagination and mystery were caught in the world of reality. How frequently this happens when confronted with the mysteries of faith!

While traveling throughout Israel and Palestine, it became my responsibility to "tailgate," making sure that everyone remained together, was not accosted by anyone, and did not wander off and get lost. At every stop, one or more would always lag behind; consequently, I was not able to hear the explanation at many of the sites and so hard to imagine what transacted at the spot some two thousand years ago.

It required much childlike faith and a lively imagination to appreciate the mystery, which was hidden from view. The little children, filled with love and excitement saw Santa, for Santa or Christmas is the personification of love. Little children and "childlike" adults have eyes that see into the mystery and go beyond reality. We must do the same with the mysteries of faith.

We just celebrated the feast commemorating the birth of Jesus; we see manger scenes all about us, but we all too frequently fail to see into the depths of the mystery. Looking at the crib we see only a reminder of an event in salvation history unless we are little children; their imagination enables them to believe. We miss that blessing because we are confused by our experience of reality; we can't reason to such an unconditional love for everyone and without limit. Babies and little children are not hampered by reason; they reach out and accept love from everyone, but we limit our love, both the giving and receiving, and share it only with those we feel reasonably deserve it.

Stretched and stressed due to the materialism of Christmas and disappointed and hurt as a result of betrayed love and friendships, we have lost the excitement of children in preparing for Christmas and are blinded to the mystery. Little children long for love; they do not judge our love on the value of the gifts received at Christmas; their eyes aglow, their smiles and laughter is contagious, and their excitement is uncontrolled when they experience our love. They believe in Santa; they believe in Jesus; they believe the mystery of love.

Children are excited at the approach of Christmas because they hope for the chance to see Santa and hope he will bring them what they want. Catholics are excited at the approach of Christmas because they hope to experience the presence of Jesus, who promises peace, love, and salvation. It is the mystery of Christmas that makes this day unique; we cannot comprehend the depth of the miracle, but with childlike faith we can believe.

The greatest joy of our peace mission to Palestine was to see the little children—children with sparkling eyes, hoping for a better future of peace, justice, and freedom. Believing their suffering and imprisonment would soon come to an end, they welcomed us, celebrated with us, and hoped in the mystery of love.

O that we could believe the mystery of love this Christmas season and all through the year convinced that our suffering will soon end, that our sins have been forgiven and that we will experience the mystery of love forever! To do this we need to close our eyes to the world and open our hearts to Santa and to Jesus, forget reality and hope in the mystery, love.

December 26, 2004

As my Grandfather clock struck midnight, the calendar year of 2004 faded like the early morning mist before the bright sun. Did we make it a year of grace, a time of spiritual growth? Hopefully we are ascending the "mountain" toward God and not merely walking around and around the base unwilling to make the climb because of the sacrifices involved. Each year we should be moving a little higher on our spiritual ascent and drawing closer to Jesus—the goal of our life.

I am amazed at the number of people who comment on my wearing sandals all year because they feel it is too cold. I am more amazed at the number of people who do not know Jesus or live what he teaches; how difficult it must be living in the cold not sharing in the warmth of Jesus's love and friendship and burdened with guilt! The world cannot know Jesus and live as it does.

There is nothing we can do to change 2004; we can only try to learn from the experiences we encountered. Much of the world simply walks around and around the "mountain," staying far from God who beckons us to come up to him. Many have grown weak in faith, have lost their sense of sin, and have become adept at rationalizing their wrong while living in denial, no longer needing a Savior.

The old year is gone; the new one is just beginning; how I wish I could convince you of the reality of Jesus and help you experience his unconditional love! Have you ever really loved someone? Did anyone have to force you to spend time together? Then how can you say you love Jesus and neglect or refuse to spend one hour with him at the Eucharist each week? Too many Catholics are walking around and around the church and not entering it; they are neglecting to climb the "mountain" to share a loving friendship with Jesus and are failing to make room in their lives for him. Mass attendance is at an all-time low; appreciation and prayerful use of the sacraments is dwindling. Immorality depicted as the normal way of living via the media, has increasingly become the norm—abortion, premarital sex, living together outside of marriage, greed, and self-gratification abound.

Pope John Paul II has designated 2005 as a year of the Eucharist; hopefully we all will strive to deepen our appreciation of the real presence of Jesus in this sacrament, receive it more frequently and carefully. Only when we acknowledge the living presence of Jesus in the Eucharist can we hope to eliminate the "culture of death" mentality and see Jesus present in every life and situation around us.

2004 was a great year, yet it was a year of great sin. 2005 will undoubtedly likewise be a year of sin, but it can be an even greater year of grace if we will only break the circle of going around the "mountain" and begin the climb, which leads us up to Jesus. I did not stay up to bid farewell to 2004 but buried myself beneath a mountain of blankets in a warm bed sound asleep. I was neither worried about the past nor anxious about the future because Jesus was with me in the past and will continue to journey with me in the year ahead. He longs to share intimately with all of us.

The New Year is upon us; we must take care not to bury ourselves beneath the blankets of materialism and secularism; we cannot "sleep" but must be awake to the needs of others climbing the "mountain" together. Convinced that sin abounds, we turn to Jesus where grace is more abounding, resolving to make this a better year as we walk more closely with him. Toss off the blankets of your comfort zone and listen to Jesus who meticulously directs every moment of our lives; trust him and make 2005 a year of grace, a time of spiritual growth! Happy New Year!

January 2, 2005

A few weeks ago I took off my sandals; some may think I did so to let them cool since I had been constantly on the go these past months. But the truth is, I went ice skating on the pond; something I had not been able to do for years. I could not help but recall my childhood days when our skates were clamped on our regular shoes (just think I could have skated with my sandals on), and how they kept coming off if you had weak ankles and did not keep your skates directly beneath you!

It was a beautiful day: the sun was shining, the temperature was unusually mild, and the ice was clear and smooth—it was a wonderful experience amid God's winter nature. The bare trees, the dead grass, the trampled weeds, and blowing leaves clearly painted the picture of life hiding from the cold, waiting for the return of warmth to renew hidden life.

As I skated on the ice, I could not help but think of what lay beneath. The thick layer of ice was preventing me from entering into the depths of the water, a pleasure which in the warm summer is so inviting, and separating me from the water, so vital for life, and from the fish, a source of food to sustain life.

Skating on the hard cold ice reminded me of how so many live their lives—separated from family and friends by a "cold" layer of "ice," hard, cold hearts, the result of some past hurt or from God because they are unhappy with the way things are going in their lives. Thus frozen in their bitterness and hurt, they experience the winter of life; everything is cold and dead, like nature around us.

Refusing to reconcile with others or accept God's plan, they "skate" through life "frozen," pretending to enjoy life, but in reality their deception leaves them empty and unhappy just like prolonged ice skating.

I truly enjoyed the moment of "freedom" and solitude, but soon the coldness began to set in, and I missed the warmth of summer with its daily surprises of beauty and new life; my ankles were tired and skating became a bit boring and routine; finally I was forced to stop when my leg muscles, pleading for mercy, sent me staggering to my car.

In like manner, when we resolve to live cut off from family and friends or worse still from God, the result can only be a cold emptiness, which leads to loneliness and unhappiness. No one can endure that coldness for long; we need the warmth of love and friendship, people who fill our lives with beauty and daily surprises, and the intimate friendship of Jesus if we are to live a healthy life, both physically and spiritually.

Healthy lives require warm and loving friendships and an intimate relationship with Jesus if we are to experience fulfillment in our lives. Living lives of separation will soon drain the life of our spirit like the bare trees, deaden our emotions like the dead grass, or break our bodies like the trampled weeds around the pond and our lives will pass as dry leaves blowing in the wind.

If you have ever skated on ice, you will recall that every time your skate blade touched the ice to glide over the water, you left a mark, you scarred the ice; you chipped away some of its beauty—a beauty that could be restored by only by the warm melting sun. So too, when we "skate" coldly through people's lives, we scar them—a scar which can only be healed by the warmth of our love and God's reconciliation.

Once the sun drives the cold away, the water will soften, offer refreshment, and become a source of life again. So too, when we forgive and reconcile with family, friends, and Jesus we will experience a newness of life. Take off those "skates" which scar; leave the cold, allow the warm love of friends, family, and Jesus to renew hidden life.

January 9, 2005

As I lay on the wet sidewalk at the foot of the steps in front of the rectory with my sandals facing up instead of being under me, I thanked God that no serious damage had resulted, no broken bones. Picking up my papers and walking on to the meeting, I realized that life could end just as quickly and unexpectedly as that mishap. It also became quite clear to me that God has a special plan for each of us, and it is most important that we keep our focus on Jesus, especially in trying and difficult times.

Why did God let me fall, why did he protect me from injury—to teach me? This past week I was a part of a Cursillo renewal with a man who was confined to a wheel chair; I celebrated the funerals of two "pillars" of our parishes, and I was deeply disturbed by the painful situation of our diocese, the increase of crime in our country, and the startling natural disasters around the world—all possible grace moments.

Why did God let me fall, to open my eyes to the love and blessings he showers upon me? God placed the man in the wheel chair—a man of deep faith and dearly loved by Jesus, in my path to bolster my courage and encourage me to persevere when the bottom seems to be falling out from under me. He teaches that even though life can end as unexpectedly as falling down a stairs, he will always lift us up. God allows the painful situations of life to show he has power to bring good out of disasters, even sin, when we live as Christians and reach out to help and forgive.

As I drove home from Springfield, through the eerie fog, following the burial service, I enjoyed a mystical experience. The trees were black and bleak, the roadsides were brown, nothing offered color or beauty, and vision was very limited; yet it brought a sense of the present. I was awestruck at the marvels of God's nature around me—resting, dead yet pregnant with new life; hidden from view but potentially active, and of the incredible way he shows his love and acts in our lives. This was extremely uplifting and spiritual; it was mystical—Jesus proclaiming his presence in the silence.

Journeying through life, injury, death, and tragedies tend to remove color or beauty and sadness and despair limit our vision; but faith brings life's happenings to the present where freed from distractions, we can focus on Jesus and see his plan. Frequently, we are caught up in everything around us—anxiously preparing for the future, distraught about our past, and vying to outdo family and acquaintances that we are unable to live the present—the only moment we can actually live.

Laying flat on the sidewalk with my face a few inches from the cement made me quite aware of the present. I could not see where I came from; I could not see where I hoped to go; I could only live the present and get up. What a marvelous analogy of life, both physical and spiritual, where we are called to trust God's plan at present!

Why did Jesus protect me from injury? He alone knows, but it taught me that even when we are experiencing life-shattering traumas, he is protecting us. Injuries, painful events, and even death have no lasting effect; physical, emotional, and spiritual injuries whether personal or affecting the total church can be mystical experiences helping us focus on the present where Jesus is forgiving, healing, and loving us.

Fog can be threatening when we try to look far in advance or behind, but calming when we look at the present and see Jesus lighting the way. Let the "fog" you're in become a mystical experience; Jesus is there. Focus on him if you fall; he will raise you up!

January 16, 2005

The surprise snow this past week, even though it was a beautiful work of God and renewed the face of the earth, was not welcomed by many. It was a cause of more work for some, a source of danger for others, a reason for joy for a few, but overall it was seen as an aggravation rather than a blessing. How like those surprise visits of Jesus!

God's snow brush painted mystery as he changed the size and form of objects; he revealed his magnificence as he replaced ugliness with beauty; his majesty could be seen in the glitter of zillions of ice diamonds reflecting the brilliant sun on the hillsides. Why are we so harsh in judging his art work, so slow to accept his special gifts?

As I swept the steps and walks, the feathery snow flew like snowbirds in flight. I could not help but think of the damage I was doing to God's work of art; how like the way we damage his greater work, our soul, all for personal convenience!

The snow caused work for some people; were they oblivious of God's blessing? It was a worry or a possible danger for others; where is their faith in God's protection? Because of our demands of convenience and speed, we fail to slow down and appreciate the moment; we even are frustrated and aggravated with God's plan. We experience those same feelings when Jesus showers spiritual snows upon us.

Each of us is a beautiful creation of God—unique, unconditionally loved, and resplendent as new fallen snow. Gifted with free will, we destroy God's work of art causing our spiritual life to wither and at times even allowing it to die buried beneath layers of crusty dirty ice and snow, our sins. That's when Jesus comes to melt away the dirty ice and snow and cover us with a beautiful "snow," his grace; we don't always welcome it.

Enjoying the "fast" life of sin, we are disgruntled with his expectations to slow down and make room for him; we sweep it aside and return to the old "sidewalk" way of life. Jesus offers to touch us with his cross, that mystery brush of renewal—not to cover over our sinful ugliness, but to totally restore us to our former beauty. He comes to renew our life, but that requires change, and we are complacent in our lethargy.

Beneath the crystallized snow, there is lifeless darkness waiting for the sun to melt the snow and warm the soil; then new life flourishes. With the passing of winter, the spring flowers beautify the hillsides and birds reverberate with songs of praise to God and life abounds. Our souls lie lifeless beneath the damages of our sins until we allow Jesus to warm our hearts, to forgive our sins, and to restore our spiritual life.

When we break from our sinful patterns and allow the presence of Jesus, the Son of life, to warm our hearts all bitterness, hatred, and division will melt so we can see beauty in people around us; join them in praising God for his blessings; and spiritual life abounds.

God's beautiful snow shrouds the ugliness of the earth until it is ready to be transformed with surprises of hidden life; so too, God shrouds us in the palm of his hands until we are ready to allow him to transform us and bring forth new life through the sacrament of reconciliation.

Fresh snow is beautiful but unwelcome; its potential for life is not appreciated; the grace of Jesus is transforming but unwelcome; we are so consumed with the enticements of the world that we neglect to appreciate our need for grace, with its potential for eternal life.

Being open to the will of Jesus is hard work, a source of danger, a cause for spiritual aggravation, but once we open ourselves to the indwelling of the Holy Spirit, it is a joy beyond words, a joy that will not melt like the snow—a taste of the life to come. Snow only covers ugliness, grace removes it; be ready as Jesus surprises us with both.

January 23, 2005

Is it winter or is it summer? The temperature changes so drastically and frequently that it becomes a bit confusing and distressing. Are you a lion or a lamb? Some personalities change so emphatically with varying situations that confusion and distress result.

On my desk is a beautiful wood carving made in Palestine; it is a lion with a lamb resting between its feet depicting the prophesy of Isaiah—there shall be no harm or ruin when people come to know God. It is a daily reminder to control the "lion" in me lest I devour the "lamb" crossing my path or seeking Jesus, the Good Shepherd.

Driving along the highway recently, I saw a herd of sheep and one looked like it had been attacked, not by a lion, maybe by some dog or perhaps it was the result of the rough underbrush around; its wool was in a sad state, hanging raggedly from its body.

Whether we believe it or not, that is what we do to those around us, even those we claim to love dearly, when we "roar" and "voice" our power heedless of the damage we are doing to the little "lambs" or the older "sheep," killing or damaging relationships.

We cannot control the changing temperatures, but we can control our temper; it may be bitter cold one day and remarkably warm the next according to God's plan. People may be like the weather changing daily or with each situation, but Jesus exhorts us to maintain our temper—to see the lamb in each person and control the lion in ourselves. We cannot control the "lion" in those around us, but we can imitate Jesus, the Lamb of God and love them so Jesus can use us to win them over, to become peaceful lambs.

Defusing ourselves of power and force, putting aside our lion role and communicating as lamb to lamb, we can maturely resolve all differences and difficulties, maintain a sense of openness through honest dialogue, and live in peace.

When a lion destroys the flock the shepherd destroys the lion. In like manner, when we carelessly or brutally destroy those around us, we are endangering our own safety for the dangerous lion will be destroyed.

Jesus invites the lion and the lamb to live together in peace. In the wild the lion is very dangerous, but when domesticated, it can be trained to be more accepting of weaker and smaller animals. Jesus came to dwell among us to prove that power is not the only way or even the best way to motivate people; love is far more effective; power lasts only until it is overpowered by a greater force, while love endures.

When we live in the "wild" of sin, not following God's plan, we, like the lion, are very dangerous and destructive to all around us, but when we come to know Jesus, there will be no more harm or ruin. Jesus has the power to destroy us, but he chooses to love us. Jesus assures us that if we love him and those around us, he will protect us from the "lions" that threaten to harm or ruin us.

Within a few days we will begin the season of Lent, a time to discern whether we are a lion or a lamb. If we find that we are a lion, we should seek ways to control and tame it; if we are a lamb, we need to trust in God's protection as we share his love with the lion.

The more we eliminate the lion in our lives, the more we will see the lamb in others and live in peace. People love gentle lambs and fear roaring lions; they respect kind and loving people and shun harsh tyrants.

What do people see in us, the lion or the lamb? What do we see in others? Will we ever live together in peace, like the lamb and lion on my desk? Only when as Isaiah says, we have come to know God. We know its winter by the signs; people will come to know who we are by the signs; lion or lamb.

January 30, 2005

Some believe whether or not the groundhog sees, his shadow will determine when spring will arrive; others believe the color of the caterpillar in the fall will determine the severity of our winter; a few believe the date of our first measurable snow will determine the number of snows we will have, and there are those who believe when the geese fly north, that warm temperatures will soon follow. Do you trust any of these forecasters to plan your life? Hopefully not; only God is in control, God determines natural events!

We laugh and joke about the groundhog seeing his shadow along with many other ole wives' tales realizing that everyone has a different version; oftentimes contradicting one another and all absolutely unreliable. The sad thing is that some people tend to carry such haphazard nonsense into their spiritual lives ignoring that God determines our faith journey and is in control.

Some people look on baptism as magic; baptism does not determine our salvation anymore than the groundhog determines when spring begins. Other people neglect to use the powerful, grace-filled sacrament of reconciliation believing that no one, not even the church, can rightly determine the severity of their sins anymore than the color of the caterpillar can forecast the severity of the winter. It seems a growing number of Catholics believe in the need for the attendance at Mass with a faith similar to their belief that the number of snows will be based on the date of the first snow. We also have those who receive the Eucharist routinely, like the instinctive drive of the geese, which migrate in search of food and not to avoid the cold, rather than with a deep belief in the real presence of Jesus.

One who perceives the sacraments in such fashion should not laugh at those who seem to believe in ole wives' tales; their misguidance only ends with some passing mishap, but those who fail to see the essential value of the sacraments are potentially in danger of far greater loss. The many wives' tales handed down from generation to generation offering guidance are not reliable or entirely beneficial, but the directives Jesus has given in his church are absolutely reliable and most beneficial when we use them properly.

The groundhog, the caterpillar, the snow, and the geese all add to the beauty and mystique of nature but do not control it or determine its outcome. The sacraments add much to the splendor and mystery of our spiritual life, but in themselves they do not determine our final outcome; God determines that according to our faith and the degree we cooperate with his grace given in the sacraments.

God is not a magician; our faith is not a magic carpet. God is a mystery and our faith is an empowerment to accept the mystery, to trust him, and live. A mystery story has tense and trying moments, exciting and elating sections, sad and disappointing times, as well as periods of joy and love. Catholics can expect the same when they live their faith; there are days when life is very trying, sad, and disappointing when we need special grace to persevere; and there are days when we are excited, filled with joy, and experience God's love—the result of living our faith, which is more than merely routinely receiving the sacraments; we must imitate Jesus's love and forgiveness in every aspect of our lives.

The groundhog, the caterpillar, the snow, and the geese do not bring spring; it is the nearness of the sun. The misuse of the sacraments does not bring salvation; it the nearness of the son. Whether we believe the "wives' tales" or not, the sun will still bring spring; but if we do not believe and carefully use the sacraments to live a deep faith the son cannot bring salvation. Does the "sun" or the "son" control our lives?

February 6, 2005

You can't believe everything you hear! This past Sunday I had my heart all set for a warm, sunny day in the woods, the promise made by the weather forecaster, but soon after I got there, gusty winds brought clouds and lowered the temperature rapidly.

Disappointed by the deception, I resolutely meandered into the sleeping woods and found a place out of the wind to sit quietly so as not to awaken Mother Nature still enjoying her winter snooze.

You can't believe everything you see! The woods appeared to be lifeless; the trees were bare, their dead leaves on the ground; the grass and spring flowers were nowhere to be seen; there were no animals frolicking around and the bird choir was silent.

After some time, I noticed several little bugs scampering along the log on which I sat; a few tiny buds on the trees; a tufted titmouse quietly flitting from tree to tree in search of food, and when I disturbed the dry leaves under my sandals, the first signs of spring, the sweet williams, were greening beneath the patchwork blanket of leaves. Suddenly I was thrilled to hear a flock of geese overhead, flying in perfect V formation, preparing to descend to the flooded field for the night. As I neared a little pond, I heard throngs of tiny frogs practicing for their spring concert, and saw deer tracks and turkey feathers along the path and around the pond. The "lifeless" woods was very much alive!

As I tried to make the best of a disappointing situation, the lack of the bright sun and the warm temperature, I saw an analogy between the weatherman and the devil, the woods and God, and the constant tug of war between the material and spiritual.

How frequently the weather forecaster promises the "perfect" day, gets us excited as we anticipate a happy experience and then leaves us disappointed when it does not happen! Not only does the warm and bright sun not shine, the clouds are accompanied by cold winds, or even worse with rain.

In similar manner, the devil makes fantastic promises, enticing us to believe him and abandon what would have been better for our spiritual development, only to disappoint us with his lies and deception. Not only does the happiness of his material promises fail to come about, but we suffer from the bitter "winds" of guilt and the "rains" of loss of the eternal happiness we forfeited. The devil, like the weather forecaster, will go out-of-his-way to convince you that he can satisfy all your cravings for physical gratification and material satisfaction, but you can't believe all you hear; he can satisfy your needs for happiness, but only for a time, and he can't prevent the bitter winds and destructive rains, which will result from your sin.

Jesus, like the awakening woods gradually revealing new signs of spring, will surprise us every day with some new grace; we must patiently await the plan God has chosen for us. Remember you can't believe all you see; worldly glitter may be very attractive, but when we appear before God, it will be drab and dull compared to the glory of sanctifying grace, our sharing in eternal life.

In the daily tug-of-war between the material and the spiritual, which side of the rope are you pulling on, social status or spiritual development? Which has priority, public school or Catholic, social and scholastic gatherings or prayer and faith sharing groups? Are you drawn to religious apathy or active participation in the Mass and parish life, amassing wealth, power, and position as you climb the ladder of success, which fails and fades more rapidly than the time spent in achieving it, or attaining grace as you prepare for a life of lasting peace, love, and happiness? Choose carefully Christ's side in the "tug-of-war"!

March 13, 2005

Many years ago I watched as some gliders, towed by small planes, were being airlifted and was amazed as they played the air currents until they were forced to land—exciting, but risky. Yet some people live a big part of their lives in a similar manner, detached from Jesus; they have lost their source of spiritual power and glide aimlessly until they are forced to seek safety or crash.

Each time I see a huge plane flying overhead, I stand in awe; how can so much weight be held aloft by two relatively small wings and propelled by a few jet motors? That in itself is a major fete, but what is even more astounding is that when it touches down only two landing gears and several small wheels support that incredible amount of weight. Still I love to fly, and I trust in the capability of the pilot.

More and more airlines are going broke; employees are demanding pay raises and expecting too many amenities, and passengers are wanting "first class" treatment while only paying regular fare along with the huge drop in air travel.

Both situations remind me of modern Catholics; a few have chosen the glider, but most prefer the plane. Many who are gliding received a good launching but once on their way, they detach themselves from the source of their power, Jesus, and glide where the modern-day current carries them, gradually losing the power of grace and their spiritual altitude as they drift and slowly descend, weakened in faith. Their "gliding" faith life might be exciting, but it is very risky where they might eventually land.

There are also those Catholics who prefer the plane but are unwilling to sacrifice to keep the plane in good condition and flying. A growing number of Catholics today expect the church to supply "first class" service, but fail to tithe or be good stewards in supporting their parish; they want more amenities and greater benefits without sacrificing or still giving the same amount they gave years ago when costs were much lower. A plane needs to be kept in good condition and requires fuel to fly or it will crash; so does a parish. The diocese, the spiritual "air line," guided by our bishop, helps to keep the parishes, its spiritual "planes," in good condition by assuring that Catholic doctrine is being supplied; the parish needs to supply the fuel for the school and faith community if the parish is to thrive; and the parishioner must make use of the church and/or school, the "spiritual plane" or like the air lines, it too will close.

Regardless of how modernized the plane may be, the air line depends on people flying, or it will go out of business; the Catholic Church faces a similar problem. Vatican II with its continual renewal has kept the church, the spiritual "air line" with its teachings of Jesus, in tip-top condition, but the increase of faith apathy, the tremendous drop in Mass attendance, the decrease in the use of the sacraments, the deficit of financial support, and the aberration from the moral law is slowly plummeting the Catholic Church into spiritual bankruptcy; resulting in its attrition and the closing of many parishes; the local spiritual "airports."

It's time we sit up and "fly" right; it's time to live our faith and abandon our "gliders," merely riding the "wind" currents of materialism and worldliness hoping all will end well; we must work with the bishop of our diocese and sacrifice to design and develop an inviting, faith-filled parish, our spiritual "air line," so present and future generations will enjoy the blessings of our Catholic faith—eternal life. The challenge is great, but possible! The challenge of maintaining an air line requires team work; so does the spiritual "air line," our parish. God uses our parish/school and all of us to make it "fly," trust him!

February 20, 2005

The puzzle is incomplete. It will never be complete until all the pieces are properly fitted together. Have you ever worked on a puzzle, one in which the colors and shapes were basically the same? It is then that you must give greater concentration and perseverance if you are to bring to completion the intended picture of the one who designed the puzzle.

God is the master puzzle maker; he has designed the most unique and complicated puzzle and patiently watches as we try to put the pieces together. You are a piece of the puzzle; everything that God has created is a part of the puzzle. That presents a problem because at times we try to put the puzzle together instead of allowing God to place the pieces where he wants, where he knows they will fit best, and where they will produce a more beautiful picture. Are you willing to cooperate?

We like picture puzzles with many vivid contrasting colors and shapes, which make our work much easier; such puzzles become monotonous in time because the pieces go together easily from repetition. We don't like those puzzles, which display only little variance in color or shape; they are too strenuous, and we tend to give up and quit. When we have the choice, we choose those puzzles that are appealing, colorful, and easy to put together.

As we look over our lives, we see that most days are routine and most of the people we come in contact with are the same; we are content even when it becomes monotonous with little change for we are in control; the pieces go together easily from repetition; but it lacks color and beauty.

We find it very difficult when God comes along with a different puzzle; one where we do not recognize all the pieces, one in which we are not sure just how we fit in the picture, one in which God is in control. This is the puzzle of life! It's up to us to let him design the puzzle, and the piece we are in the puzzle; and it is our responsibility to let him use us as he chooses, or the puzzle will never be complete.

God's choice of the puzzle often breaks with the routine; he adds colors and shapes that are quite out of the ordinary to see how we will react. Our routine lives are often shocked by the glare of a broken home, a child born to an unmarried couple, a scandal, someone abandoning their faith, or a loved one diagnosed with Aids.

We love puzzles with bright colors or distinguishing shapes until we find them in the puzzle of life and then we do not know how to handle them. We try to force pieces together, bending, tearing, and nearly destroying those forgetting that God knows where each piece goes and quietly offers us grace to work it out. The flashing colors cannot be hidden; but with God's help, we can lovingly blend the colors in ways that embellish the beauty to the total picture.

When we find ourselves in a new puzzle, it may take some time and prayer to find out how we are to fit in; but we can be sure that we have an important place, or God would not have placed us in the situation. We can try to force the colors or shapes to fit into our plan, but that will only lead to greater problems distorting the finished project. We can even refuse to be a piece in the puzzle, and it will never be complete.

Our shape and color may differ from puzzle to puzzle according to God's plan. In one we may be a big piece, in another we may be a very small piece; but both are equally necessary if the picture is to be complete; one day we may be bright, loving, and forgiving; another day we may be less colorful, patient, and supportive.

Life is a continuous puzzle; generally routine but highlighted from time to time with splashes of color and challenging us to discern what piece God has for us in each situation. No puzzle is too hard to piece together. Every piece is valuable; every puzzle is designed by God, and when we let him place the pieces where he chooses, it will bring to completion a picture of eternal beauty.

February 27, 2005

This past Sunday evening, my Sandals journeyed to Jerseyville with a few of our youth to see a religious presentation: "Heaven's Gates–Hell's Flames." Live people with the aid of multimedia props sought to convey the message that we all shall die, at a time, place, and in a way we least expect, and appear before God. Will we be ready, will our name be written in the book of life—*where are we choosing to spend eternity*?

Most of us live under the presumption that we still have time to prepare; but do we? Death is no respecter of age; it may be an infant drowning, a child killed in an accident, a youth consumed by cancer, a young man dying from a heart attack, or the result of failing health and age.

The "real-life" presentations clearly depicted situations where people foolishly risked their very salvation chasing after fleeting worldly pleasures, where they put off committing their lives to Jesus, hoping to do so later only realizing their mistake when it was too late as they met with an untimely death. Are we making the same mistake?

Lent is a special time for a reality check. Has the conniving devil manipulated you into placing a higher priority on sleeping, fishing, sports etc., than gathering to celebrate the Sunday Mass? What place does Jesus hold in your life?

Each Sunday night our youth leaders sacrifice their time to help our young people grow in faith and to enjoy wholesome, Christian activities; only a few take advantage of our youth program; each Sunday many are missing Mass, risking salvation.

I regret that only a few of our youth experienced the presentation of "Heaven's Gates—Hell's Flames" because it clearly conveyed the reality of hell and the consequences of our actions, which many have come to discredit. The devil is very clever, and we are so gullible; he has almost convinced us that hell is a myth or mechanism to scare us into living moral lives, deprived of freedom and fun.

Parents, what do you find when you make a spiritual reality check? Are you living your Catholic faith, what place have you given to Jesus? We cannot relegate his role in our lives simply to an occasional cry when in dire need; he deserves the pivotal position in every aspect of our lives. Your way of living motivates and inspires your family to choose the spiritual things, or to take foolish risks. You reveal the importance of committing yourself to Jesus by the way you live each day. Young people are like leaves on a branch, parents, which is grafted to a vine, Jesus; when the branch is spiritually healthy, the leaves will flourish; when the branch is sick, weak, or broken from the vine, the leaves will suffer and eventually die.

The vine is alive; what is the condition of the branch? Many leaves are in dire need and about to fall from the branch. It is time we refocus our lives; following our natural desires will lead us and our young people to hell's flames, but focusing on the spiritual faith and fully committed to Jesus will lead to heaven's gates.

My Sandals experienced another "grace-filled" gathering this week as the local ministers, school leaders, and businessmen and women united to launch "Project 7," a Christ-centered program to help our young people make the right choices.

Our youth are facing difficult choices; it is up to us to guide and encourage them in making the right one. We need to help them commit their lives to Jesus by going to church with them, urging them to participate in our parish youth gatherings, and encouraging them to experience "Project 7."

"Heaven's gates" or "hell's flames" awaits our choice—it's a lasting choice, make it good!

March 6, 2005

Lent is a time to turn off the "lights" of the world and review the "spiritual video" of our lives. We are so busy and blinded by the flashing attractions of the world that we seldom scrutinize our spiritual progress. Lent offers us the opportunity to withdraw from the material glitter and glare and seek the solitude of the "desert" where Jesus will reveal the spiritual status of our souls. What would your DVD show? Are you among those on a merry-go-round, those in an elevator, or have you chosen the escalator?

We are all on a faith journey; but where is our journey taking us? It seems that some are on a merry-go-round simply going around and around, faster and faster each year, but never rising to a higher level of spirituality. They are unwilling to make any change to become more Christlike neglecting to achieve a higher level of spirituality each year.

There are those who use the elevator and rise up for a short time only to descend, often to a lower level than when they began. Their misuse of life and time ends with the sad awareness that they have failed to rise to a higher level than the year before.

Maybe your video will show you "walking up" on a "going down" escalator, walking fast enough that you remain in the same spot, never getting any higher or improving but gradually tiring in your efforts to live your faith. A few will simply ride the escalator up or down and never do anything to make changes, simply wasting their time and missing the blessings of a close friendship with Jesus.

Hopefully your DVD will show you both rising to greater heights of faith and drawing nearer to Jesus like the person who begins at the base of a huge mountain, gradually climbing upward always getting a little higher and closer to the center until eventually you reach the peak to share peace, love, and life with Jesus forever. This requires sacrifice, honesty, and a desire to change—a willingness to die to self and sin and allowing Jesus to renew us spiritually.

This past week we enjoyed a beautiful snow, which covered over the ugliness of winter and transformed the panorama into a winter wonderland. Soon it will melt, reveal that nothing has changed, and the ugliness is still there. We can no longer just cover over our old self, hiding our sinful inclinations like snow covers over the earth; we must undergo a conversion of heart.

It is time to get off the merry-go-round, out of the elevator, or leave the escalator; our faith journey requires personal effort and sacrifice as we "climb" the mountain. Jesus is always there to assist us, but we must partner with him; we can't do it alone, and he is not going to do it for us. This Lent, let us look up the mountain to see Jesus, our goal; look down and keep our eyes on the path, humbly accepting God's plan; look inside to see what we are trying to cover over with a false veneer of piety and ask God for the grace to die to our sinful self and ways; look around to see who we need to forgive or ask forgiveness, where we are failing to love, and how we can bring peace and unity to our personal lives, families, parish, and community.

When the snow melts with the return of the bright, warm sun, the moisture will transform the ugliness of winter into the beauty of new spring life. In like manner, when the "snow" of Lent passes with the Resurrection of the "son," the "moisture" of our prayers, fasting, and alms giving will bring new spiritual life to our souls. Participating in the Paschal Mystery will transform our souls; help us to climb up the mountain, and make us more Christlike as we undergo a change of heart.

Jesus calls us up the mountain; he uses Lent to show us the way; will we follow?

February 13, 2005

Mr. and Mrs. Rich Garden had worked long and hard to prepare the soil and carefully planted the vine as soon as the temperature had maintained above freezing levels. The vine could not control itself as the gardeners planted it in the rich soil; its excitement was visible as it drank in the spring rains and basked in the warmth of the sun. Within weeks the vine was spreading rapidly covering large areas of the melon patch, pleasing the gardeners who were carefully tending its every need—watering, fertilizing, weeding, and spraying for insects anticipating delicious melons.

As the months passed, the vigor of the plant began to slow; its fresh green leaves were a bit dry and spotted with ugly holes ravished by hungry bugs and disease; its vines were hardening and overgrown with weeds as the gardeners became occupied with other pressing matters. Their preoccupations resulted in the neglect of the vine and only a few melons matured, and they were of inferior quality.

Gradually, the vine withered due to lack of water, the summer's heat, the invasion of destructive bugs, and the overgrowth of weeds. With the vine's original excitement for life waning, the production of fruit ceasing, and the involvement in other frivolous matters, the gardeners lost interest in the vine completely.

This is comparable to the spiritual lives of some today. Parents are very excited about having a baby. They go to great extremes getting everything ready for the new arrival. They are very anxious about having the child baptized, care for it as s/he draws near to First Communion and then things begin to wane as they and their children get more involved in other things.

Without the careful encouragement and example of the parents, these little ones begin to lose their excitement about the sacraments, gradually fail to receive them, and their spiritual growth diminishes. Parents, like the gardeners, need to be alert to the dangerous attractions of the world and modern times which, like the bugs and other plants' diseases, continue to attack and destroy the spiritual health of these growing children.

Family prayer time, reception of the sacraments, and participation at Mass together are powerful means of maintaining the spiritual life of young and old alike and a "spiritual spray" to control diseases of the soul. What choice will we make?

This past week, the Ministerial Alliance of Carrollton, sponsored "Project 7" to assist our young people on their faith journey, to encourage them to make the right choices, and to never give up in their efforts to improve. It was a wonderful presentation by a group of young people sharing their lives, revealing how they made bad choices, and the consequences in order to motivate our youth today to make the right choices.

The presenter and his team did their part; they chose to come to help us in our work of preparing our young people to make the right choices as they face the difficult future ahead. Some of our youth made the choice to attend the presentation; while others chose not to participate; now the responsibility rests on us to nurture the seeds planted at that gathering, by making the right choices ourselves.

This "spiritual gardening" seems easier and more accepted when the "plants," the children, are young and excited about Jesus and few things affect their spiritual life when the parents are "good gardeners" by living their faith; but it requires more effort when the heat of summer, "those teenage years" along with the insects and weeds, "drugs, alcohol, sex, and peer pressure" begin to choke and kill the life of the soul.

We cannot give up; they must not give up; only right choices bear lasting, good "fruit"!

March 20, 2005

As spring continues to invade our area, we see more and more signs of new life—the flowers blooming, the grass greening, the birds mating. All new life, both physical and spiritual, is a result of death; Easter is a result of death!

Walking across the yard, one may find an empty bird egg shell, the empty tomb—what was dead or lifeless has broken forth with new life.

Have you ever gone to the cemetery the day before a funeral and seen an empty grave? If it was being prepared for a family member or loved one—one who died suddenly or who was very young, then your heart was likely heavily burdened. We still do not see; we do not understand; we question the plan of God.

We celebrate and rejoice when a baby is born; we dream of great accomplishments or fame totally blotting out of our minds that from that moment on they will experience pain, failure, and rejection constantly faced with death. We find it very hard to believe that life leads to death while death leads to life.

Jesus called Lazarus's lifeless body out of the tomb to help the people believe; he beckons us to enter his tomb to see the truth and believe. The world has duped us promising that if we enwrap ourselves in a cocoon of materialistic fantasy, just like a caterpillar, we will come forth as a butterfly enjoying freedom and happiness; it only leads to death. Jesus raised Lazarus from physical death, knowing fully well that he would die again, to prove he was God with power over sin and spiritual death; he invites us into the tomb to show his power to restore life—life that is eternal.

When Jesus was born on Christmas day, there was rejoicing, for a child was born. When Jesus died on Good Friday, there was much sorrow, great dreams had been thwarted and darkness reigned. The Resurrection, the empty tomb of Easter, turned the tide from pain and sorrow into peace and happiness for those who believe.

Jesus invites us to come into the tomb away from the busyness, the glitter, and the distractions of the world. We are so bombarded at Christmas with preparations that we can't find time for Advent and so fail to appreciate the importance of his birth; we are so immersed in worldly pursuits that the purpose of Lent, for the most part, is excluded from our lives. We need to leave the world and enter the tomb away from the brightness of the world into the darkness of the tomb if we are to see the glory of the Resurrection.

A teacher gave each of her class of second graders a plastic egg with the instructions to take it home and bring it back with something in it that helped them to understand the meaning of Easter. The next day each child presented their egg filled with candy, money, a flower, or some object connected with Easter except for the one little poor boy whose egg was empty. When asked to explain, he said the empty egg reminded him of the empty tomb and Jesus's Resurrection, which brought him new life.

The empty bird shell, the empty grave, and the empty plastic egg teach us the real meaning of Easter—life has conquered death. Easter is here. Have we emptied ourselves and made room for Jesus or are we still buried in the tomb of worldliness and sin? Jesus cannot enter into cluttered lives. We cannot begin a new life until we die to the old one;

we cannot live lives of grace until we come out of the tomb of sin. Jesus has died for our sins, passed through the tomb, and made room for us; will we enter the tomb believing that life does not end with death, but that death is our birth to life?

Jesus says, "I am the Resurrection and the Life, whoever believes in me will never die." If you believe, you will have a happy Easter today and a happy Easter at Resurrection!

March 27, 2005

When I was a child, a huge tree stood, like a giant, in the middle of our country road, with one lane on each side, extending its long branches to offer shade to those who rode past on their horses, to the teams of horses pulling wagon loaded with hay, grain, or other supplies, and to farmers working their fields. It was a spectacular sight to see this stately sentinel hovering over the road, but it was a blessing to the tired horses and the farmers who rested in its cool shade and drew refreshing water from the deep well nearby.

Over the years, as the horses were replaced by tractors and more cars used the road, the tree, in the middle of the road, was considered a hindrance; no one needed its cool shade and when the dirt road was replaced with gravel, they removed the beautiful landmark all in the guise of progress; it was an inconvenience and a possible cause for an accident.

As I look at the picture of that tree on the shelf in my office, it reminds me of Jesus, who stands in the middle of our lives offering his love and extending his arms, waiting to embrace us when we are weary and life becomes burdensome. If only we will stop and rest with him, there he will refresh us from the "grace," well of living water.

The need for Jesus in the center of our lives is far more essential than any need that tree could supply to the horses or farmers years ago; yet Jesus faces the same challenging threat as the tree. Years ago we had a need for the "tree of life" because things were not as convenient as today and we turned to God for help; our days were not so filled with outside distractions, and we shared some of our time in prayer; worldly attractions were not so available and overwhelming, so Jesus and his church became a major part of our spiritual and community life. We had a need for God, and we made room in our lives for Jesus who refreshed us and nourished us by means of the sacraments and the Mass.

With the deluge of "conveniences," the development of rapid transit and our "egotistic" secular intellectualism we have little need for God; we have become self-sufficient and act like we are totally independent. We feel Jesus, the "tree," in the middle of our lives is no longer needed; he is truly an inconvenience to our freedom and even a source of danger threatening our plans of material happiness; so we have removed him from our lives.

We may live in palaces, drive fancy cars, have sizeable bank accounts with our "security bins" fully packed, but without Jesus, the "tree," we have nothing. We may enjoy an abundance of worldly happiness and live long lives, but what do we have at the end of the "road," if we have removed Jesus, the "tree," who is the way to life?

They removed the tree from the middle of the road; they widened the road destroying the beautiful landmark with its refreshing shade turning this unique scenic road into a speedway, which became more dangerous than driving around the tree. Their gain did not equal the loss.

In like manner, those who remove Jesus from their lives deprive themselves of the most beautiful friend, who offers peace, rest, and perseverance to the tired and burdened, and a needed guide along the dark and confusing faith journey, and are now rushing recklessly on a dangerous speedway, which will end in spiritual death.

The tree of life in the garden through the disobedience of Adam brought death to the world; the tree of death on Calvary through the obedience of Jesus brought life to the world. Removing the tree in the middle of the road may save the life of the careless driver; removing the tree of life, Christ, from the middle of your life only leads to death. Keep Christ in the center of your life, and you will enjoy the refreshing water and nourishing food of eternal life.

April 3, 2005

I have never been really hungry for food or for love! Don't get me wrong; I like food, and I love to eat; I crave for love and appreciate sharing in loving relationships; but I have never been deprived of food or loving friends. I have never experienced the pains of starvation or isolation, for God has blessed me abundantly with food and friends.

This past week in the play "Annie," the students of North Green High School including a number of young people from All Saints Parish were used by God to proclaim his Gospel Message to live the two great commandments, love God above all and your neighbor as yourself, and to perform the corporal works of mercy, caring for the needs of the less fortunate and the marginalized.

I am not sure what the play writer had in mind when writing this play, but it certainly brought home the point that we are rich, and we often ignore the poor and that no matter how much you possess, if you have no one you truly love, life is merely a glittering sham.

Many rich people are starving for love; many poor people are starving for food; many, both rich and poor, are starving for God. In the play, we saw the long lines of people, who were in desperate need, hungering for food, shelter, and the basics of life, but no one responded to their plight; we saw the inhuman treatment of orphans, enslaved by a legal system, hungering for love; and we saw the emptiness of possessions in the lives of the rich hungering for God. When God entered the picture, priorities were realigned; the obsession for possessions was supplanted by the sharing of personal love with others.

"Annie" was only a play, but it clearly conveyed the discrepancy in society then and today portraying the urgency of social reform. The chasm between the rich and the poor is widening at a disturbing pace and few seem to care resulting in an even greater disaster, spiritual blindness. Those who "possess" are blinded by the glitter and glare of their gold to the dire need of the poor forgetting that all they have is a gift from God; as stewards, they are to use their gifts for his glory and the good of all his people.

The play is over, but life goes on! The costumes are removed; the stage settings are dismantled, but the "actors," including all of us, are still performing on the stage of life "acting" out reality in our present day settings. What part are we playing?

In truth, we are all orphans huddled in the long line of the needy—desperate for shelter, starving for food, and pining for love. God, our loving Father, has adopted us and supplies our every need. He sent his son to offer us shelter from the evils of the world, while feeding us on the bread of life, the Eucharist. His love is so intense that he sacrificed his son to renew and deepen this love relationship, but it is a choice we must make.

In the play, a greedy couple pretended to be Annie's parents just to get the huge amount of money promised by the real parents; they had no love or compassion for Annie. Their deception was discovered; they were punished, and Annie was adopted by a loving couple who had come to realize that love was more valuable and fulfilling than things.

Millions hunger for food and a great number of people hunger for human love; we all have an unquenchable hunger for a personal love relationship with Jesus—a love that can be experienced only when we live the Gospel Message. It is not easy, because the devil, like the evil couple in the play "Annie," is trying to entice us by promising to answer all our needs with material things so as to draw us away from God, who longs to adopt us and share love and life with us—that life, which God alone gives and a love, which he alone can fulfill—eternal life!

April 17, 2005

On a small table in my office, under a couple of plants there is a little boy sleeping; next to him is a small dog keeping watch and close by stands a little lamb. Is the sleeping boy in charge or the small dog? Which one is shepherding the lamb?

Some people might think that would be a good depiction of the Catholic Church today; from the way things are developing in the church, the Holy Spirit must be asleep, the hierarchy, like the dog, just looks on, and the sheep are left on their own. If that is how they feel, then they are the ones who are asleep, for the Holy Spirit is awake, alive, and active among us.

In the past two weeks, my "Sandals" have accompanied the Holy Spirit visibly acting; I was present as the Spirit gave spiritual birth to several through baptism, healed the brokenness of some by means of reconciliation, came to a group of children in their First Holy Communion, empowered the youth of our parishes to live their faith more fully as they received confirmation, witnessed as a couple committed themselves to a life of fidelity and love in matrimony, prepared a man for his entry into eternity, and prayed with a large number of parishioners as the Spirit Anointed them with the sacrament of healing. The same Holy Spirit brought peace and consolation to a family mourning the loss of a loved one. Who would dare say the Spirit was asleep, as the Church gathered in prayer, while the cardinals discerned a new pope? If the Holy Spirit is that active in my life, to say nothing about everyone else, how can we say that the Spirit is asleep?

The problem people have in perceiving the action of the Holy Spirit is summarized in their lack of faith. Demanding great signs and wonders and looking for external changes, they fail to appreciate the internal spiritual transformation resulting from the powerful gifts of the Spirit or the presence of the Spirit acting in the daily events of life. We are so accustomed to seeing that we have a hard time believing when we see no visible change.

A few weeks ago the Spirit of God was seen in the outpouring of love by millions of people and the endless hours of TV broadcasts reminding the world of the place of God in their lives—offering strength, peace, love, and life.

This past week we saw the Holy Spirit at work in a powerful and visible way when the Spirit of God guided the cardinals in their selection of our new pope. Mixed reactions abounded as news of the selection was announced; some likely thought that the Holy Spirit was right on top of things and others may have felt that the Spirit was certainly asleep. How could they make such a choice? They were guided by the Spirit!

We choose by visible and tangible qualifications, while God sees within the heart. God knows what is facing the faith life of the church; we don't! God knows who is best suited to lead and protect his church, just as he chose David, the youngest and most unexpected son of Jacob, to be king of his people, and God made that choice known as the Spirit led the cardinals in their selection.

If anyone is sleeping, it is not the Holy Spirit! If anyone is sleeping, like the little boy on the table, it is those whose faith has gone dormant; those who have closed the minds and hearts to the will and activity of God in our present-day world; those who do not want to be told "this is good, this is bad; this is right, this is wrong," for the Holy Spirit, like the little dog, is keeping careful watch over the church, his sheep. Wake up! Be open to the Spirit acting in your life!

April 24, 2005

What do people think of us? How sad that we are far more worried about what others think of us than we are about what God thinks of us! We are concerned about being a part of the "in" group, donning the "mod" hair styles, wearing the latest "fad" in clothes, and engaging in life-endangering and immoral actions; we are goaded by what others might think of us ignoring what God thinks.

This past Saturday, I went to see the Carrollton High School play "Do black patent leather shoes really reflect up?" True, it joked about some of the things we did in years past, but it clearly emphasized morality and living the essentials of our faith; something which modern society fails to acknowledge.

What people say or think about you matters little; what God knows about you determines your eternal salvation. The world may judge you and reject you for adhering to the teachings of Jesus, but that is only temporary, but those who are more concerned about what others think than what God thinks and ignore the directives of Jesus face eternal condemnation. The choice is not easy, but the end result is eternal; think about it.

Everyone wants to get to heaven provided they do not have to believe, think, say, or do anything that Bible says or as long as they do not have to imitate Jesus; that is impossible!

I am appalled at the indecent attire, which has made its way into church; it is scandalous. Low-cut dresses or blouses, bare midriffs, and skimpy shorts are unacceptable in church and to many even on the street; they are tempting. This is true for men as well as women. Each time we say the Lord's Prayer, we pray "lead us not into temptation"; our actions certainly do not verify our words.

I urge everyone to make a reality check as I am doing; are we more concerned about what others think or what God thinks? I too am concerned about what people think of me, but God has been prodding me to face my responsibility to shepherd reminding me that I need to become more concerned of what he thinks (expects) of me and less concerned of what others do. I condemn no one; but if I fail to guide you, then I condemn myself.

The devil is clever as we read in the book of Genesis and as we know personally from the experiences of our daily lives; he can trick us into rationalizing our choices; he can turn our hearts away from our loving God; he causes us to become more concerned about what others think, while ignoring what God thinks.

It is time we forget what people think of us and begin to concentrate on what God thinks of us. God loves us; he sacrificed his Son, Jesus, to show his love and free us from sin and established a church to help us on our faith journey to attain eternal life. Our faithful participation in Mass, our frequent reception of the sacraments, and our observance of the Commandments of God and the church show that we are more concerned about what God thinks of us than what people do. Neglecting these powerful spiritual helps, out of fear of what people will think, will lead to disappointment and spiritual disaster, for the world only gives us passing pleasure; it cannot forgive our sins; it destroys life.

The message of the high school play is something we all need to consider. The moral fiber of today's society has been stretched, even severed, because we have chosen to be guided by what people think and living the essential teachings of our faith have been ignored because we are more anxious about winning the approval of people than God. "How far is too far" was a song in the play; we have gone far too far—we have chosen the standards of the world and the opinion of people over those of God.

May 1, 2005

"O when the saints coming marching in . . . O Lord, I want to be in that number" are the beautiful words of an old spiritual; will we be found among that number? Absolutely! I want to tell you about some saints marching in my life.

This past Sunday, nineteen little saints came marching into church, happy, excited, and beautiful as they prepared to receive Jesus, their Lord and Savior, for the first time in the Eucharist. What a wonderful day for our parish family! What a great responsibility for us to guide and support them by our example of living faith! They are a marvelous example showing their deep appreciation of this sacrament; we are to be an example and help them grow in faith, so they will remain holy and pleasing to God and be among the saints when they come marching in on the last day.

The next group of saints that I have encountered recently is those people who, during their days and even months of "testing," clearly manifested their trust in God's plan and patiently accepted his will and persevered in witnessing deep faith; they have been an inspiration to me. Such people are a living example of the Paschal Mystery—suffering, death, and Resurrection.

Their agony in the garden was their sickness; their scourging, the pain of immobility; their crowning, their confinement; their carrying of the cross, the uncertainty of the outcome of the illness; and their crucifixion, the humility of dependency. Their death is dying to self-desires and being open to God's will; and their Resurrection comes with their growing in faith as they recover, or their sharing in the fullness of life if God welcomes them home. They have passed the "test" and will certainly be among the saints marching into glory.

Another group of saints are those who so faithfully live out the corporal works of mercy tending to the sick and dying—spouses, family members, and hospice workers. It is a special blessing to witness their long hours of ministering, their peaceful acceptance of the demands made of them, their belief that Jesus is with them and empowering them, and the deep love motivating them. They are living saints exemplifying the true presence of Christ among us.

Every day, saints pass through our lives, but we frequently miss them because we have the misconceived idea that saints are found only among the dead. Whether Pope John Paul II is ever declared a saint by the church or not does not deny the truth that he was a saint. His compassion, love, and care for the least as well as the greatest attracted millions around the world to recognize this leading them to Jesus. He lived a saintly life and now marches with the saints!

The life of a saint reflects the life of Jesus and inspires us to do the same. There are a great number of saints in our parishes—individual and families who, like Jesus, touch my life and hopefully many others, by their deep faith, moral living, and involvement in parish activities. I am inspired by the tremendous sacrifices they are willing to make proving the high priority of their faith and the place of God in their lives, insuring that their children and future generations will realize that nothing is more important than their intimate, loving, relationship with Jesus, maintaining a Catholic School, which is a great source of truth, a guide for moral living, and an opportunity to share the many blessings of our Catholic faith.

O when the saints come marching in they will be there; take note of their presence in your life today; imitate them as they imitate Jesus, and you will march with the saints.

May 8, 2005

This past Saturday night, twenty-six young people gathered for an all-night "lock-in." It began with a beautiful Mass at which the youth had an active part in the singing and the ministries and then continued with food, games, a spiritual video, and three stimulating presentations—a married man who was greatly handicapped as a result of an accident, a college girl and a male high school student who shared personal life experiences to show us where we needed to place our "locks," what to keep out of our lives and who to let in, how to avoid wrong choices, how to handle and work through mistakes, and the importance of God in our lives. Our first speaker, confined to a wheel chair and nearly totally dependent on others, amazed the group by his efforts to live and to enjoy life. They were surprised to see him drive his own van and manage his motorized wheel chair, since he had no control of or use of his legs and very limited use of his hands; his sense of optimism and positive attitude was amazing. He never complained about his mishap, the months of pain and rehabilitation and the drastic changes in his life; he only witnessed his trust in God and tried to impress on all of us the security and blessings of Jesus in our lives.

Even though many of us, young and old, have physical problems, what are they compared to the "cross" in his situation? Splinters! We complain when things are not the way we want them or life is a bit difficult, and we fall into the "Why me?" syndrome. He clearly conveyed the message that we can carry on under any difficulty when we have faith and trust in the help of God.

Our college student reminded us that all too frequently we live in a daily "lock-in." We have established our personal whims as our pattern of life; we have locked ourselves in a state of rebellion, lashing out at anyone who opposes us, and ignoring the experiential advice of parents or teachers while totally severing relations with Jesus.

She warned that such a head-strong "lock-in" would lead to much suffering, shame, and regret, and encouraged them to keep open the lines of communication with parents and teachers, to listen and learn from their experiences. Exposing the myth that alcohol, drugs, sex, fame, or possessions do not really satisfy their inner longing for happiness and love, she stressed the essential need to develop a real, intimate relationship with Jesus, without whom they would never find true peace and love in this life or lasting happiness in the next. She made it quite clear that all too often we "lock ourselves in" by foolishly and blindly "locking out" those who love us and want only to help us, especially Jesus.

The high school student encouraged us to walk with Jesus as we make our choices and to set our goals high. He set before us the model of an athlete who was quite mediocre but became the "star" of a game because of his motivation. He warned against buckling to peer pressure and assured us that when you say "no," you are not an outcast; people will come to respect your boundaries and life will be safer and more rewarding and many will welcome you into their lives. He exhorted them to respect themselves and others, to listen to their parents and teachers, and to be open to the Word of Jesus assuring them of many unbelievable blessings and benefits, both physical and spiritual.

All three were emphatic about the importance of Jesus in their lives—the need for honest and open communication with parents, peers, and God, establishing moral and ethical boundaries, counting their blessings, living deep faith, and trusting God completely. The "lock-in" urged us to "lock out" what is spiritually destructive, and to "lock on" to Jesus who offers peace, happiness, love, and life, now and forever—a grace-filled experience.

May 15, 2005

It's time for us to build a new church! The church in Pawnee was struck by lightning, which gutted the inside leaving only the skeleton, an empty shell. They will not be permitted to rebuild due to the lack of enough active parishioners willing to sacrifice their time, talents, and treasures to sustain a viable faith life. How sad to see a church burn! How tragic to see the church disintegrate! A building does not make a church, it is merely the place designated where the Church, the people gather to pray and worship as one.

There are tiny and not very fancy churches where the Church, the people are active witnessing their faith as a parish family and throughout the community, and there are huge beautiful buildings where only a few gather as church—no longer life-giving spiritually and doing little if anything to embellish their faith life or live the corporal and spiritual works of mercy. It appears that the spirit of Catholicism is slowly diminishing as we fail to instill the message of Jesus in the hearts and lives of each coming generation; the result is similar to the fire in Pawnee.

The devil, like lightning, continues to strike individuals with extreme flashes for luxury or worldly accomplishments and their inordinate desire burns out their love for God and leaves only an empty shell or a spiritual skeleton—no longer enthusiastic about things eternal, Catholic in name, but not in action; only a skeleton of faith, no longer practicing.

Lightning can destroy a church, but only the devil can destroy the Church.

It's time for us to build a new Church, not a new building, but to build up the faith life of our Church. It costs much to build a new church and many sacrifices are required; it costs even more to build a new Church. Carpenters, plumbers, electricians, architects etc., are a must when you build a church building, time and effort is necessary; but when it is completed, their work is finished. Priests, ministers, musicians, teachers, and parishioners are needed to build a Church, and their work is never completed.

When the parishioners fail in living their faith or their responsibility to support their parish financially, the Church begins to collapse. When they lose their deep appreciation of a Catholic School, the foundation weakens. If the parish family neglects to pray for and encourage their children to become priests, sisters, or brothers or refuses to use their talents and time for the evangelization of its members and community, it will soon "burn" up all its potential and suddenly find an empty church.

It's time to build a new Church—one with enthusiasm, compassion, and concern for others patterned after a close knit loving family willing to tithe while being good stewards. We have a beautiful church building; we need a Church (people) actively living their faith. We need to reach out to the many parishioners opting to go elsewhere, or worse, nowhere, to welcome and actively involve our youth, to witness our conviction of the Catholic faith by willingly sacrificing to assure future generations that a church building will be maintained for the Church to gather.

An empty bird shell has no more life; the life it gave now lives on to give new life or has died. An empty "burned-out" church offers no life; it must be rebuilt or it is useless; the Church can offer life only when Jesus is acting in and through the people, or it is an empty shell. It is time we build a new Church—people who treasure their faith, who enthusiastically share it, who willingly sacrifice for the growth of a life-giving Church.

May 29, 2005

Two young men, preparing to leave college following graduation, were packing their belonging. As they removed pictures and certificates from the wall, they joked about who had the most, what good were they, and how would they benefit them in the future.

How many more would they add to their collection of certificates from preschool, kindergarten, eighth grade, high school, college, and their doctorate degrees? Neither had any assurance of work; in fact, one or both of them would be working in fields unrelated to their scholastic preparation. Hopefully, they would eventually find employment corresponding to their degrees. In the meantime, all their awards and certificates would be packed in a box, hopefully, to be hung on their office walls at a later date. All too frequently, one has little control over the situation of employment, due to an excess of qualified professionals seeking the same position; parents, family, and friends share these disappointments and continually try to remedy the situation.

Facing such an outcome, after years of scholastic preparation, can be very disheartening even when it is out of our hands; but what is far more disheartening is the number of people who have placed their spiritual certificates, their Baptism, First Reconciliation, First Eucharist, Confirmation, and Matrimony along with other spiritual recognitions such as for serving, choir, or some Liturgical Ministry, in a box and are not using them. What good are they if one neglects to use them on their spiritual journey?

Because of uncontrollable factors, we may not be responsible if we are unable to acquire a desired type of employment, but we have no excuse for the way we live our faith life. The certificates are not simply documents of accomplishments, but they are guarantees of "grace" helps. Baptism envelopes us with the restored life of God; the other sacraments are supportive and empowering gifts to maintain and help us grow in divine life.

If we merely place these "spiritual certificates" in a box and neglect to use the powerful graces of the sacrament, we are only fooling ourselves; they have no value. No matter how many scholastic certificates or awards we may attain as we go through life, they have value only in so far as they aid us in living our faith. In like manner, no matter how many sacraments we receive, they are useless empty signs, unless we use them to bring about an inner change, to become more loving, forgiving, and caring for others.

Graduations are the focal point of young and old this time of the year, but for many, it means the end and not as the word implies—a gradual movement upward or a step up the ladder of life. That is a sad decision for one intellectually gifted by God because we should always work and live in a manner that betters things around us; it is an even greater tragedy when we neglect to live Christian lives.

Society places great emphasis on intellectual accomplishments, but very little on spiritual development. We seldom feel the same disappointment when our loved ones do not practice their faith as we do, when they are unable to get a specific position or choose another type of work than they were schooled for. How often do we encourage our children, youth, or others to live their faith? Success is measured by our income and possessions and is oblivious to our need to live moral and ethical lives—to practice our faith. Religious or priestly vocations are no longer encouraged, and money seems even more desirable than a permanent commitment in marriage; the egocentric doctrine of the world is quickly undermining the doctrine of God—many with scholastic awards and certificates as well as many with spiritual certificates will "fail,"; only those who use them to become more Christlike will "graduate" and be a success now and forever.

June 5, 2005

Did God make a mistake when he created humans? God made all things; all living animals, all vegetation, water, earth, fire, wind, and all that has been, is now, and will ever be, and God has never made a mistake. All creatures, except for humans, are true to their nature; only people rebel, sin, and turn away from God—a mistake, but not God's.

They say that water falling on a rock long enough will eventually wear it down; is that what has happened to truth? When was the last time you veered from the truth, even just a little? Why?

One drop of water will not change a rock, likewise one "little" untruth, a lie, will not destroy us, but it weakens us. It is the beginning, and gradually the size will increase and the number will multiply until they will eventually destroy reputations and institutions. Little untruths lubricate the way for devastation—white lies soon turn gray—then black.

Certainly God did not make a mistake when he made us; we are the epitome of his creation made in his image and likeness and gifted with an intellect and free will, which sets us above all other creatures. The sole creature that can reason and choose has untold blessings as well as grave responsibilities; we can lie and become slaves of sin, or we can tell the truth, and the truth will set us free.

Years ago, at a gathering, we played a game. We sat in a circle, and the first person whispered some short story to the person next in line, which was passed on until it got back to the one who started it. No one was allowed to ask it to be repeated; they had to tell the next person what they heard, right or wrong, and by the time it got back to the first person, it usually was far from the original truth. Many play this game in real life!

Life is not a game; it is living reality honestly considering all the facts and upholding the truth. Jesus makes it quite clear that he is the Way, the Truth, and the Light; whoever hears his Word and lives the truth has the light that leads to life. Do we believe him?

Frequently, the truth is distorted; it may be fictitious, exaggerated, or destructive depending on the individual and the situation. Some make up stories, that have little if any truth content in order to excuse their failures; others exaggerate the truth in order to appear equal or better than those around them; and then there are those who deliberately deviate from the truth hoping to destroy someone.

Once you tell a lie, you will need to tell another, and another in order to protect yourself and cover the previous falsehood; unable to remember what "story" you told the first person, you will tell another spinning a web of falsehood until you are caught in your lie.

Those making up stories or exaggerating the truth are slowly "wearing down" people's trust like water wearing away a rock destroying their own reputation. Worse still, for those who deliberately destroy the good name of others, "It would be better," says Jesus, "had a mill stone been tied around their neck, and they were dropped into the sea."

Rumors, half-truths, and lies saturate our lives; great is our need of Truth, Jesus. Jesus clearly demonstrates the value and benefit of the truth; he taught the truth, he lived the truth; his love and compassion for everyone witnessed to that truth. All who follow the way of truth will enjoy the light of Christ who leads to life.

God did not make a mistake; we make a mistake when we enter the "quicksand" of so-called "white" lies, which quickly pull us down into "gray" lies and eventually we sink into those destructive, deadly "black" lies. Isn't it time we stop playing games?

June 12, 2005

The great Prophet Elijah, was waiting for God to reveal himself; he expected the "mighty" God to manifest himself in some powerful way; so he searched for him in the mighty wind as it destroyed the great mountain, in the violence of an earthquake, and in a huge fire, but God was not there; he revealed himself in a tiny whispering sound. God is mighty, but he speaks to us and reveals his message in simple ways.

A couple of weeks ago, while on retreat, I went out into the wooded yard to reflect on the message of the spiritual director and to enjoy the beauty of nature. As I sat on a bench, I looked down and saw the tiniest ant crawling between my sandals, and through this, I was reminded of God's incredible plan of creation and total control over all things.

The ant was less than one-sixteenth of an inch long; yet it dared to crawl between my sandals rushing on its way to accomplish some mission to better self or to help the ant colony as a whole. I had the power and the freedom to move my sandal and destroy the little creature or to choose to let it live; I chose the latter.

In those few moments of prayer and contemplation, I became quite aware of a similar parallel between God and me, all of us. God, the creator of all, the one who governs all things, looks down on me as I hurry about seeking personal gain or working for the good of others. When considering the totality of creation, I, like the tiny ant, am totally dependent on God, who can end my life as easily as I could that of the ant.

That tiny ant was undaunted as it climbed huge cement walls unaware of what danger it might find on the other side; it made its way through tall grass and even taller weeds; unable to see what might be hidden a few inches ahead it scurried across vast areas of hot and barren blacktop. With no relief in sight, risking the possibility of being trampled by humans or smashed under car tires, it was instinctively motivated to accomplish the task of bettering its life and that of the ant colony.

Each of us can learn much from that happening; we are far greater than any ant; we are highly intelligent beings capable of reasoning and discerning a solution for our problems and planning for the future; yet we are often tempted to give up when life becomes difficult or unknown. We too face walls of the unknown—failure, sickness, and death; we get lost in the busyness of the world, which causes the spiritual blessings to become hidden right before our eyes; we experience dry and barren times when friends and family and even Jesus seem so distant. Traveling the "fast track" we are in danger of being destroyed physically, mentally, emotionally, and spiritually due to the pressures society imposes on us to be a part of the "in" group. Are we bettering our lives or others?

The great problem we face today is "control"; we want to control our lives, everybody, and everything around us and even God. We love a powerful God as long as he uses his power according to our plans and empowers us to remain in control; we shudder when God tells us that if you want to be first, you must become the last, and that whoever humbles himself will be exalted while the one who exalts himself will be humbled.

The little ant was powerless, yet it sought to achieve its goal trusting in God; we too are to trust that God will guard and guide us as we seek to achieve our "goal"—a personal, loving friendship with Jesus. We do this best through our awareness of his presence and actions in the daily events of life, and being open to his message in the simple experiences around us, even an ant. Jesus, the all powerful God, began his life as a helpless baby and appeared to end it as a helpless person. But he was in total control of the world and the plan of our salvation at every moment. Listen as he whispers to you!

June 19, 2005

While on retreat, I met two people I did not like; one was Jesus and the other was me. The weeks preceding had been very busy, and I had anticipated a week of quiet time to rejuvenate, rest, and pray. That was not God's plan!

During the first night, I was awakened several times by unusual noises in the adjoining room, which were disrupting my sleep, and then at 5:30 a.m., I heard someone knocking on the wall, so I went to check—no longer a happy camper.

Due to previous evening engagements, I arrived late at the Retreat House, and was unaware that the priest in the next room was physically impaired until I entered the room. As a result of a stroke years earlier, his left arm and leg no longer functioned and so was confined to a motorized wheel chair. And now during the night, he had lost his sight—he was totally disoriented. I helped as much as I could and then "crashed" until morning prayers, after which I, upon his request, returned to help him get to breakfast, which was a difficult and lengthy undertaking. This unexpected infringement of my time was beginning to disturb me as I anticipated a tiring and exhausting week.

Fortunately, the staff was able to convince him to see an eye specialist and took him to the hospital where it was discovered he had suffered a hemorrhage or something behind his eyes, causing a temporary blindness, which was gradually restored throughout the day with the help of medication.

Later, as I reflected on the events of the previous night, I was shocked as I realized that I did not like Jesus, embodied in this disabled priest and asking for help, because it was an inconvenience; I was ashamed and humbled. Following this, I experienced a feeling of dissatisfaction; I did not like myself; my reaction to the situation was anything but Christlike and the Words of Jesus "whatever you do for the least, you do for me" were burning in my heart. Remorsefully the incident led to a time of in-depth self-analysis, which is what a retreat really should be.

With the increase of physical disabilities associated with aging, I am still greatly blessed, more than many others; why then should I fail to graciously help those afflicted with disabilities much worse than mine? This "eye-opening" experience alerted me to the need of trusting and accepting God's plan hidden in mystery and surrounded with suffering exhorting me to take up whatever cross Jesus chose for me. It is so easy to like Jesus when all goes well, to become self-complacent with regard to our spiritual way of living, but the truth is seen when we are tested as gold in a furnace.

The priest with physical impairments, accepting of his unending burdensome cross was a greater example of a follower of Jesus than I, who became impatient with God for disturbing my night's sleep. Many of you are an inspiration to me as you lovingly and generously care for the needs of others in your lives day after day. Once again God uses simple experiences to teach; ordinary situations to test our faith and regular events to prove our love; if we remain alert to his presence in the mysterious, accept his will in suffering and believe when he tells us he loves us. Let us live in such a way that we prove our love of God in one another.

June 26, 2005

Breinigsville, PA USA
05 July 2010
241177BV00007B/61/P